PLATS DU JOUR

PLATS DU JOUR

BY

PATIENCE GRAY AND PRIMROSE BOYD

WITH ILLUSTRATIONS BY

DAVID GENTLEMAN

Prospect Books

1990

© Patience Gray and the estate of Primrose Boyd
Illustrations © David Gentleman

Published by Prospect Books, 45 Lamont Road, London
SW10 OHU

Additional typesetting by Crypticks, Leeds

Printed and bound by Smith Settle
Ilkley Road, Otley, West Yorkshire

ISBN 0 907325 45 9

CONTENTS

(after the above added material comes the facsimile reprint of Plats du Jour, with its own Table of Contents and with its original pagination preserved)

INTRODUCTION

If I cast my mind back to 1954-55, when this book was being written, I have to work hard to recreate in my memory the paucity of interesting food in England – and of interesting books on food in the bookshops. So much has the scene changed since then.

Publication of *Plats du Jour* in 1957, the first such book to start life as a mass-circulation paperback, was an important and early milestone along the road of change.

It was not the earliest. Rays of sunlight had been shining on the bleak British gastronomic landscape since 1950, when Elizabeth David's *A Book of Mediterranean Food* appeared; and her three next books, including *Italian Food* (1956), had made a further impact. But this was still only the start; and at this time only one of her books, the first, was in paperback on the Penguin list.

Other works which helped point people towards the pleasures of foreign food, such as those of Boulestin, Sir Harry Luke's *The Tenth Muse* (1954), Lesley Blanch's *Round the World in Eighty Dishes* (1956), and the series of André Deutsch books (including Sheila Hutchins' *What's Cooking?*, 1954, whose title failed to indicate its enterprising international content) were for hardcover customers only; a category which didn't include me – though I had made an exception for a second-hand copy of *The Gentle Art of Cookery* by Mrs Leyel and Olga Hartley, that truly extraordinary work of 1925.

Plats du Jour was different. It was born as a paperback; and that is the only 'back' it has ever had until now. It sold phenomenally well, outstripping sales of hardcover books by a factor of 25 or so to 1. In just the first ten months of its existence almost 50,000 copies were sold; and the total number in circulation, even now and with their pages growing ever browner round the edges, is therefore considerable. It is remarkable how many people, whether or not they were

INTRODUCTION

cooking in the 1950s and 1960s, treasure a copy of it, although it was in print only from 1957 to 1961.

The explanation is simple. It is a very good book indeed. Its principal ingredients, the knowledge and amiable enthusiasm of the authors, have given it a lasting value. It is a comfortable book to settle down with, and to cook from. And the breath of inspiration which emanates from it is still fresh, although the scene in Britain has changed so much since it was written.

The delightful and eye-catching jacket by David Gentleman – once seen, never forgotten – has ensured that it is always easy to spot in the kitchen or in a second-hand bookshop . . . or in a jumble sale. Jane Grigson once told me that she was in the habit of picking up any copy of *Plats du Jour* which she found at church jumble sales, and then giving them as presents.

I have done this too, but I have also thought for many years, and especially since I became the editor, and Prospect Books the publisher, of Patience Gray's recent (and third*) book on food, *Honey from a Weed*, that it would be good to put *Plats du Jour* back into the bookshops, and this time on good paper inside a hard cover.

Now the moment has come. With the cooperation of Patience Gray and of Lorna Hubbard, sister of Primrose Boyd (who died, alas, in 1982), we can relaunch what can rightly be called a 'classic'. It could also be called a 'period piece', since it is so patently a product of the 1950s.

We considered briefly whether it could be updated. The answer was 'absolutely not'. Any attempt to do this would have destroyed its fabric and integrity. Even such details as the choice of fish for seafood recipes mirror the situation as it was then, and could not be changed without distorting the picture. So we have the reprinted the book in facsimile, enlarging it very slightly by photography for ease of reading, and asking our printers to carry out a few tiny surgical operations to remove incidental blemishes from the original text.

So here it is: a book which, almost 35 years ago, helped to establish what were then faintly discernible trends but have since become

---

* the second, which is exceedingly rare, bears the title *A Book of French, Italian, Greek & Catalan Dishes for Blue Funnel Ships*, was written in Naxos in 1963, and then printed for use by the cooks in those ships

INTRODUCTION

irreversible changes in the way British people look at food and cookery.

One may wonder whether to count the authors, and other pioneers, as wave-makers or as surf-riders. The answer, I suppose, is that they were both. There was a wave to ride on, but they made it bigger. As I see it, there was in the 1950s a crucial and threefold combination: a stronger current of interest in foreign food than had existed before the Second World War; the activity of a few really good writers on the subject; and the fact that these writers could begin to reach a really large audience through the Penguin paperback list.

Of these three factors, the last was wholly new. Lorna Hubbard has told me of a friend who assured her that *Plats du Jour* had a 'seminal influence' on young women who were beginning to cook in the period just after wartime austerity and rationing. Just so. But few of those young women would have been exposed to the influence if it had not been available for three shillings and sixpence. And the influence would not have proved to be so enduring if the book had not been of first quality.

It is a privilege for Prospect Books to introduce *Plats du Jour* to a new generation.

Alan Davidson
World's End
Chelsea
March 1990

PREFATORY NOTE

I sometimes wonder at the presumption, ours, in embarking in 1954 on a cookery book. But looking at David Gentleman's delightful drawings in the original now battered little Penguin book, the thought consoles me that they reflect the spirit of adventure which informed the undertaking.

In Prospect Books' new edition this period piece has changed its size but not its content, though some typographical errors and mistaken spellings have been excised and, when possible, insupportable gaffes obliterated.

It is sad that Primrose cannot add to mine her own account of this mutual enterprise. We met in 1950 in the design studio of F. H. K. Henrion, where we had been summoned to work as research assistants on the Country Pavilion he was creating for the Festival of Britain. Breadwinning being a common concern, when the Festival opened in May 1951, we formed a research partnership which operated in the afternoons. In the mornings Primrose painted while I worked for several years for Professor Guyatt at the Royal College of Art. Although this has nothing to do with cooking, it had to do with our future illustrator, a gifted student then in the School of Graphic Design.

The research jobs on which we separately engaged were concerned with food, drink, plant life, the history of market gardens, the cultivation of exotic plants and vegetables, among other subjects; with olive oil campaigns, reports on the design of fuel appliances and refrigerators, and the search for illustrations, including food and wine. Where I was concerned, the work embraced 'ghost writing' for patrons who had only time to polish and sign the fruits of ghostly labours. All services were paid at the rate of five shillings an hour.

Primrose, the living image of the 'professional woman' before her time, who sometimes lectured me on the importance of 'women's

PREFATORY NOTE

rights' and 'executive dress', smarted under these working conditions. She often urged me to invent a more substantial source of
home-based income. And this is how the proposal emerged to write a
book – directly inspired by the practice we both favoured at the time
owing to our many occupations – a book which was to contain a
series of recipes concentrating on a *plat du jour* – the preparation of a
single dish in terms of nourishment.

Working on this idea, a framework was evolved, to which we each
contributed recipes. The synopsis that ensued was rashly proposed to
Miss Eunice Frost, the *éminence grise* at Penguin Books. To our
surprise Miss Frost offered us a contract and an advance of £200 – the
equivalent perhaps of £2,000 today. Just at this moment, David
Gentleman had won a travelling scholarship at the RCA. Miss Frost
swept down to the Senior Common Room, examined his drawings
and later commissioned him to illustrate the book. David cheerfully
set off on his European journey, and we set off on ours.

Travel, the hard way, was closely connected with our aim to
broaden the post-war approach to island cooking at a time when
rationing and 'austerity' were petering to an end. My grand-daughters
maintain that it was their great-aunt Elizabeth Haimendorf and I who
had, by hitch-hiking to Budapest in 1937, pointed their youthful steps
in the direction of Katmandu, Peru and Mandalay today. My sister
and I were also apparently to blame, in fanning travel fever by vanish-
ing through the Danube's Iron Gates on a three month exploration of
Romania with a student's Quaker grant in 1938. I suspect that
Primrose's peregrinations occurred in France, Holland, Spain; in any
case, travel-starved after the war, France, Italy and Yugoslavia were
my immediate destinations.

While working on the book in 1954 in children's schooltime, travel
was confined to London buses and the Underground. In the little
Public Library at Camden Town in a damp basement on open
shelving I came across a splendidly illustrated 1848 edition of Brillat-
Savarin's *Physiologie du Goût*, the artist being Bertall, his full page
drawings engraved on steel by Ch. Geoffroy, those in the text engraved
on wood by Midderigh; this light-hearted edition published by Gabriel
de Gonet, rue des Beaux-Arts 6 (Paris) contrasted with this period of
revolution. Although today people affect to be bored by this book, to
me it was a source of inspiration, and certainly the fungi featuring in

typographical chapter headings induced me – just as much as Monsieur A. Maublanc's treatise – to devote a final section of *Plats du Jour* to this neglected subject.

Escaping at lunchtime on a 19 bus from the Royal College, a remarkable collection of culinary works awaited me in the stack-room of the London Library, among which the volumes of Carême and Urbain Dubois. From Carême I suspect the recipe for *Carpe à la Chambord* was stolen, and cooked, to his surprise, for Irving Davis. How pretentious, how absurd!

How scandalous it seems today that, by rendering a recipe into one's own words, no obligation was felt to declare its source! Other grounds for shame: the *paella* recipe induced a lady at a dinner party to hurl invective at me across the dinner table, and almost the knives, the plates. *Touchée*: at the time neither Primrose nor I had been to Valencia.

We held to a basic rule: no recipe could be included without the proposer having cooked it. One cannot but be appalled today by the number of times a sauce is 'thickened' with flour, egg yolks, butter. Fortunately these days, by common consent, are past. But at that time, English cooks, so used to 'thickening' the juices from the roast, may have felt encouraged or at least tranquillized by this procedure.

Primrose cooked for her hard-working husband Donald Boyd, director of Talks at the BBC. He seemed to thrive on dense pea soups, casseroles slowly cooking while she painted, on excellent *terrines, pâtés, quiches*, on pickled tongues, salads and French cheeses from Roche in Soho, in perfect condition because freshly imported and never refrigerated. I wonder now why we assumed that every English cook knew how to make a salad.

Some things shock me beyond measure: the suggestion that left-over wine should be indiscriminately poured into a bottle for cooking purposes – a sure way of making vinegar. I have counted at least ten asbestos mats as aid to slow cooking. Then, no one knew that heating asbestos produces noxious fumes; wire mats are safer.

Today the detection of errors in *Plats du Jour* could become a 'parlour game'. Quite apart from the lady who longed to stab me at the dinner table, I have drawn my editor's attention to a few astonishing mistakes which remain embedded in it. Cereals and pulses confused! Italian *prosciutto* described as smoked!

PREFATORY NOTE

Naturally one finds the detailing of cooking procedures tedious. We assumed then and perhaps correctly a certain ignorance. The aim was to *define* the actions involved, as opposed to naming them. In spite of everything, while scanning the chapter Cuts & Joints for errors, I felt quite nostalgic for English beef as it was then, and for my little kitchen in the converted billiard-room on the heights of Hampstead.

At the time it was a surprise to hear that the book was to be found on shelves in lofts in New York's Greenwich Village. More than thirty years later, the surprise is that Prospect Books thinks it is worth republishing. Both I and Primrose's sister Lorna Hubbard thank Alan Davidson for his Introduction to the new edition.

Patience Gray
Spigolizzi
November 1989

xiv

THE FACSIMILE

A PENGUIN HANDBOOK

PH 32

PLATS DU JOUR

PATIENCE GRAY AND PRIMROSE BOYD

THIS is not intended as an armchair cookery book. It is designed for action in the kitchen. The underlying theme is a concentration of excellence in one main dish, rather than dissipating thought and care on several, and it contains a collection of recipes, mainly French and Italian, for dishes which can be served with no further sequel than salad, cheese, and fruit. The authors have imparted in the description of these dishes some of the enthusiasm which naturally belongs to the preparation of continental food. They have taken care to define the methods and operations involved, to discuss the contribution made by aromatic herbs and spices, and to suggest the kind of pot or pan most suitable for the creation of each dish. But it is as well to remember that no Provençal, Italian, or Spanish dish, however carefully prepared away from its home, can do more than approximate to its original. As wine is now both fairly abundant and reasonable in price and it is no longer an extravagance to use it in cooking as well as at table, some brief accounts of *vins ordinaires* are included in the text, with an accompanying chapter on the great variety of cheeses now available. The chapter on edible fungi, whose culinary aspects are largely ignored in this country, is an especially new departure for a cookery book.

PATIENCE GRAY AND PRIMROSE BOYD

Plats du Jour

Illustrated by

DAVID GENTLEMAN

->->->->->->->-> * -<-<-<-<-<-<-<-<

PENGUIN BOOKS

Penguin Books Ltd, Harmondsworth, Middlesex
U.S.A.: Penguin Books Inc, 3300 Clipper Mill Road, Baltimore 11, Md
CANADA: Penguin Books (Canada) Ltd, 178 Norseman Street,
Toronto 18, Ontario
AUSTRALIA: Penguin Books Pty Ltd, 762 Whitehorse Road,
Mitcham, Victoria

—

First published 1957

Made and printed in Great Britain
by Butler & Tanner Ltd,
Frome and London

+>+>+>+> * +<+<+<+<

CONTENTS

'Music and wine make even slavery bearable'

IL SERAGLIO

+>->->->> * <-<-<-<<

ACKNOWLEDGEMENTS

W E have consulted a great many works in the course of preparing this book, for guidance and correction. But in particular we would like to acknowledge our debt to two sources
of inspiration, the works of Austin de Croze and Reboul.
Austin de Croze's *What to Eat and Drink in France* may perhaps be reprinted one day and become accessible to those who
seek a guide in gastronomic adventure across the Channel;
Reboul's *La Cuisine Provençale* is an object lesson in the
art of setting down meticulous directions. We are indebted
to Pellegrino Artusi's *La Scienza in Cucina*, and to Marcel
Boulestin's books which introduced us long ago to the
French approach to cooking. We are extremely grateful to
Mr John Ramsbottom for kindly reading the chapter on
Fungi and correcting our mycological errors. A. Maublanc's
Les Champignons comestibles et vénéneux gave us the courage
to devote a separate section to this subject. We wish to
thank Michael Joseph, Ltd, for permission to print an extract
from *Stay me with Flagons* by Maurice Healy, and Mr Bailey,
butcher, of Manningtree, and the Boucherie française, of
Messrs Harrods, for help given to Mr David Gentleman in
preparing the illustrations. We are grateful to Mrs Stanley
Murdoch for reading and criticizing the text.

PATIENCE GRAY
PRIMROSE BOYD

2

INTRODUCTION

In this book we have tried to set down the recipes for a number of dishes of foreign origin, in the belief that English people may be stimulated to interpret them, and in doing so find fresh interest in the kitchen. The difficulty lies in the diversity of methods used to achieve similar results, in conveying the timing in preparation and the texture and appearance of the finished dish. If the cook has not some vague conception of what it should be like, some recollection to fall back on, it is unlikely that a recipe is sufficient to act as an infallible guide. The operations of reducing the sauce for a braise or effecting a liaison of egg yolk and lemon juice require judgement and vary with the occasion. It is hard to give exact directions in the preparation of things even as simple as rice, for example, as the speed of cooking and the absorbent qualities of rice are variable. Between the written recipe and the finished dish there are many such variables which determine its success. A great deal must always depend upon the cook.

But looking at the original dish, contemplating for a moment a preparation as ancient and simple as *cotriade à la bretonne*, for instance, in which a variety of fish are poached with onions, potatoes, and herbs, and daily served in the cottages of Breton villages not a stone's throw from the sea, it must be clear that the natural qualities which give this dish its flavour are with us partially absent; besides, the air we eat it in, the stove we cook it on, and the pot we cook it in are different. This is a dish which involves only fresh fish, waxy yellow potatoes, and Breton onions; how much more variation enters the picture when the oil used comes in question, or the wine added to a casserole, or the herbs that we include. It is in a rather cautious spirit that we set down these recipes, and, in order that their recreation should not be only a ghostly semblance of the original, we have paid particular attention to the kind of pots in which to cook the dishes, the kind of store

9

cupboard that they suppose, and the contribution that specific aromatics, herbs, spices, and condiments can play in cooking.

What culinary achievements we can claim are the result of enjoyment and the wish to reproduce tastes which have been first experienced in foreign places; perhaps in a little railway inn at Coutances, in Normandy, in a *trattoria* behind the *Piazza della Signoria* in Florence, in a courtyard in Sienna shrouded by oleander pots, or in some colonnaded inn in Calabria. This explains why most of the dishes in this book are of French or Italian origin, and why, on the whole, the recipes are of quite humble extraction. We have never eaten a three-star meal at Les Baux or at *Les Trois Faisans* in Dijon. Pre-war periods of truffled woodcock and champagne in Berlin, and an all too brief encounter with caviare in Bucharest, have given place to Italian journeys where lack of means has sometimes eliminated meat from the menu, and French excursions where plates of limpid oysters have set the tune of the Sunday midday meal.

But lack of means is just as much a familiar feature of our daily life here in England, and long before this book was thought of, we had separately evolved a system of cooking by which a variety of dishes was replaced by a single *plat du jour* accompanied, as a rule, by a green salad, a respectable cheese, and fruit in season, and, wherever possible, by a bottle of wine. This conception of a meal underlies this book.

It is a personal point of view encouraged by the experience of simple meals abroad where attention is given not only to the *vin du pays*, but to the kind of bread, the choice of cheese, and the crispness of the salad, as well as to the preparation of the principal dish. It is borne out in everyday life by the limited time available for cooking, the consequence of preoccupations outside the family. Some of the dishes given here do not amount to a *plat du jour* in the substantial sense outlined; the *Brandade de morue* is too rich to be eaten beyond a few spoonfuls, fried gudgeon are too slight, some of the soups call for a sequel; some discretion must be used. Where the occasion is a special one, a *pâté*, or an extravagance in the form of Dublin Bay prawns or smoked salmon, may be called for to precede a *Daube à la provençale* or *Poulet à l'estragon*. But barring such exceptions, the liberating idea prevails, a concentration of culinary activity, a close attention to a particular dish, which, once composed, can often be left to combine its flavours in a slow oven, later to be enjoyed with a glass of enhancing wine.

Pots . Pans . Stoves

POTS, PANS, AND STOVES

IN this country most cooking is done on gas and electric stoves, slow combustion stoves, coal ranges, combination stoves (particularly in the Midlands) incorporating open fires with oven facilities, and, in country places, on kitchen ranges, paraffin stoves, and calor gas.

A number of very satisfactory solid fuel continuous burning stoves combine excellent cooking and oven facilities with water heating and an open fire which can be fitted with an attachment for grilling. Such stoves are in a moderate price range (between £40 and £60). The heat generated by solid fuel and wood is dry and probably, in many ways, more satisfactory than gas or electricity. This type of stove is appreciated by country dwellers whose kitchens are warmed and water heated while the bread is baking, a return to the old-fashioned range in a new, smokeless, economical, and labour-saving form. Perhaps, before long, some of the casseroles, *daubes*, and other slow-cooking peasant dishes described in this book will find their way into the lower, slow-heating oven to cook all night without trouble or expense; or the owner of such a stove may be prompted to throw a bunch of rosemary or juniper onto the glowing coals while grilling some lamb chops.

Experiments are constantly being made by manufacturers to improve, both in design and performance, these different appliances, and since gas stoves are so ubiquitous it is to be hoped that the manufacturers will produce, before long, a gas grill on the cooker, which is not only improved by being at eye level (three models are, at present, equipped in this way), but is also efficient.

The problem of the grill crops up in connexion with a continuous burning coke fire, and a possible solution* involves an oven shelf supported by a sandwich of three bricks, the oven shelf in turn supporting a wire-mesh grid six inches above the red-hot

* See *Architect and Building News*, 23 December 1954.

coke. The intensity of heat given off by red-hot coke is very much greater than anything at present produced by a gas grill and full advantage should be taken of it.

In southern France and in Italy there is a far greater use of wood for fuelling cooking stoves. The fragrance of burning wood not only contributes to the delicious aromas of the southern kitchen, but imparts its smoky flavour to the dishes simmering on the – to us – archaic stoves.

Charcoal is also in fairly common use, providing an economical device in the form of a brazier for grilling fish and meat. These rustic conditions contribute to the foreignness in foreign food, and partly account for the missing qualities in a dish made here using the same ingredients, following the same method, but turning out a more or less shadowy image of the original. This is not a plea for a return to rustic stoves, but a note that an element is already lacking in the picture when we try to resurrect the form and substance of a dish on a modern cooker.

*

Among new kitchen utensils there is one of Danish origin, solid in appearance and simple in design, which exactly expresses the present-day requirements for culinary implements. It consists of four parts, a deep, cast-iron enamel-lined two-handled casserole, a shallow two-handled lid, a detachable wooden handle, and a four-legged cradle in wood, with split cane covered handles, in which to bring the casserole to table. The casserole lid, reversed and fitted with its handle, fulfils its second function as a heavy frying- or sauté-pan. It would hardly be an exaggeration to say that armed with this utensil it would be possible to produce most of the recipes in this book.

This design expresses clearly, in terms of use, the abolition of the barrier between kitchen and dining-room in the open planning of a modern house or flat. Today, we either live in our kitchens or our kitchens are a part of the living space. The *batterie de cuisine* must, therefore, be scrutinized from this point of view. The Swedes and Danes, who were the first to revolutionize architecturally many aspects of ordinary living, have also produced new kitchen equipment. The Danish casserole is not only an object which can pass through the screen dividing the kitchen from the dining-table, but it is the modern equivalent of the copper pan, which is heavy to prevent burning, slow to heat, capable of retaining heat, with the lid closely fitted, and large enough to braise a chicken.

We know perfectly well that many people live in far from modern homes and are cooking daily with possibly ancient but serviceable weapons. In discussing pots and pans here the intention is not to revile old equipment but to run over a basic list of utensils for the sake of those who are setting up house for the first time or need to replenish.

It is always disturbing to be confronted with the listed regalia of kitchen implements, a natural reaction to the disparity between an ideal condition and the existing facts. If one examines the *Batterie de Cuisine* in *L'Art Ménagère de la Cuisine Française*, for instance, a feeling of despair is more likely to take possession of an English woman rather than an immediate resolution to acquire some of the articles mentioned. We therefore recommend a visit to a shop such as Cadec's in London's Frith Street where in an ordered chaos all the essentials are displayed.

*

Saucepans should be bought with a view to solidity and durability, with fitting lids. Three heavy saucepans in forged aluminium of 3-pint, 5-pint, and 7-pint capacity are more use than several less substantial ones. 'Falconware', temporarily out of production, 'Crown Merton', or 'Sphinx', stainless steel, with aluminium base, are a standard. Besides these, a larger pan, of 4-quart capacity, with a lid and two handles is useful as it will go into the oven and can also be used for boiling *pasta* and rice, for cooking large pieces of ham or a pig's head, and for jam-making in the absence of a preserving pan. Added to these essentials are a small double saucepan for sauces and a little pan for milk.

A good, heavy aluminium frying-pan or enamelled-iron pan, between 10 and 12 inches across, is needed for shallow frying in oil, butter, or lard, and for sautéing meat and vegetables before they are transferred to an earthenware casserole. This heaviness cannot be too greatly stressed as a light frying-pan communicates the heat to its contents so rapidly that there is no time lapse between browning and burning. A lidded sauté-pan should be on the list, a shallow-sided pan which combines some of the qualities of a frying-pan with the fitted lid of a saucepan. A special iron omelette pan, kept only for its purpose, which has curved sides and costs about 17*s*., is not a luxury for anyone who appreciates the difference between an omelette and scrambled eggs.

A *marmite*, which is a rare utensil in English homes, is the traditional French stock-pot, its form corresponding to the dual requirement of accommodating a piece of meat several pounds in weight and allowing room for a quantity of liquid with a minimum of surface evaporation. In France earthenware *marmites* used to be employed universally but have been largely replaced by tall aluminium cylinders with a lid and two handles, which can be obtained here.

The choice of the appropriate size of vessel is nowhere more important than in braising, when a piece of beef, a bird, a hare, or a golden carp is submitted to a method of preparation which conserves all their natural taste and, in the final result, presents the object dressed with its own rich and aromatic sauce. A braise is only possible in a heavy iron enamelled *cocotte* which will stand the application of heat from below, and which will only just contain the piece of meat, game, or fish on its vegetable bed, so that the minimum of liquid is required to immerse it. The oval *cocotte* is, therefore, the best shape for braising a chicken or pheasant, the round *cocotte* for beef, but as these cost about 44*s*. in Swedish or Belgian ironware a choice will have to be made. This is far more important than letting the mind dwell upon fish kettle or *saumonnière*, which each costs about 63*s*. and are more limited in use. These can sometimes be found among junk stalls or in street markets for a few shillings.

A wider choice of utensils is offered in earthenware and heat-resistant china. Earthenware lidded casseroles, for stews cooked in the oven, and more sophisticated Swedish chinaware in clear colours are to be found in good department stores. Large oval earthenware dishes about 2 inches in depth and 15 inches long are best for oven-cooked sliced potato dishes, for cauliflower *au gratin*, or for preparing baked fish with an accompaniment of vegetables. These are also invaluable for *Gigot à la bretonne*, a roasted leg of lamb to which haricot beans in a rich onion and tomato sauce are added towards the end of the cooking. *Gratin* dishes of a similar size and shape exist in ovenproof china.

Deeper earthenware vessels are not often found here. Such is the kind of earthenware pot which is sold on Sundays in the *piazza* at Portofino, glazed inside and out, circular in shape, with a handle, an ideal receptacle for all kinds of *pasta*, for *risotto*, for a *cassoulet*; a capacious object which lends an air of authenticity to an Italian dish.

This emphasis on earthenware may seem outmoded when people are, perhaps, collecting glass ovenware and plastic containers, but earthenware has certain properties which give it a natural superiority. It is slow to conduct heat and provides an excellent receptacle, in the form of a crock, for fresh vegetables, for keeping milk or stock cool in jars or *pâtés* in *terrines*. It is slow to cool, and a dish of beans or potatoes cooked in the oven and taken to the table will retain their heat longer than when they are transferred to a china serving dish. Glassware is capable of the same use, but by displaying the contents of the dish on the table loses its function as a frame. Using a material as ancient as earthenware may be old fashioned but it has some bearing on the art of cooking.

These are some of the utensils which should inhabit the kitchen. A self-basting dish for use in the oven has not been mentioned because we are in some doubt as to its merits other than keeping the oven clean. As it can only operate by employing a small quantity of liquid in the form of water, stock, or vinegar, which condenses on the inside lid of the pan and drips onto the joint below, it produces a moist atmosphere which is very far from the dry conditions required for roasting. The meat is, to some extent, steamed rather than roasted, with a consequent loss of crispness and juice. This can be mitigated in the case of beef, by roasting without the lid in a very hot oven for the first quarter of an hour to seal the meat, and in the case of mutton by starting with the lid on in a moderate oven and removing it in the last twenty minutes to crisp the outside. It can be used with advantage in cooking a pheasant, whose flesh tends to dryness.

The pressure cooker really deserves a book devoted to its potentialities. We do not regard it as a centrepiece in the cook's armoury, but as a weapon with rather special range which must be used with painful exactitude. Its chief function is to reduce, in the initial stage, the cooking time of cereals such as haricot beans, chick peas, lentils, so that one can, at short notice, be ready to incorporate them in soup or casserole, and it dispenses with the need for soaking them overnight. It is excellent for curtailing the cooking time of an oxtail, which is normally about four hours and reduces it to one. In this case, the oxtail must be prepared, seasoned, and sautéd with vegetables beforehand, and it will be found that a great deal more flavour needs to be imparted initially, and much less than the normal amount of liquid used in preparing a stew which is to cook slowly. It can also be used for cooking substantial pieces of ham in a relatively short time. At the other end of the scale there is no better way of cooking potatoes in their skins or fresh green vegetables which retain their colour and taste. Merely from personal observation it seems that vegetables which are best treated by rapid boiling benefit from the pressure system, and things like haricot beans and lentils, which normally take a great deal of soaking and preliminary cooking, are effectively broken down by the pressure. In the first case the flavour is perfectly retained; in the second the flavour has, in any case, to be imparted. As a rapid stock-maker and for soups it is very good indeed.

Apart from pots and pans, there are a number of subordinate devices which are of use and without which it is often difficult to achieve the desired results. A 10-inch chef's knife is probably the first of these; it is of steel, to be kept clean with steel wool, and is expensive at about 22s. This is not to be confused with the stainless steel variety which is much cheaper but far less sharp. Then wooden spoons in different sizes; a metal spoon with perforations for skimming broth; a palette knife for sautéing and omelettes. 'Prestige' have a range of kitchen instruments with a bracket to hold them, including a palette knife, a potato-mashing device, a fish slice, and egg and batter whisks. A pestle and mortar cost about 14s. 6d. and are particularly important for making *pâtés* as well as for pounding the ingredients for stuffing fish and *ravioli*, for home-made curry powder, and for reducing herbs, spices, and shallots to a molecular state. Equally useful are a *mezzaluna*, a moon-bladed chopper, or an *háchoire*, a two-handled chopper with a straight blade, for vegetables; a *mandoline*, a slicing device with adjustable blades (13s. 6d.);

a colander, a wire sieve, a *chinois*, which is a pointed strainer for sauces, and a vegetable *mouli*, which is now sold everywhere in several sizes, for soups and *purées* (middle size about 18*s*. 6*d*.); a pepper mill (13*s*. 6*d*.), and a salt mill for *gros sel*. We would also like to put in a word for a larding needle. A pastry cutter (a fluted wheel pinned to a handle) is useful for cutting *ravioli* and *lasagne*. A glass rolling-pin and a slab of marble for pastry, found in a junkshop, are our last claims for the kitchen.

These claims may be criticized on the grounds of omission rather than of opulence. We have, in fact, left out all mention of electric mixers, coffee machines, and meat grinders, not out of prejudice, but for reasons of economy. One can make a good mayonnaise without the mixer, a good cup of coffee in a jug, and, if minced beef is required, the butcher can produce it.

To us, the most promising point of departure is the gleam of a sharp steel knife or moon-bladed chopper, the sight of an iron *cocotte* which can stand the heat of flame and hot-plate, an oval *gratin* dish which will emerge from the oven with gilded *pommes savoyardes*; objects which stimulate the imagination and yet confine our culinary thoughts to distinct possibilities. One cannot separate the *plat du jour* from the vessel it is cooked in.

The Store Cupboard

3

THE STORE CUPBOARD

WHAT the store cupboard contains is rather a personal matter, the consequence of individual habit and taste, of the size of household, and of the weekly food budget. But if this book is to be of any practical use it depends to some extent on many of the ingredients, specified in the recipes, being ready to hand in the kitchen. So we would like to propose the inclusion of certain commodities, assuming a family of four. But first it is necessary to stress one essential point.

Instead of a cupboard lined with ranks of tins – tinned soups, tinned meat, tinned vegetables and relishes – it should rather contain a collection of seasonings, spices, aromatic herbs, olive oil, beef concentrate, tomato *purée*, Spanish onions, garlic, fresh root vegetables, a bottle of wine, a flask of brandy – culinary accompaniments which can at any time be called into play, and added to these, a few pounds of staple commodities, spaghetti, rice, haricot beans, which with the minimum of trouble can be transformed into substantial dishes, a reserve against the many moments when shopping is impracticable. That really is the main object of the store cupboard, to provide meals at short notice without shopping, and, equally important, to leave one free to select carefully the piece of beef for a *gulyas* or *bœuf à la mode* without having to search at the last moment for paprika pepper or a handful of juniper berries.

It is very easy to fall into a system of hypnotic habit where shopping is concerned. The reiteration of last week's grocery order, the alternation between rolled rib and loin of lamb for the weekend joint, the attachment to a greengrocer who for some reason avoids red peppers and aubergines in season, and clings to frosted lettuce when endive, batavia, and chicory are at their best, are habits which fetter an experimental frame of mind.

But living in London the pleasures of Soho stores and street markets can distract one from the monotony of housekeeping. The wine shops, the shops loaded with different kinds of cheese, varieties of *pasta*, *salami* sausages, the jars of dried herbs and spices, the packets of fungi, the displays of vegetables and fish, can provoke almost as much interest as an early-morning saunter through the market beyond the Rialto bridge in Venice. That is an exaggeration, but there is the same sensation of variety, of unfamiliarity, and of exciting possibilities.

There are many things in this book which are easily found in any Soho store, but which the English grocer does not usually stock. Some shops, like Parmigiani's in Old Compton Street, and Schmidt's in Charlotte Street, are willing to send orders by post. For people living in the country it is a good idea to place an order from time to time with such a shop. Continental delicatessen shops are another widespread source of supply. These shops have arisen by now in many different parts of Britain. We must not leave out of account the all-embracing potentialities of Selfridges' Food Store and Harrods' Food Department. Bearing these in mind, it should be possible for those who are living in town or country to keep many of the ingredients mentioned in these recipes in the store cupboard.

Among the staple provisions are different forms of *pasta*, rice, semolina, haricot beans, and other pulses such as chick peas and lentils. In the *pasta* section there is a diagram of many types which can be bought here. They are best bought freshly made, but the packets of Italian make, for instance Buitoni and Bellolio, are excellent. Besides soup *pasta* it is worth having a few pounds of *spaghetti* to serve *al sugo* or *alla bolognese*, *lasagne*, *tagliatelli*, or *fettuccine*, plain or coloured green with spinach, and some of the larger *maccheroni* to serve *au gratin*.

Rice should be bought in two kinds: Italian rice, which has particularly absorbent qualities and a rather short and rounded grain, for *risotto*, and Patna rice for *paella*. Semolina is required for *gnocchi* and occasionally for dumplings.

Several pounds of haricot beans should be kept, particularly as one has to decide the day before to soak them. There are several kinds, but those of medium size and rather flat shape are best for *Gigot à la bretonne* or a *cassoulet*. Brown and red beans make an excellent soup, chick peas are needed for an *olla*, lentils for soup or to accompany a partridge.

Beef concentrate, dehydrated chicken *bouillon*, and some of the Knorr dehydrated soups can be used in emergency to provide stock for casseroles and braises. One of the most indispensable things is Italian concentrated tomato, *Estratto di Pomodoro*, obtainable in tins which contain sufficient to make a sauce for four people. Not only for Italian *pasta* dishes, but for soups, for fish and poultry, and for various casseroles, this tomato essence has a sweet sharp quality which cannot be replaced by any number of English tomatoes. If you can only make an occasional expedition to Soho or the larger provincial towns these are best bought in quantity. Concentrated tomato can also be bought in tubes, 1s. 9d. a large tube.

Anchovies in oil are also valuable as an ingredient for stuffing poultry, as well as for judicious use in sauces and sometimes salad dressings. Roasted pimentos are excellent in tins, to be used as a salad, as well as in some dishes in these pages.

Danish pork is one of the few tinned meats which does not taste of tin and preserving matter. It is contained in its own fat which is good for sautéing vegetables prior to making a dish. There are also small tins of *pâté de foie* which are quite inexpensive and can be used as an ingredient in a stuffing for fish or fowl.

Parmesan cheese and matured *Pecorino* will keep indefinitely, and though expensive, are economical in use, and are needed to impart their special flavour to *minestrone*, rice, and *pasta* dishes.

Olives should be bought by the pound, far cheaper than in bottles, and can be stored by immersion in olive oil. Black olives, particularly, are recommended for use in cooking.

These imperishable stores are complemented by a string of Spanish onions, a head or two of garlic, a pound of shallots, a few small leeks, carrots, celery, and, needless to say, potatoes, although they do not properly belong to the store cupboard, but rather to an earthenware crock in the kitchen or larder. Together they represent some staple stores which with plain flour, for a *quiche*, *pizza*, or ribbon *pasta*, can be regularly bought.

There are a number of preserves which can best be made at home and which are excellent accompaniments to meat and game; besides

red currant and mint jelly, quince jelly with venison, marmalade
with cold veal, cranberry jam with turkey, gooseberry jam with
pork, and apple and tomato chutney for lamb and mutton are some
of them.

The cupboard should of course contain Demerara as well as
granulated, lump, and castor sugar; Demerara or Barbados sugar
is used for boiling ham, and for *soupe à l'oignon*. Block salt is to be
preferred for most culinary activities, the refined salt being relatively
tasteless. For the table sea salt (grey salt), which can be obtained
from Roche's in Old Compton Street (or Tidman's Sea Salt from
chemists) and requires a salt mill, tastes sharper than rock salt and
is a noticeable improvement on all other table salt, though more
expensive.

Red and white wine vinegar are needed for cooking, malt vinegar
can be reserved for pickling; red for salad dressing, for adding to
braises and casseroles, a good substitute if wine is lacking, and
sometimes to complement it, and white for a fish *court-bouillon*, for
sauce tartare, sauce remoulade, and for French mustard. Tarragon
vinegar which can be made at home by steeping tarragon leaves for
a few hours in white wine vinegar is used for sauces for fish and
poultry.

Certain fats are suitable as a cooking medium for particular
dishes. What a feeling of distaste is inspired by those amorphous
bowls of fat that contain the sediment of frying-pans, the dregs of
mutton from the baking tin, the skimmings of the boiled bacon.
The fat of pork, beef, veal, ham, and bacon have each their different
taste, which should be kept separate. Mutton fat has a taste of sheep
when used in cooking. The fat parts of a pig's head or belly when
rendered down is purer, whiter, and better tasting than lard bought
from the grocer, though an exception might be found in the best
Danish lard. It is better to cook with bacon fat, or pork fat, or beef
or veal dripping, when preparing meat dishes, even if it means a
little extra labour in rendering or clarifying, than to cook with lard
or margarine, both of which can be used for pastry. The proposals
in most of these recipes cannot be considered as extravagant, and
there is not an exaggerated use of butter. But when butter is one
of the ingredients there is no hint of margarine acting as a substitute. The same applies to olive oil. Olive oil, apart from its merit

of attaining a greater intensity of heat without burning than animal fats, is economical in use and more digestible. But presumably owing to the expense of canning, it is progressively cheaper as the size of container increases. It is therefore best to buy it in gallon cans and never in little half-pint salad bottles. In fact the oil sold in bottled form is not infrequently adulterated with tea-seed or nut oil. Italy, Spain, and Greece produce oil which is canned and imported. Spanish oil has only recently come back into general distribution since the war, and is cheaper than the Italian brands. Greek oil is rather thinner and more delicate, but if you enjoy the actual taste of the olive, Spanish and Italian oil is hard to equal, and oil from Lucca is the best. Few English people realize the variations in quality of olive oil. Buying a demijohn of oil in Florence is as serious a matter as buying a dozen bottles of claret here, and a great deal of consideration precedes the choice. It is wise therefore to economize in buying by the gallon oil of Spanish, Italian, or Greek provenance, and it will be found far more agreeable in cooking and hardly more expensive than the sum of all the margarine and packets of lard which it replaces. Those who actively dislike the taste of olive oil might try ground-nut oil which is effective and cheaper.

Many of the recipes in this book call for the use of wine. One of our objects is to outline meals which are simple in conception but to which a glass of wine naturally belongs. This provides a chance of accumulating what is left in the kitchen, red wines being decanted into one bottle, and white wines into another. When preparing a meal for a special occasion there is nothing for it but to buy a cheap bottle of wine for cooking. For some dishes, for *Alose à la piquerette* or for a *matelote*, one should buy the best wine one can afford. White wines used in cooking should be on the dry side. Perhaps a reasonable point of view in the matter of table wine versus kitchen wine is to slightly overestimate table needs, and spare half a pint of wine to cook the *plat du jour* which it is to accompany. In general, a dish in which a particular wine has been used requires a wine of a similar nature to accompany it. On the same principle fish or rabbit cooked in cider can very well have cider served with it. As far as brandy is concerned some fish and meat dishes are enriched by its use, provided that the alcohol is volatilized by setting light to it, either in a spoon before pouring it over the object or in the pan itself, but it doesn't mean that the dish is ruined if it is omitted. It is an improvement and it sometimes has the effect of removing a trace of oiliness which may appear for instance in a *matelote*. We are unfortunate in that wine in this country cannot be taken as a matter of course. We can only use it with economy but it is no exaggeration to say that it alters the whole complexion of cooking, and provides an inspiration to the cook. Olive oil and wine both draw one out of the pedestrian path of Irish stew and shepherds' pie into the realms of culinary invention and imagination.

Aromatics

AROMATICS

Salt

SALT is, before all, the first essential in the preparation of food. As a culinary agent its principal effects are the imparting and release of flavour, and its action as a preservative. In the *pot-au-feu*, for example, salt is used to hasten the extraction of the juices of the meat, while *gros sel* (sea salt) is served with the resulting *bouilli* to impart some flavour to meat which has been deprived of its juices by long simmering.

To taste sea salt ground from a salt mill is to have the impression of tasting salt for the first time. And yet most people put up with refined rock salt for table and culinary purposes because it runs easily and the grocer sells it. Let us hope that more people will discover the merit of sea salt even if they restrict its use on grounds of trouble and expense to the table. Rock salt in block is already an improvement on table salt, and should be used both in the kitchen and at table in the absence of sea salt.

Sugar plays a smaller but useful part in releasing flavour, even in savoury dishes, in sauces and soups.

Onions, Shallots, and Garlic

But, if salt is the first essential, it is the onion in its many forms whose discreet use is at the base of the fugitive aromas which emanate from the kitchen, used in association with a variety of fresh herbs and their fruits, root vegetables, citrus fruits, mushrooms and toadstools.

The onion tribe are all included in the genus *Allium* which belongs to the plant order *Lilliaceae*. The principal species, *Allium Cepa*, comprise a number of onion varieties which are characterized by their hollow fleshy leaves and prominent bulbs at the base of the stem, and range between large, good-keeping onions, like 'Bedfordshire Champion' and 'Giant Zittau', to the small clustered red shallot which is so much more in use in French kitchens than in ours. The Spanish onions cultivated for export by the Bretons round Roscoff are quite different in quality from the harder, better-keeping but more pungent onion varieties grown here. They are more fleshy, milder in flavour, with a mauve or pinkish tinge resembling the shallot, and though more expensive bought by the string, are more valuable in the preparation of a sauce or braise than their English counterparts. The little flat white bulbs, 'Paris Silverskinned' for instance, usually imported from France, are to be found in Soho greengrocers, and these are the variety which should be used for *poulet bonne femme* and *matelotes*. The flat white bulbs, medium sized, 'White Lisbon' and 'White Portugal' varieties, are best for pickling.

Several onion species are grown for their leaves alone, particularly perennial tufted chives (*Allium Schoenoprasum*), and the Welsh Onion. Chives are usually included in the category of culinary herbs, probably because their bulbs are practically nonexistent, and because they undergo the same treatment of fine-chopping as herbs such as parsley, chervil, mint, and savory, with which they combine so well. The flat-leaved alliums, the leek and garlic, are less highly prized here as sources of flavouring, leeks more often being treated as a vegetable, and garlic being used either too flagrantly or not at all. To the French it would be inconceivable to dispense with leeks, which have a sweeter and more delicate flavour than onions, and impart it to many braises, *mirepoix*, as well as to the *pot-au-feu* and *la soupe aux poireaux et aux haricots*.

Garlic probably has the most remarkable properties of the onion genus. It has a benevolent effect on the human system, encouraging transpiration and clearing the respiratory organs. Any one who has attempted the recipe for *Lièvre à la royale* described in every detail by Senator Couteaux in Elizabeth David's *A Book of Mediterranean Food*, which contains 20 cloves of garlic and twice that quantity of shallots, will be aware of the invasive powers of this extraordinary bulb. Some hours after eating this dish, there is a peculiar sensation of liberation in the head, and it is as if one had acquired a completely new sense of smell. This is also experienced when preparing an *aïoli*. But as a rule garlic must be used with discretion. Its use in *Lièvre à la royale* is exceptional, and is an example of how, even when used in large quantities, both garlic and shallot can conceal their presence. In M. Couteaux' own words, 'the chopping of the garlic and the shallots must be so fine that each of them attain as nearly as possible a molecular state. This', he says, 'is one of the first conditions of success of this marvellous dish, in which the multiple and diverse perfumes and aromas melt into a whole so harmonious that neither one dominates, nor discloses its particular origin, and so arouse some preconceived prejudice, however regrettable.'

Let us not be prejudiced against the garlic, but take trouble to reduce it to a molecular state at the point of the knife or in the mortar, to combine it with basil and parmesan cheese in a *pesto* for flavouring a *minestrone*, to fry thin slices of it in olive oil with mushrooms or *cèpes*, so that it may impart its extraordinary properties to savoury dishes.

Herbs

There is usually a rather confusing distinction made between pot-herbs and sweet herbs, which was originally enforced by Mr Loudon in his *Encyclopaedia of Gardening* and persists in gardening catalogues. Pot-herbs included parsley, purslane, tarragon, fennel, borage, dill, chervil, horseradish, Indian cress, and marigold. Sweet herbs were thyme, sage, savory, clary, mint, marjoram, basil, rosemary, lavender, tansy, and costmary.

As there is no logical basis for these two categories, it is much easier to remember that culinary herbs belong, with a few noteworthy exceptions, to two botanical families, the *Labiatae* and *Umbelliferae*. The members of the *Labiatae* group have their leaves impregnated with little glands containing a volatile oil, which is present to some extent in the flowers as well and produces a characteristic fragrance when rubbed or crushed. Marjoram, basil, rosemary, lavender, sage, mint, savoury, thyme, and balm belong to this order. In the plants belonging to the *Umbelliferae*, the oil is present chiefly in the fruits (seeds), though in the case of parsley, fennel, chervil, and lovage the leaves or fronds are very fragrant and widely used in cooking, while dill, annise, caraway, coriander, and cumin are used chiefly in seed form. The principal exceptions to this division of culinary herbs into two families are tarragon which belongs to the *Compositae*, borage to the *Boraginaceae*, and sweet bay to the *Lauraceae* families, each of which contain their fragrance in their leaves and flowers.

As the source of the fragrance of culinary herbs lies in this volatile oil, certain practices have been evolved to release it. Fine chopping, bruising, pounding are obvious simple ways of doing so. So is the application of heat, in its simplest form by putting a faggot of herbs in with the roasting joint, or in a soup or casserole. The Italian practice of finely chopping basil or marjoram with garlic, and putting it into the pan in hot olive oil before sautéing some pieces of meat for a stew, or the rice for a *risotto*, is an excellent way of flavouring a dish, as the fragrance of the herbs and garlic is more readily extracted by the action of the hot oil than it is by long simmering or boiling. But this method prevents one removing the actual herbs from the dish, and may be a reason for the French criticism of Italian cookery for being too highly seasoned, implying that herbs should be savoured but not seen.

There are customary combinations of herbs which have acquired a name (usually French) through long association, the faggot of parsley, thyme, and sweet bay, the *bouquet garni*, being the most familiar, and even the English cook's indispensable addition to soups and casseroles. There is *ravigote* which brings together tarragon, chervil, parsley, burnet, and chives, and which derives from the verb *ravigoter*, 'to cheer or strengthen'. This invigorating combination is used finely chopped in salads, for *ravigote* butter to serve with steaks or fish, and for *sauce ravigote* and *sauce tartare*.

Fines herbes do not represent a special collection of sweet herbs, the *fines* referring to the fine chopping required, and not to the delicacy of particular plants. *Fines herbes* can consist simply of parsley and a blanched shallot, or include chives, a little mint, basil, tarragon, chervil, and savory, and are used principally as a flavouring for an omelette, for *sauce rémoulade*, and for stuffing fish.

More often herbs are made to associate with onion, shallot, garlic, or leek, with carrots and sometimes celery, for flavouring stews and braises. A *mirepoix* is the name for a convenient collection of herbs and vegetables answering this purpose. Two carrots, two onions, two shallots, two bay leaves, a sprig of thyme, and a clove of garlic are minced very small with a quarter of a pound of fat bacon and a quarter of a pound of raw ham. The concoction is then set on the fire with a little oil or butter and after a few minutes is ready to impart its flavour to soup, braise, or stew. If wine is to be used in the dish, a glass of red or white wine is added to the *mirepoix*, the heat being raised for a moment to evaporate the alcoholic content of the wine and allow it to diffuse its aroma. In the case of *Carpe à la Chambord* a bottle of wine is added to the *mirepoix*.

Clearly, much depends for culinary subtlety on the combination of different herbs with the onion family, and with root vegetables. Italians, both in Tuscany and Venezia, use carrot and celery with garlic, shallot, or leek, as a point of departure, and many of their recipes begin with an instruction to make a *battuto* (hash), or *soffritto* (literally, under-frying) of these vegetables, sautéing them in a little oil as the preparation for a dish. In the back streets of Venice, greengrocers display a small still-life, two carrots and half a celery plant, all ready for the cook. Italian celery is smaller, greener, more fine-leaved, and in fact more herb-like than the forced celery sold here.

A triumphant combination, which as far as we know has no name, is a garlic clove teased to a pulp with the point of a cook's blade, slid into hot olive oil with some fresh mushrooms and chopped parsley, to be served with a steak, or as a dressing for baked fish. The French would probably maintain that better still is the combination of mushrooms, parsley, and shallots which they have named *Duxelles*. This was an invention of La Varenne, the first great French cook of modern times, who in his cookery book published in Paris about 1650 described himself as *Escuyer de Cuisine de M. le Marquis d'Uxelles*. The mushrooms for *Duxelles* are washed and quartered, pressed between two plates with a slice of onion over heat to remove any moisture. They are then sautéd with fresh butter, parsley, and shallots, and allowed to simmer until tender. Cream may be added, and is particularly suitable when the *Duxelles* is used as a relish for fish cooked in a *court-bouillon*.

Very few enthusiastic cooks rely on the half-dead mint, the wilting parsley to be found at the greengrocer's. The fragrance withers with the plant's exposure. The smallest garden usually contains these herbs, with thyme, chives, sage, and fennel, and sometimes lavender and rosemary. Sweet bay is also usually to hand. Winter and summer savory, marjoram, borage, chervil, tarragon, and basil are more rarely found. Basil, without which no dish of *pasta* can approach the Italian original in flavour or fragrance, is not always easy to grow in our climate. In a wet summer, though the seed germinates, the plant makes little growth unless removed to a greenhouse, and if left out of doors it is killed by the first frost. It is worth taking trouble with it, before having recourse to the dried and powdered form which can be obtained at Culpeper House or at Roche in Old Compton Street. Borage, on the other hand, is a hairy, vigorous annual, which hardly requires any cultivation. Its limited use in salads, into which its tender shoots and blue flowers are sometimes put to add a taste of cucumber, is compensated for by its very pretty appearance in the garden, and its habit of self-propagation.

There are two varieties of marjoram which can be grown for cooking purposes, *Origanum Onites*, and *Origanum Majorana*. The first grows wild in Mediterranean areas, thriving on poor mountainous soil, and is the herb referred to as *Oregano* in Italian cookery books. It is gathered when coming into flower in May, dried, and sold in fragrant spiky bunches by Italian greengrocers. *Origanum Majorana* is a native of North Africa. Both are grown here as annuals, being liable to wither in the frost. Neither has the sweet strong fragrance of the wild plant, but this lack of intensity must be familiar to anyone who has compared plants growing in their native habitat with those transplanted to different climates and soil conditions.

Chervil is rather a neglected herb, perhaps because it is not used alone as a source of flavouring. But as one of the ingredients of *fines herbes* and *ravigote* it deserves to be grown more, particularly as it is simple to cultivate and the leaves can be used six to eight weeks after sowing. Savory, of which the annual summer variety and the perennial winter kind are both particularly useful with meat and fish, can be used with chervil and parsley in casseroles and soups.

The summer savory, apart from germinating very slowly, is quite simple to cultivate.

No attempt has been made to go into botanical details or outline the requirements for the cultivation of these plants. There are several excellent books on the subject, for instance *Culinary Herbs and Condiments*, by M. Grive, F.R.H.S., Heinemann, 1933 (with one serious omission: saffron). There are seed merchants who specialize in the supply of seeds for culinary purposes. Thompson and Morgan, of Ipswich, who have a very full list, come particularly to mind, and Herb Farms, which supply the plants themselves (see list of suppliers, p. 291). We have only wanted to make the point that herbs used for the fragrance contained in their leaves are best in fresh condition, with its obvious corollary that a wider selection of culinary herbs could be grown along many garden paths.

TARRAGON VINEGAR

Tarragon is esteemed by the French; we are inclined to pay lip service to this plant by having a bottle of tarragon vinegar in the kitchen and forgetting to use it. It is its peculiar tartness which makes it an ideal accompaniment to fish. It does not often ripen its seeds in this country, and is best grown from an existing root or cutting. The variety for use in cooking is French tarragon, which has dark, smooth green leaves, and not its paler relation, Russian tarragon, which lacks sharpness.

Tarragon vinegar:
Fill a wide-mouthed vessel with tarragon leaves, picked on a dry day, when the plant is coming into flower, when the leaves contain the maximum flavour. Cover the leaves with white wine vinegar, and allow the concoction to infuse for five or six hours. Then strain the vinegar through a cloth and bottle it, corking tightly.

This vinegar can be used for mixing mustard, for *sauce tartare*, and as an ingredient of fish sauces. (See also *Poulet à l'estragon*.)

SAGE IN CLARET

Sage is too well known and too easy to grow for discussion. It must be used with discretion as it has a very pungent flavour. *The Cook's Oracle*, 1821, proposes a little-known use for sage.

2 oz green sage leaves, 1 oz fresh lemon peel pared thinly, 1 oz salt, a pinch of cayenne pepper, and a few drops of citric acid (obtainable from the chemist) are steeped for fourteen days in a pint of claret. The bottle is shaken every day. After this period the contents of the bottle should be allowed to settle, when the infusion is decanted into a clean bottle and tightly corked.

This can be used to add to the juices of roast pork, duck, or goose, when the fat has been poured off, to make a gravy, as an addition to a veal goulash or to an onion sauce for haricot beans.

SAGE SAUCE FOR ROAST PORK

A small handful of sage leaves, two onions, a teaspoonful of flour, a teaspoonful of vinegar, 1 oz of butter, ½ pint of gravy, salt, pepper.
Scald the sage leaves and chop them with the onions to a fine hash. Melt the butter in a pan, put in the sage and onion hash, sprinkle with flour, and allow to cook for ten minutes. Add the vinegar, gravy, and seasoning. Cook gently for half an hour.

Drying Herbs

If for lack of greenhouse facilities a supply of herbs cannot be kept up beyond the limited range of those which will survive the winter, it is a good thing to dry your own in summertime rather than buy the rather colourless herb packets in grocers' shops. Garden herbs, picked straight out of the garden (early morning, sunny day) when the plant is coming into flower, dried in the airing cupboard, rubbed through a sieve and put into airtight glass jars, with a little salt and a scrape of dried lemon peel, and stored in a dark place, not only keep their fresh green colour, but retain their flavour. But not for ever. The oil is fugitive, the fragrance lasts a winter through. This is perhaps the explanation for indifferent shop-bought herbs. This method of drying is much better than merely hanging up bunches of marjoram, mint, and thyme in the kitchen, where though they look pretty they collect dust and lose much of their strength.

A HERB MIXTURE

Gather ¼ lb parsley, ¼ lb lemon thyme, ¼ lb sweet marjoram, ¼ lb winter savoury, and 2 oz sweet basil. Dry these herbs in the airing cupboard. Strip them of their stalks and put them through a wire sieve. Take 2 oz dried lemon peel and pound it with ¼ oz celery seed and a teaspoonful of salt. Pound 6 bay leaves to a powder and add them to the other finely powdered herbs, with the lemon peel and celery seed. Mix all together and pass through a fine sieve. Put the resultant powder into bottles, stopper them well, and keep them in the dark.

A FRENCH RECIPE FOR A HERB MIXTURE

3 oz dried thyme, 3 oz dried bay leaves, 1½ oz dried marjoram, 1½ oz dried rosemary, 3 oz nutmeg or mace, 3 oz paprika pepper, and 1½ oz ground black pepper.

Strip the stalks from the herbs. Pound all these ingredients to a powder in a mortar and then pass the mixture through a fine sieve. Put into bottles and stopper them securely.

Herb Fruits and Spices

The fruits or seeds of plants used in cooking have their own peculiar uses, and are on the whole more ignored by English cooks. A dislike of seedcake in childhood makes some people reject caraway for other purposes. An addiction to curry powder in tins produces an unfamiliarity with its refreshing and pungent constituents. Herb fruits known and grown in this country such as caraway, coriander, dill, and juniper (which is properly a shrub), originate in more favourable climates and are usually grouped with condiments and spices grown in the Mediterranean, the Levant, and the Far East, when discussing their culinary merits. These are nutmeg, mace, capsicum (from which cayenne pepper is derived), black and white peppers, ginger, cinnamon (which is the rolled bark of the cassia tree), cloves, wholespice, saffron (which was once grown in quantity round Saffron Walden), cumin, and anise.

These spices are used in association by Jewish people who appreciate pungent food. They are employed a great deal in Alsatian cookery, and to a rather lesser degree in Provence. They operate not only as tastes, but as stimulants to appetite and aids to transpiration in warmer climates. In our own climate their use is largely a matter of personal taste and experiment.

The main principle is to avoid packets of mixed spice, and to buy, in their whole state an ounce at a time, some of the spices mentioned here. Experiments can be made with dill and potato salad, caraway and wholespice with red cabbage, coriander crushed with juniper berries and knobs of cloves for a beef casserole or as a garnish for baked fish. The most effective way of communicating the flavour to the meat is to roll the pieces in the crushed fruits before firing the meat in hot oil. This is similar to the *entrecôte au poivre* in which raw steak is beaten and rolled in crushed peppercorns and quickly grilled or fired in a red-hot pan. Both have a very tenderizing effect on the meat, and there is a delicious flavour without too much heat. Something of the same effect occurs when coriander, cumin, caraway, or anise are pounded together with a little garlic and used as a dressing for fish which is to be baked in olive oil or grilled.

Herbs and condiments must be used in this way to produce a subtle flavour. Cloves can be quite disgusting if used in excess. It is preferable to use only the knob of the clove, which can be powdered between the fingers, in *ragoûts* and stews and to confine the nail end of the clove in an onion when boiling ham or preparing a *court-bouillon*. Cinnamon, on the other hand, is not used enough in meat dishes. A fragment of cinnamon bark, broken off and ground with a rolling-pin or in a mortar, can be used in stews, and a piece of bark should be put into the saucepan when boiling ham. Nutmeg is a spice which is used more freely on the Continent than here, particularly in Italy where potatoes mashed with butter and milk are flavoured with nutmeg and a little sugar, and it is used in the stuffings of milk-curd cheese for *ravioli*, and sometimes with veal.

As a rule herb fruits, condiments, and spices are employed as culinary stimulants. This is borne out very clearly in the effects of a *soupe à l'oignon* which is highly peppered and reviving, and in the preparation of a home-made curry powder. Tinned curry powder is a poor thing in comparison with the pleasure of pounding these olfactory stimulants. It is worth making about 6 ounces at a time, as it is vigorous work.

A CURRY POWDER

$2\frac{1}{2}$ oz powdered turmeric, 2 oz coriander seed, $\frac{1}{2}$ oz powdered ginger, $\frac{1}{4}$ oz whole black peppers, $\frac{1}{4}$ oz powdered cayenne pepper, $\frac{1}{4}$ oz whole cardamom seeds, 13 cloves.

Turmeric (which provides the colour for a curry powder), ginger, and cayenne are best bought in powdered form. The other ingredients should be pounded separately in a mortar, before combining all the other ingredients and mixing them into a homogeneous powder. The knobs only of the cloves should be used or, if preferred, half the quantity of wholespice.

This commentary on the possibilities of combining aromatic flavours in the preparation of food does not pretend to be comprehensive. We have tried to establish the importance of imagination and experiment applied to the many sources of taste at our disposal. Cooking is mere chemistry if it is concerned only with the correct application of heat to different foods. In the consideration of flavours, released or imparted, it approaches art.

Applying the Heat

APPLYING THE HEAT

THE object of cooking is, to put it in its lowest terms, to bring about a transformation in food which would offend were it presented in its natural state. The alteration of taste and texture, the transformation of what is by nature tough into something tender, the development of a crude taste into a delicate flavour, are the result of chemical changes brought about by the application of heat, in the form of grilling, roasting before the fire, baking in the oven, immersion in boiling water or hot fat, and similar processes.

Most culinary disasters are the result of a failure to apply the proper intensity of heat, for the proper length of time – misjudgements arising from a lack of experience which only practice and an understanding of the chemical changes brought about in cooking can rectify.

Some people may quarrel with this attempt to define culinary operations. It is intended to serve as a guide to those who consult these recipes.

Boiling

Water boils at a temperature of 212 deg. F. The term 'boiling' is commonly misused, 'boiled ham', 'boiled beef', 'boiled mutton', for instance, being in fact only submitted to boiling temperature for a few moments to seal the surface of the meat, before being gently simmered at a temperature well below 212 deg. F. Actual boiling is usually of short duration, and followed by a period of simmering or poaching in respect of meat or fish. It is maintained:

1. For the rapid reduction of a sauce, for instance when the liquor, in which a joint of meat or piece of poultry has been braised, is to be reduced before serving as a sauce; or to concentrate the liquor of a *court-bouillon*.

47

2. For blanching green vegetables, i.e. green peas, cabbage, broad beans, *haricots verts*, which are boiled for eight to ten minutes according to size and age before being tossed in butter.

3. For cooking *spaghetti* and other forms of *pasta* before they are treated with a sauce; for boiling rice.

4. In the preparation of jams and preserves. After the sugar has been added, rapid boiling is enforced to set the jam in the shortest possible time without loss of flavour.

Poaching

This has a far wider application in culinary practice, and refers usually to a process which has been called 'a boiling which does not boil'. It is best illustrated in the use of a *court-bouillon* for fish, in which an aromatic liquid is prepared in advance by simmering water and wine, or water and wine vinegar, with root vegetables, herbs, and spices, and allowing it to cool. When the time has come to poach a fine fish, the *court-bouillon* is brought to the boil, the fish is put in, the heat raised until boiling is re-established, to seal the outer surface of the fish and conserve its juices. The heat is then turned down while the fish is gently poached with the lid on, the surface of the liquid only just being disturbed by a bubble rising here and there. With small fish the process is of course curtailed. The chief points to watch are:

1. The vessel in which the fish is cooked should be of a size to permit the complete immersion of the fish in the liquid.

2. The poaching liquid should be used after reduction as the basis of an accompanying sauce, being not only well-flavoured in advance but enriched by whatever juices have escaped from the fish.

Simmering

Simmering is in effect much the same as poaching, but the term is used with regard to meat, and because of the coarser texture of meat it is often a prolonged operation. Simmering can take place on top of the stove or in a low oven, and is a term which applies equally to the slow process by which the juices are extracted from meat and vegetables in the preparation of broth, or the slow cooking which breaks down the fibres of meat in a stew or casserole, although this latter process is better known as stewing.

Stewing

Stewing applies to a preparation of meat and vegetables which have first been sautéd in a suitable fat to seal the meat and conserve its juices, and to allow it to take on some colour which not only improves the appearance of the dish, but develops the roasted flavours which only appear when meat is subjected to a high temperature (i.e. through frying in fat or grilling). Some liquid is then added and the casserole or heavy pan is lidded and allowed to stew very slowly until the meat is tender. In this twofold process the flavours which are at first contained by sautéing are later released in the process of stewing. Irish stew is probably one of the few exceptions to our definition of a stew, in that there is no previous sautéing of either onions, lamb (or mutton), or potatoes. Stewing temperature is 170 deg. F.

Sautéing (sauter)

This term covers a fairly wide range of operations and temperatures. The initial sautéing of meat when making a stew is done in either oil, bacon fat, butter, or lard, not only to prevent its juices immediately escaping when the stewing or simmering is instigated, but to produce the roasted flavour brought about by slightly carbonizing the exterior of the meat. The meaning of the word, to jump or toss, refers to the shaking of the pan and the disturbance of its contents to bring about the browning of the meat without allowing it to burn. When the meat is cooked the pan is swilled out with wine or stock.

The word also applies to the preparation of mushrooms, onions, and green and root vegetables, either as a preliminary to their inclusion in a stew or braise, or for serving on their own. In the case of mushrooms and green vegetables, the process is carried out by gently cooking in butter with a lid on the pan to minimize evaporation, and shaking from time to time to prevent sticking. In the Italian kitchen the term *soffritto* exactly expresses this latter process, meaning under-frying, and is used a great deal in the creation of *risotti* and in the preparation of sauces for *pasta* dishes (q.v.).

Braising

Braising is an operation referring to joints of meat, saddle of hare, whole chicken, duck, and smaller birds, in which they are contained in a heavy lidded iron or copper *cocotte* and cooked very slowly in a minimum of liquid, stock, or wine, after an initial firing in hot oil, butter, or lard. As a rule, the meat, hen, duck, or fish is laid on a *mirepoix* or vegetable bed of chopped and sauté onions, shallots, herbs, and root vegetables, and a little bacon, which are to communicate their flavour both to the object braised, and to the sauce. After cooking, the sauce is then strained and reduced by rapid boiling, and is served with the meat or bird. Sometimes, as in *Canard aux olives* or *Canard aux navets*, an additional condiment is prepared apart, and added to the strained sauce. Braising was originally carried out in copper *braisières* which were capable of sustaining live charcoal on their lids. In this way the heat was applied from above as well as from below, on top of the stove, producing a combination of stewing and roasting. Now that this is no longer the case, the braise is usually started on top of the stove and completed in the oven, which is awkward as it requires basting. This is necessary because the liquid in which it cooks tends to reduce and there is the danger of the meat drying. For this reason, and perhaps formerly as a protection against the heat from above, the piece of meat, or whatever it is, is usually larded.

Larding

Larding bacon should be bought and sliced into neat pieces two to three inches long, ⅜ inch wide, and ⅛ inch thick. The strips of bacon should be dusted with salt, pepper, nutmeg, and appropriate spices, and if possible soaked in a little brandy for an hour before use though this is not essential. The strips are used in the proportion of three ounces of fat to each pound of meat, and are inserted horizontally into the meat by means of a larding needle.

Marinading

If the meat is of rather poor quality or the bird shows signs of age, or you think the flavour of some river fish would be improved by immersing it for some hours in a preparation of wine and aromatic vegetables, this does not substantially alter the method of braising. The vegetables for the marinade should include thickly sliced onions and carrots, in the proportion of one ounce of each to one pound of meat, with four ounces of bacon skin, a clove of garlic, and a bouquet of herbs. The meat (whether larded or not) is seasoned with salt, pepper, and spices, placed on some of the vegetables in an earthenware vessel, covered with the rest, and wine poured over, ¼ pint being allowed per pound of meat. The meat should be left in the marinade for about six hours, and should be turned about three or four times in it, the vegetables being replaced on top of the meat, after turning.

When it is removed it must be well dried in a cloth before being browned in oil or fat. The vegetables and bacon skins are likewise removed, and dried before sautéing to accompany the meat. The marinade itself is put in a pan and reduced by boiling before providing the liquid for the braise.

Braising is complicated and requires care. But the result should be meat or fowl which is more tender and delicate in flavour than can be attained by any other method of preparation. The cooking utensil must conform to the size of the meat or bird to be cooked, as only in this way can one economize on the wine or stock required to cover the meat, and at the same time ensure a sauce which is both concentrated and well-flavoured. Larousse's definition of a braise is: '*Faire cuire au feu doux, sans évaporation, de manière que les viandes conservent tous leurs sucs.*'

Cooking en daube

This is a very similar process to braising, only it usually applies to pieces of beef or chicken which have been cut up or jointed, cooked with vegetables and herbs in the slowest possible way, the lid being hermetically sealed (see *Bœuf en daube*).

Cooking à la poêle

This is a method of preparation which is sometimes referred to in cookery books in rather vague terms. A *poêle* is an iron frying-pan. But *à la poêle* usually refers to a dish prepared in a covered casserole. The method is applied to the better cuts of meat and poultry, i.e. those which merit roasting, and is akin to braising, but instead of using wine or *bouillon* to immerse the braise, butter only is used and the object is frequently basted.

The meat or poultry is placed on a *mirepoix* of finely minced carrots, chopped onions, and two chopped sticks of celery, a table-spoonful of lean diced ham or bacon, with half a bay leaf and a sprig of thyme, all of which have been previously sautéd in butter, the sauté-pan being swilled out with a little Madeira or sherry. The meat is seasoned and covered with melted butter. The cover is then put on the pan and the *cocotte* placed in a moderate oven, being allowed to cook for approximately the same time as it would normally take to roast, that is, 15–20 minutes per pound of meat. When the meat is tender, the lid is removed so that the surface can brown. It is then moved to a serving dish and kept warm while a sauce is prepared, using the vegetable base as a foundation to which a little good stock is added before passing it through a sieve. Any fat must be skimmed off the surface of the sauce, and it is then served separately in a sauceboat.

Grilling

Grilling generally applies to the finer, most tender, and smaller cuts of meat or fish and to small birds like pigeons when young and tender. Also to vegetables or fungi which contain a high degree of moisture. Two factors must be borne in mind. The object is submitted to a fierce heat. To prevent the surface exposed to this fierceness from drying, the meat or fish should be brushed over with olive oil or melted butter beforehand. If there is any doubt about the tenderness of meat, it will be improved by preliminary marinading in wine vinegar and olive oil, or in olive oil and lemon juice (particularly veal or mutton). Steaks or *schnitzel* cuts should be beaten with the blunt edge of a chef's knife. The grill must be so hot that it immediately produces an outer coating on the meat through which no juice can escape. The seizure should be effected on both sides before the heat is moderated to complete the cooking. When turning the meat a spatula or tongs, rather than a fork, must be used to avoid piercing the tissue and freeing the juice. If the grill is incapable of producing this instantaneous effect through lack of intensity, pan-grilling can be substituted, particularly in respect of fillets of steak and *schnitzel* cuts. A frying-pan is heated till it is nearly red hot. When the steak has been beaten, flattened, and seasoned, pour a very little oil on the bottom of the pan, sufficient only to prevent burning, and slap the steak into the pan. Leave it for a few moments before turning it over, but be careful not to let it burn. This produces practically the same results as grilling, though more perilous in execution. Electric grills are better than gas grills, red-hot coke or coal is better still, and charcoal is best.

Frying

Frying is the immersing in very hot fat or oil of various forms of food. All the merit of good frying consists in *la surprise*, which is the term applied to the seizure of the boiling oil on the exterior of what is being fried at the moment of immersion. This carbonization of the exterior forms a protection which prevents the grease from penetrating, conserves the juices, and allows the object cooked to retain all its taste. The oil or fat must be well heated in advance in a receptacle which, to prevent accident, should be twice as large as the quantity of oil employed. The temperature can be tested by dropping in a few crumbs of bread. If they brown, crisp, and fizz instantly, the oil is hot enough. Whatever is to be fried should receive a coating of egg and breadcrumbs, batter, or in the case of very small fish a dusting of flour. Salt is applied only after frying, and whatever has been cooked must be thoroughly drained on absorbent paper, so that no trace of oil or grease adheres. Olive oil is the best frying medium as it is capable of reaching the highest temperature, nearly three times the temperature of boiling water, 554 deg. F. to be precise, without burning. Clarified beef fat is good. So is ground-nut oil. Lard, though used a great deal, invariably makes the food look and taste greasy. Mutton fat should never be used for deep frying on account of its penetrating smell. Unless there is a large volume of hot fat, the objects to be immersed should be put in one at a time, so that the temperature of the fat is not abruptly lowered. Food that is deep fat fried should not be kept waiting before serving.

Suitable subjects for this process are:

Fish – Whole whiting, fillets of sole, plaice, cod, gudgeon, sprats, Dublin Bay prawns, *scampi*, scallops, fresh pilchards, whitebait.

Meat – *Croquettes*, jointed poultry or rabbit, veal *schnitzel*, breaded lamb cutlets, brains.

Vegetables – Potatoes in many forms, sliced aubergines, hearts of globe artichokes, Jerusalem artichokes cut in chips, small pieces of cauliflower.

Shallow Frying

Shallow frying has long been recognized as a particularly English form of cooking, and is the only culinary accomplishment of many people. It is successful for bacon, egg, and sausages, in spite of the fact that bacon is often improved in flavour by grilling. But it is not so effective for frying flat fish, where there is a risk of mutilation in turning them over. Lamb or mutton chops are better grilled or cooked in earthenware in the oven than in a frying-pan where they are subjected to only partial heat. Liver is an exception, provided the pan is very hot, the liver is seasoned, and the amount of oil or butter used is very small. Effective frying must take place at the same intensity of heat as grilling heat. At such a heat when the pan is very hot indeed, a steak can be adequately cooked, liver can be browned outside and remain tender within, pancakes can be tossed, and omelettes can be achieved with the proper rapidity.

Under-frying or sautéing, which takes place at a lower temperature and which is such an important part of cooking, is dealt with under the separate heading, SAUTÉING.

Roasting

Roasting temperatures vary between 350 and 450 deg. F. which is about double the heat of boiling water. Roasting means the direct application of heat to joints of meat, poultry, and game before a clear fire, basting the while, at a temperature sufficient to brown but not burn the meat. Meat enclosed in an oven and submitted to indirect heat of the same temperature is not properly roasted but baked. However, as this is what we all do and continue to talk about the 'roast', we will not start calling it 'baked' beef. Different types of meat require different treatment. Beef should go into a hot oven so that a strong heat seals its surfaces and drives the juice inwards, after which the oven temperature can be moderated. Mutton and lamb, in the form of leg, shoulder, or loin is improved by cooking in a moderate oven, and it is not necessary to heat the oven in advance. As the oven heats, the joint of lamb or mutton renders some of its excess fat, and it will be found in practice that very little valuable juice escapes. The oven temperature should not exceed 350 deg. F. Whereas only beef of inferior quality should be marinaded before roasting, or beef which owing to hot weather might begin to go off, lamb and mutton are improved in flavour by rubbing the fat coating with salt, and pouring over it the squeezed juice of a lemon and a little olive oil. A *bouquet* of herbs should roast with the meat, a sprig of rosemary is an especially good aromatic for lamb or veal. Poultry need to have their tender breasts protected with a bard of bacon. Large capons and geese especially should be stuffed and trussed, fired in very hot olive oil, wrapped in several layers of greaseproof paper, and baked very slowly for a long time, on a grid over a baking tin. The goose should be pricked all over after firing in oil, so that the excess of fat can seep during this slow cooking into the pan. An astonishing amount will be collected, and can be saved for the many dishes which specially call for its use. Joints should be placed on a grid over a baking tin, and not put directly into the tin.

Baking

Baking refers to the application of diffused heat in a closed oven, at a sufficient temperature to brown whatever is being cooked. In the case of some *quiches* and *tartes* the temperature required for cooking the pastry is too hot for the nature of the contents, and in such cases the pastry has to be cooked beforehand and the heat reduced before the filling is put in. In some fish dishes, the baking heat is counteracted by the addition of liquid, wine, or fish stock to partially immerse the fish, a combination of baking and stewing being the result. *Pâtés* are also baked in a somewhat distorted sense, the *terrine* containing the *pâté* being first placed in a tin containing boiling water to ensure a gentle and overall application of heat. Some vegetables, after a preliminary blanching, are baked in a little butter in the oven, being basted with their juice from time to time. Tomatoes, aubergines, *courgettes* (little marrows), and onions can be treated like this, so can red peppers, soaked with olive oil, and the bases of globe artichokes. Vegetables cooked in this way are improved if a little lemon juice is poured over them before serving. Mushrooms and fungi are also baked, but usually after being sautéd in oil or butter first, or oiled and put under the grill, otherwise they would be in danger of drying.

Cooking au gratin

Cooking *au gratin* applies to preparations baked in the oven, in open receptacles of earthenware or china, which are finished with a sprinkling of breadcrumbs and oiled butter or olive oil, which turns a crisp golden brown and contributes to the texture and the appearance of the dish.

Note

The recipes in this book are for four people unless other recommendations are made.

Specific oven temperatures have not been given but as a general guide the table overleaf may be useful.

ELECTRIC AND SOLID FUEL	GAS	Heat of Oven
Centre Oven Temperature ° F.	Thermostat Setting	
240°	¼	Very Slow
260°	½	
280°		
	1	Slow
300°		
	2	
320°		
	3	Moderate
340°		
	4	
360°		
380°	5	Fairly Hot
400°	6	Hot
420°		
	7	
440°		
	8	Very Hot
460°		
	9	
480°		

Soup

6

SOUP

THE soups in this section bear no relation to delicate *consommés*, those transparent creations of French chefs which, as Grimod de la Reynière suggested, should appear at the beginning of a dinner to prepare the palate and reflect the wealth of dishes which are to follow, rather in the same way as an overture announces the main themes of an *opéra comique*.

They are country soups, peasant soups, soups belonging to *la cuisine bourgeoise*, which, followed by a salad, good bread, and a respectable cheese, can provide a satisfying meal.

Although we start off with the *pot-au-feu*, the foundation of so many soups, sauces, and meat dishes, we do not imagine for a moment that English cooks maintain a continuous supply of broth derived from pounds of gravy beef, marrow bones, and knuckles of veal. The disappearance of the stock pot is linked to the departure of the domestic cook. The kitchen is no longer the scene of continuous activity, but a place for sporadic effort.

With this in mind, we have tried to provide a short-cut where feasible, by suggesting the use of beef extract or beef concentrate in some recipes, but there are certain dishes whose point of departure is the true beef broth, the extracted virtue of beef and marrowbones produced only by respecting the simple rules of chemistry underlying the *pot-au-feu*.

Soup does not play as fundamental a role in this country as it does in the diet of the French people. But, with the price of meat at its present level, it seems worth while to experiment with some of the substantial soups which have provided a generous if simple diet for country people in different parts of Europe, whose supplies of meat have always been more restricted, and who have used other sources of protein – haricot beans, chick peas, lentils, for instance – which tend to be neglected by us, perhaps out of ignorance of the methods of preparing them.

There is, instead, a general addiction to soup in cellophane packets and a too-constant recourse to tin opening, which result in a disagreeable monotony. Such soup is seldom worthy of a soup tureen, and this capacious object has become an uncommon feature on the supper table. The soups in this book really need a tureen from which to serve them, preferably one that can be put in the oven; *Cotriade à la bretonne* or *la Garbure* cannot be served furtively from a saucepan.

POT-AU-FEU

The *pot-au-feu* is fundamental to French cooking. This is what Brillat Savarin said about it in 1826.

'One calls *pot-au-feu* a piece of beef destined to be treated in lightly salted boiling water in order to extract its soluble parts. *Le bouillon* is the liquid which remains after the operation is terminated. The meat despoiled of its soluble parts is called *bouilli*. The water dissolves at first a part of the osmazone; then the albumen, which coagulates before a temperature of 50 deg. Réamur is reached and forms the scum which is ordinarily removed; then, the surplus osmazone with extractable part, the juice, and finally, some part of the envelope of the fibres, which are detached by the continuous boiling. *To have good bouillon the water must heat slowly, so that the albumen does not coagulate inside the meat before being extracted; and the water should only just boil, in order that the diverse elements which are successively dissolved can unite gently and without difficulty.*'

Although the chemical constituents have since been more accurately determined these are still the simple rules which ensure a good stock or *bouillon*. 'One adds to the *bouillon*', he says, 'vegetables or roots to improve the flavour, and bread or *pasta* to make it more nourishing; that is what one calls a soup.'

One of the ways in which the boiled beef resulting from the *pot-au-feu* is served in Normandy and Brittany is to chop it into little cubes in a potato salad with finely chopped shallots and fresh herbs. It is also eaten hot with potatoes, gherkins, and *gros sel*, or sliced cold and served with a mustard sauce. (See *le Bouilli*, page 176.)

The ingredients for the *pot-au-feu* on a small scale are:
    1 lb of lean beef (shin), 1 lb of lean skirt beef, one beef marrowbone; the neck, pinions, and giblets of a fowl, 2 carrots, 1 turnip,

2 leeks, 1 celery heart, half a small white cabbage, salt, 4 pints water, 1 onion, 1 clove, and a *bouquet garni*. (It should really be made in larger quantities. The proportion of meat to water remains constant – 1 lb of meat to 2 pints of water.)

Tie the meat into shape with string. Put it into the *marmite* with 4 pints of cold water and some salt, put the *marmite* on a moderate heat and bring the contents slowly to boiling point, reduce the heat, and simmer gently. Remove the scum as it comes to the surface; the final broth must be clear. After two hours, add the vegetables, the carrots sliced, the turnip cut in pieces, the leeks chopped finely, the celery, and the onion into which the clove has been stuck. Put in the *bouquet garni*, the herbs being tied together for subsequent removal. The cabbage should be sliced and blanched for five minutes in boiling stock in a separate pan before putting it into the *marmite*, or, failing stock, into boiling water with beef dripping added, before it finishes cooking in the *marmite*.

When the cabbage is cooked, test the soup for seasoning. Take out the meat, and keep it warm if it is to be served hot after the soup. Remove the necks, giblets, and pinions of the fowl, and the marrowbone. Spoon out the marrow and either drop pieces of it into the soup, or keep it to serve separately on toast. Skim off any fat which may lie on the surface of the soup. Normally the soup is passed through a sieve and served clear and transparent with a little soup *pasta* or rice, cooked in it at the last moment, with the pieces of marrow.

Larger pieces of meat will require considerably longer cooking. A 4-lb piece of beef should be simmered for not less than 4 hours.

CONSOMMÉ

We do not imagine that many English people take the trouble to make a double broth or *consommé*, but it is as well to know how to achieve it. It is in fact a beef broth or *bouillon* doubled with veal and fowl, the former to give it suavity, the latter to improve its flavour. A calf's foot can be substituted for the veal to introduce the gelatinous quality. Instead of a fowl's carcase, a stuffed fowl can be simmered in it.

The resulting liquid, clear, smooth, and flavoured, is served with a little soup *pasta* cooked in it, a fine *mirepoix* of vegetables, or some other soup garnish; sometimes with a little sherry or Madeira; sometimes darkened with caramel, or made golden with saffron.

¾ lb shin of beef, ¾ lb lean beef; 1 knuckle of veal; ½ lb fowl carcase; 2 carrots, 1 turnip, 1 small stick of celery, 1 leek, a small piece of parsnip, 1 small onion with a clove stuck in it, and 2 quarts of beef broth (from the *pot-au-feu*), salt.

Put the beef, knuckle of veal, and the fowl's carcase into the *marmite* or stockpot, pour on the beef broth, from which all particles of fat have been removed, add sufficient salt, put the pot on a moderate heat, and bring it slowly to the boil. Then adjust the heat, so that a bubble rises to the surface now and then. Skim the liquid very carefully and remove the scum as it surfaces, keeping the sides of the pan clean with a damp cloth. Put in the vegetables, remove any further scum that rises from time to time, and clean the sides of the pot. The lid should then be put on at a tilt to allow the steam to escape, and the pot simmered for 3–4 hours. Take it off the fire, pour ¼ pint of cold water into the broth and leave it to allow any fat to congeal on the surface. Remove the fat, strain the liquid carefully into an earthenware crock, and let the *consommé* get cold before covering it.

VEGETABLE BOUILLON

When there is no beef for stock, an excellent *bouillon* can be made from fresh vegetables at any time of the year, the vegetables used depending upon the season. The method is simple and the resulting broth should be clear, well-flavoured, and golden in colour. It takes under an hour to prepare, and can be served with a little soup *pasta* or rice, or used instead of beef stock in the preparation of a sauce for *spaghetti*.

Ingredients can be chosen from all or any of these vegetables: leeks, carrots, a small piece of turnip, a celery heart, peas, tomatoes, the heart of a white cabbage; 1 shallot, ½ bay leaf, a slip of lemon rind, a sprig of thyme. For 2 pints of *bouillon*, 1½ lb of vegetables will be required, just over 2 pints of hot water, and 2 oz fresh butter.

Melt the butter in a stewpan, and then add the chopped shallot and finely sliced white part of the leeks to it, and cook for a few minutes. Put in the sliced celery, the carrots, the turnip, peas, tomatoes, cabbage, whatever else has been included, and the herbs. When the vegetables are heated through, pour on the hot water and bring the contents of the stewpan to the boil. Lower the heat and simmer for 45 minutes, by which time the flavour should be extracted from the vegetables. Taste for seasoning, and strain the liquid into a tureen. Don't press the vegetables against the sieve, as the *bouillon* should be clear. If *vermicelli* or rice is to give body to the soup the strained liquid will have to be returned to the pan, and the *bouillon* cooked for another 10–12 minutes.

LA BISQUE AUX LÉGUMES

The *bisque* has gone through a whole series of culinary mutations; this *bisque aux légumes* retains only the shade of the original. In seventeenth-century French cookery books the *bisque* is a soup made of pigeons or small birds – quails, partridges – with a rich garniture. The important thing seems to have been to make the broth red, and crayfish were added to produce this effect. The crayfish finally displaced the pigeons and the *bisque d'écrevisses* (crayfish stewed in white wine, shelled, pounded, incorporated with crayfish butter, made from the pounded shells and claws, the whole thing passed through a sieve and re-heated) held the field and the word *bisque* came to mean a *purée* of shellfish. This soup retains two characteristics of this history, it is a *purée* of lentils; it is red, thanks to the paprika. It is extremely simple to prepare, which its elaborate antecedents are not.

1 lb of lentils, 3 leeks, 3 carrots, a piece of celery, 2 egg yolks, ground pepper, 1 teaspoonful of paprika, 4 pints of stock (water failing stock).

Soak the lentils overnight. Simmer them for two hours with the white part of the leeks, the carrots and celery cut up, and salt, in four pints of stock. Pass the contents of the saucepan through a sieve (or twice through a *mouli*), and re-heat the *purée*. If you are using a tureen from which to serve the soup, have it already warmed. Then beat up the egg yolks in the tureen, season them with the paprika pepper, add a little hot soup to thin out the yolks after which you can pour in the rest of the hot soup without the risk of curdling the egg. Line the soup plates with slices of French bread which have been slightly toasted under the grill and rubbed with garlic.

BORTSCH

There are a very great number of recipes of Russian, Ukrainian, and Polish origin for this delicious soup. The more elaborate ones contain both beef and duck stock and the meat is finely sliced and served in the soup. Others are based on *kvass*, which is a sour alcoholic liquid obtained from beetroots soaked in warm water and fermented by the addition of rye bread. A very good *bortsch* can be made with stock from beef bones alone, the recipe for which is given here. *Bortsch* should be accompanied either by sour cream or by pastry patties filled with chopped beef or duck.

3 pints of good beef stock with all the fat removed from it; 5 large uncooked beetroots, salt, pepper, a squeeze of lemon juice, about 1 gill of sour cream.

Wash the beetroots, in fact scour them. Put the stock into a large saucepan, and shred the beetroots into the stock, using a slicer with a fine shredding device. Put the saucepan on to a low heat, heat the stock up slowly, and let it simmer for an hour, when the beetroot should be cooked and all the colour extracted. Add some lemon juice, salt and pepper. Strain the stock through the sieve to remove the beetroot and serve the *bortsch* in deep white soup plates to set off the colour. The sour cream is served separately.

BOUILLABAISSE DU PAYS DE CORNOUAILLES

The quantities are given for 10 to 12 people, as a variety of fish are used.

4 lb of fish chosen from red mullet, gurnet, whiting, mackerel, little turbot, rock salmon, fresh tunny; 4 or 5 leeks, 2 lb medium sized waxy potatoes, 5 tomatoes, 3 celery hearts; salt, pepper,

thyme, bay leaf, chopped parsley; 5 pints of water; 3 egg yolks
4 tablespoonfuls of cream.

Use the white parts of the leeks only, and cut them up into
fairly thick rounds. Scrape the potatoes, and remove the skins,
pips, and juice from the tomatoes. Cut the hearts of celery into
small pieces. Put all these into an earthenware stewpan with the
water and herbs. Bring to the boil and let the liquid simmer for
25 minutes. Clean the fish, and cut them into slices 1½ inches
thick. Put them into the pan, and cook very gently for fifteen
minutes. Beat up the egg yolks in a bowl, add a little of the hot
fish stock to them, stirring well, and then return the blended
yolks and broth to the pan. The heat should be reduced to avoid
the possibility of curdling, and the soup must be gently stirred
to effect the thickening. At the last minute, add the cream.
This Breton *bouillabaisse* is sometimes served with hot French
bread. If preferred, small squares of dry bread fried in butter
can be tossed into the soup when it is put on the table.

CAPELLETTI NEL BRODO DI CAPPONE

In the *pasta* section the Italian enthusiasm for all types of *pasta*
enveloped in fragrant and aromatic sauces, and sometimes enclosing
delicious stuffings of cream cheese and spinach, or *mortadella* and breast
of chicken, is described. *Capelletti*, little envelopes of *pasta* in the shape
of a half moon, are often served on feast days in the broth in which a
chicken has been cooked.

3 pints of chicken stock and half a breast of chicken (boiled),
½ lb *mozzarella* (which can be bought in Soho) or home-made
cream cheese (see page 118), 1 egg, 2 oz grated parmesan;
2 oz butter; grated nutmeg, a pinch of allspice, salt, 1 tablespoonful of finely chopped parsley or basil. For 5 or 6 people.

Put the piece of chicken in a sauté-pan with two ounces of
butter and let it cook gently with the lid on, while you prepare
the paste. For the paste you need ¼ lb of flour, 1 egg, 1 egg white,
salt. Make a mound of the flour on a wooden board, press a hole
in the centre of it, break the egg into the hole, and work it in with
the white with a light quick circular movement of the fingers.
Work the dough on the board, adding a little more flour if it is

at all sticky. The paste should be elastic and should neither adhere to the board nor to the fingers. Roll it out to the thinness of a sixpence, and leave it for half an hour. Meanwhile, remove the chicken from the pan, and slice and chop it up as finely as possible, mixing it with the cream cheese, from which every particle of moisture has been extracted, and the parmesan, the egg, spice, parsley, and seasoning. These should combine into a mixture which is fairly firm. Take a round pastry cutter, 2½ inches in diameter, and perforate the paste in a series of circles. On each of these put a spoonful of the chicken mixture, wet the outside edge of the circles with a brush, fold them over into half-circles, pressing the edges together. Put them into boiling chicken stock in a wide saucepan (so that the *capelletti* don't bombard each other) and cook, if they are freshly made, for 5–8 minutes but longer if they have been prepared some hours beforehand. This should make about 30 *capelletti*. Serve the soup in a tureen with grated parmesan.

COLD ASPARAGUS SOUP

1 dessertspoonful of butter, 1 dessertspoonful of plain flour, 1 cup of milk, 4 cups of asparagus water, 1 egg yolk, 2 table-spoonfuls of cream, ½ cup of cooked asparagus heads, a grate of nutmeg, and a little cayenne pepper.

Heat the butter in a stewpan, add the flour to make a *roux* and stir well over a gentle heat for a few minutes. Heat the milk, pour it onto the butter and flour mixture, stirring until smooth, and cook for 15 minutes. Heat the asparagus water and pour it onto the white sauce, stirring well, then add the asparagus heads. Cook for 20 minutes, and strain through a sieve. Mix the egg yolk with the cream, beating them well together, and add them to the strained soup. Put the soup back onto a gentle heat and stir to effect the thickening. When it is smooth take it off the stove. Chill in the refrigerator before serving.

COLD CUCUMBER SOUP

½ lb chopped cucumbers, 1 tablespoonful of chopped dill leaves, 1 tablespoonful of very finely chopped onion, ½ lb chopped cooked young beetroot with the leaves on, 1 tablespoonful of parsley, salt and pepper, two bottles of yoghourt, 2 hard-boiled eggs.

Peel and chop the cucumbers. Scald them and rinse in cold water. Put them in the refrigerator for 3 hours. Mix all the other ingredients together, except for the hard-boiled eggs. Put the mixture into the refrigerator. When you want to serve the soup, combine the cucumber with the rest of the ingredients and serve with slices of hard-boiled egg in each soup plate, and one or two cubes of ice.

COLD SORREL SOUP

The ingredients are: 4 handfuls of sorrel leaves which have been washed and have had the centre stalks removed, 1 clove of garlic, half a small cucumber which has been peeled and sliced, the juice of 1 lemon, 2 hard-boiled eggs finely chopped, 2 raw eggs, salt and pepper, 1 teaspoonful of finely chopped tarragon leaves, and 2½ pints of boiling water.

Chop the sorrel, and throw it into the water already boiling in a pan. Adjust the heat and simmer for 10 minutes. Crush the garlic with some salt and put it into the pan. Add the sliced cucumber, the lemon juice, salt, and plenty of freshly ground black pepper. Beat the raw eggs together, remove the pan from the heat, and pour a little of the liquor from it onto the beaten eggs, stirring vigorously. Return this mixture to the pan and continue to stir the liquid over a very low heat until the *liaison* is effected. Take the pan off the heat, add the chopped hard-boiled eggs, and let it cool, stirring now and then. Chill in the refrigerator. A small lump of ice can be put in each soup plate before serving this soup. Sprinkle finely chopped tarragon leaves on the surface.

COTRIADE À LA BRETONNE

In the little villages and ports of Brittany a variety of fish is the chief article of diet, and the *cotriade* is a kind of northern *bouillabaisse*, invented to accommodate the poaching of a fisherman's catch and the making of an excellent soup in one vessel, usually an earthenware pot.

The Breton housewife relies upon the carrots, onions, and herbs to flavour the soup and improve the fish, and these, together with the potatoes which are particularly waxy, yellow, and good, are served separately with a dressing of cider vinegar and pepper.

You need 1 pound of cleaned mackerel, the same quantity of whiting, and a slice of conger eel. Fresh sardines and coalfish are used by the Bretons as well. A slice of cod can be included (cut from the shoulder) and fresh pilchards when available. At the least, whiting and mackerel should be used.

For four persons the ingredients might be: 2 lb cleaned fish, 1½ lb potatoes, 4 carrots, 2 large Spanish onions, 1 clove garlic, thyme, parsley, 1 clove, 2 oz butter, saffron, 3 pints of hot water, and some slices of grilled French bread.

Heat 2 ounces of butter in a large casserole or earthenware *marmite* standing on an asbestos mat on top of the stove. Slice the onion very finely and cook it in the heated butter. After a few minutes add the hot water, pepper, a little salt, and bring to the boil. Slice up the potatoes into thin rounds and cook them for 20 minutes in the boiling liquid with the sliced carrots, the herbs tied together, the garlic clove, and the clove. Then add the fish, a pinch of saffron, bring the broth once more to the boil and simmer gently for 15 minutes. Remove the fish and vegetables onto a hot dish, pour the soup into a tureen in the bottom of which some slices of grilled French bread, lightly rubbed with garlic, have been placed. The soup is eaten first from deep soup plates, and the fish and vegetables afterwards.

ERWTENSOEP

This thick pea soup should be made the day before it is wanted, as it takes a long time to cook – about six hours – and in any case the flavour improves with waiting. When cold it is very thick indeed, so care must be taken not to burn it on re-heating.

1 pig's trotter (fresh or salt; if salted it must be soaked for a few hours), 1 pig's ear (fresh or salt; soak if salted), a pint of dried peas, 1 lb potatoes, 1 celeriac or heart of celery, some green celery leaves, 4 leeks, 8 pints of water, salt.

Wash and soak the peas for 24 hours in cold water, then boil them in the water in which they have soaked for 2 hours. When they are soft, push them through a sieve, leaving the coarse outer skins behind. Put the trotter and pig's ear and the *purée* of peas in a heavy pan, and simmer them with the lid on for another 2 hours. Then add the diced potatoes, chopped celeriac or celery heart, the leeks, cleaned and cut up in rounds, the chopped celery leaves, and simmer the soup until it is smooth and thick. The longer it cooks the better the taste and texture. Two hours is a good estimate for a successful blending. When re-heating taste for seasoning and add more salt if necessary. *Croûtons* of bread fried in bacon fat can be put in each soup plate on serving.

This is the kind of soup which is best suited to a slow combustion stove, the cooking of the pig's ear and trotter in the *purée* of peas being carried out in a covered earthenware pot in the slow oven.

GULYAS

Gulyas soup resembles *Gulyas* proper (page 175) in its ingredients, except that less excellent beef or veal is used, and instead of the reduced sauce it presents the appearance of a rather liquid stew.

2 lb shin of beef, 1 lb onions, 2 oz lard or pork fat, 1 tablespoon-ful of flour, 1 lb potatoes, 1 lb tomatoes, green peppers when in season, 1 clove garlic, a *bouquet garni*, salt, 1 dozen coriander seeds and half a dozen wholespice, 1 oz paprika pepper, a glass or two of red wine if available, 2 pints of water (or stock).

Slice the onions, and brown them in a heavy saucepan in the melted fat, while you are preparing the meat. This should be cut into 2-inch cubes, trimmed of fat or gristle. Grind the coriander seeds and the wholespice in a mortar, add the garlic crushed, salt, and the paprika pepper. Roll the pieces of meat in this preparation, then in flour, and fry them for a few minutes with the onions. Cut up the tomatoes, slice the green peppers, and put them in the pan. Pour on the red wine, let it reduce a little, then add the 2 pints of hot water or stock, with the *bouquet garni*. Bring to the boil, lower the heat, and let the *gulyas* simmer gently for at least 2 hours. Half an hour before serving the soup, cut up some potatoes into rounds about half an inch thick, and cook them in the soup.

Stewing veal can be used for this soup, or very lean pork. Paprika pepper burns very easily, which explains the instruction to roll the meat first in the spices and then in flour. Some people, for this reason, prefer to add the paprika when the liquid has been poured in, but in this case very little of its flavour is communicated to the meat.

HARE SOUP

On some occasion when the preparation of *lepre colle polpette* (page 234) has deprived a hare of everything but its head and bones, an excellent soup can be made with these remains.

Fresh hare bones (including the head), 2 ounces of bacon fat or its equivalent in bacon rinds, 1½ ounces of plain flour seasoned with black pepper and salt, 12 chestnuts which have been both peeled and skinned, 3 onions, 2 carrots, 1 stick of celery, a small piece of cauliflower, 3 mushrooms (dried ones will do very well), 2 bay leaves, 1 teaspoonful of thyme, 1 teaspoonful of marjoram, 1 blade of mace, 2 clove heads, a pinch of brown sugar, 4 pints of beef stock.

Put the bacon fat in a deep pan over a good heat, and when it is hot drop in it the hare bones which have been dipped in seasoned flour. Fry the bones in the fat until they are brown. Then throw in the chestnuts and the vegetables, which have been roughly chopped up. Shake the pan to prevent burning and add the herbs, mace, sugar, and clove heads. Sprinkle on the rest of the seasoned flour and mix it in. Adjust the heat, warm the stock and add it to the hare bones and chopped vegetables. Stir well. Put the lid on the pan and simmer for 2½ to 3 hours. Strain the liquid into another pan, remove the bones, and push the residue of vegetables and meat through the strainer (or through a sieve) into the soup. Taste for seasoning, and if there is any red wine left over from preparing the *lepre colle polpette* pour it in. Bring the soup to simmering point once more and after 2 or 3 minutes it will be ready to serve.

LA GARBURE

La Garbure is a savoury and solid soup produced with different variations in Gascony, Béarn, and the Basque country, a dense concoction of fresh vegetables in season, pickled pork, ham, sausages, and haricot beans, transformed into a memorable experience by the addition of *confits* of various kinds, preserves of meat and poultry.

The Gascon *garbure* starts off with onions fried in goose dripping, and should be remembered for an after-Christmas occasion when this may be available.

Cut up 2 onions, 2 or 3 turnips, 3 or 4 potatoes, and half a cabbage which has been scalded, drained, and sliced. Put a few spoonfuls of goose fat in a casserole, brown the onions, and then add the turnips, the cabbage, and after a few moments the potatoes. Pour on 3 quarts of water, put in 1 pound of salt pork which has been blanched beforehand, and simmer the soup slowly till the pork is tender. Remove the pork onto a wooden board, and slice it thinly. If you have a large enough casserole or tureen which will go into the oven, the traditional way to prepare the soup for serving is to cut some thin rounds of French bread, put a layer in the bottom of the tureen, covered by a layer of sliced pork, followed by another layer of sliced bread and again pork. The soup is poured over, grated cheese is sprinkled on the surface and the casserole is put in the oven for the top to brown.

Confit d'oie should ideally be included in this *garbure*. This is a preserved goose leg, which is sliced and added to the soup with its accompanying fat before it is put in the oven to brown. Pieces of a duck or goose which have already been roasted and a little additional goose fat would do as a replacement. The soup is sufficiently solid to be eaten with a fork. When nothing remains but the broth, a little red wine is poured in, and the soup bowl is emptied at a draught.

LA GARBURE HENDAYAISE

1 lb haricot beans, 2 lb shoulder end of belly of pork, fresh vegetables in season, ½ lb peas, ½ lb broad beans, ½ lb tomatoes or ½ lb leeks, 1 lb red peppers, ½ lb runner beans, salt, pepper, grated cheese, slices from a large French loaf.

Soak the beans overnight. Put them in a large pan and bring them to the boil with twice their quantity of water. Simmer them for half an hour, then immerse the piece of pork, and cook gently for a further hour with the lid on. Then, having prepared the vegetables and cut them into slices (peas and beans excepted), put them into the pan and let the cooking proceed until the vegetables are tender. Remove the pork, cut it into slices, and lay these on toasted slices of bread, cover with a heap of the vegetable mass, sprinkle with cheese, and brown in the oven or under the grill. This may not sound like a soup but *garbures* are eaten with a fork.

LA HABADA

La Habada might be considered as a Spanish counterpart of the *pot-au-feu*, using salt beef and smoked ham instead of fresh beef and fowl, and replacing the root vegetables with the more substantial haricot bean (*Haba* = bean). But both these cornerstones of Spanish and French cookery probably have their origin in the *olla podrida* which combines different meats and vegetables on a gigantic scale

Prepared for twenty people in a farmhouse kitchen, the *olla* would include, besides a great piece of beef, a leg of mutton, a raw smoked ham and salt pork, the ears, feet, and tail of a pig, a hen, two partridges, and *chorizos* (Spanish smoked sausages), as well as carrots, leeks, onions, cabbage, potatoes, garlic, herbs, and *garbanzos* (chick peas). This encyclopaedic meal was prepared in two enormous earthenware vessels.

Even though *la habada* may seem a dwarf beside the parent *olla*, it will, made in a large French *marmite*, provide a substantial soup followed by a dish of salt beef, ham, sausages, and beans for about eight people, with cold meats left over. It is not really worth making for less.

2 lb salt beef, a piece of ham or bacon weighing about 2 lb (this should properly be the smoked Estramadura ham), 1 lb black pudding, 6 smoked beef sausages, and 2 lb haricot beans, water to cover.

The beef and ham (or bacon) should be soaked in water for several hours to remove some of the salt, and this can best be done the night before, the haricot beans being put to soak likewise, in twice their quantity of water. Next day put the beef and bacon into a large *marmite*, cover them with fresh cold water and bring it up to the boil, lower the heat, and simmer for 2½ hours in all. During this time the haricot beans should be cooked separately in the water in which they have been soaking, for at least 1 hour, or until they are tender. When the meat and bacon have been cooking for 1½ hours, add the black pudding, the sausages, and the cooked haricot beans. After a half hour, taste for seasoning and add fresh black pepper if you wish. Salt will, probably, be unnecessary. At the end of 2½ hours the meat, bacon, and beans should be well cooked. The soup should be strained off, and served while the dish of beef, bacon, pudding, sausages, and beans is kept warm for the next course. A good, strong full-bodied wine such as *Côte du Rhône* will be needed to wash it down.

LEBERKLÖSSE FÜR SUPPEN

If we are to believe Joseph Wechsberg, the author of *Blue Trout and Black Truffles*, dumplings are for all practical purposes the Czech way of life. The Italians have let imagination run in the creation of many frivolous forms of *pasta*, and the Czechs put their whole hearts into dumplings – soup dumplings, dumplings instead of potatoes, dessert dumplings, dumplings round, flat, and oval.

Not to be eaten thirty at a time, occasionally a few meat dumplings in a clear beef broth or vegetable *bouillon* are acceptable.

1 lb calves' liver, 1 slice of dry bread, ¼ lb beef suet, 4 yolks of egg and 2 egg whites, parsley, salt and pepper, a pinch of thyme, half a bay leaf chopped or pounded, 2 oz dried breadcrumbs.

Remove all the skin and tubes from the liver, and chop it as finely as possible with a heavy kitchen knife. Liver is improved and chops more easily after soaking for a little while in milk. Soak the bread in a little stock, or in the milk in which the liver stood, and when it has absorbed it, squeeze out the moisture. Mix the chopped liver and bread, the herbs, seasoning, and suet. Beat the 4 egg yolks and the 2 whites together and add them to the liver mixture. Sprinkle in a little of the dried breadcrumbs and form a sample dumpling, the size of an egg yolk. Drop it into boiling broth from a wet spoon and simmer for 8 minutes. If too soft in texture add more breadcrumbs. If too solid, another egg yolk should be added to the mixture. When the adjustment has been made cook them in the stock, and serve about three or four for each person in a soup plate of *bouillon*.

MARROWBONE SOUP WITH MARROW DUMPLINGS

Economical, nourishing, and cheap, the broth is thin but well flavoured with herbs and vegetables, and the little dumplings are rich and light in texture.

For the broth – about 2 lb beef marrow bones, 1 carrot, 1 onion, 1 leek, 2 sticks of celery, the heart of a white cabbage, herbs, salt and pepper, 5 pints of water.

For the dumplings – the beef marrow from the bones, 1 cup of breadcrumbs, 2 teaspoonfuls of finely chopped parsley, 2 eggs, salt, pepper, and a little plain flour.

To make the broth: Get the butcher to chop the marrow bones into several pieces, so that they will go into a large pan. Put the bones into the pan with the vegetables which have all been cleaned and chopped up. Put on about 5 pints of cold water and bring to the boil. Add salt, ground black pepper, and simmer the soup for at least 4 hours. Strain off the liquid, without pressing the vegetables so that the soup is clear. Remove the marrow from the bones. Put the soup back and heat it up again.

The dumplings: Chop the marrow, or mash it. Add the dried breadcrumbs, salt, pepper, parsley, and the beaten eggs. Make into small dumplings, roll them in flour, and then drop each one carefully into the broth which should be simmering gently. They will take about 5–6 minutes to cook, depending on their size, and when they are firm the soup is ready to be served. The broth should be ladled into soup plates and a few dumplings put into each. As they are very light they need rather careful handling.

MINESTRONE ALLA GENOVESE

This *minestrone* is a soup of vegetables and rice or *pasta*, which is distinguished from a mere vegetable stew by two culinary operations. In the first place some of the vegetables and herbs are gently sautéd in olive oil before adding the stock in which they are subsequently simmered, and in the second, it is enriched by the addition of *pesto*, a Genoese invention which consists of grated parmesan, finely chopped basil, pine kernels, and a garlic clove, all pounded together, and combined into a soft paste with a little olive oil. Dried basil can be used in the absence of fresh basil, but to less good effect.

The vegetable ingredients can be varied according to the season, celery and leeks being replaced in summer by French beans, runner beans, broad beans, young carrots, etc.

A typical *minestrone* needs ¼ lb haricot beans (already soaked overnight), 2 tablespoonfuls of olive oil, 1 garlic clove, 1 Spanish onion, a pinch of basil, the white part of a leek, 2 carrots, 2 potatoes, 1 turnip, a handful of peas or finely chopped spinach, a handful of rice or soup *pasta*, a pinch of sugar, salt, a small tin of tomato *purée*, and 4 pints of hot water.

For the *pesto*: 2 tablespoonfuls of grated parmesan or *reggiano*, 2 tablespoonfuls each of pine kernels and finely chopped basil, 1 pounded garlic clove, and 1 tablespoonful of olive oil.

The haricot beans will need some previous cooking; meanwhile the other vegetables can be prepared and sautéd. Heat the oil in a heavy frying pan, cut up and slice the onion, the leek, and the garlic clove, and sauté them on a low flame without browning. Add the sliced carrots, the potatoes cut up into little cubes, the turnip, and sprinkle with a little basil.

After a few minutes empty the contents of a small tin of tomato *purée* into the pan, dilute it with a cup of hot water, season with a pinch of sugar and a little salt, and transfer the vegetables to the saucepan in which the haricot beans are cooking. Add the rice or *pasta* and simmer the soup for an hour.

Put in peas or spinach 20 minutes before the meal, and have the *pesto* ready pounded to stir in at the last moment.

Stock can, of course, be used when available, or the liquid in which a piece of bacon or a boiling sausage (*ʒampone, cotechino*) has been cooked, provided it is not too salt.

MUSHROOM STALK SOUP

A delicious and economical soup which can be made in a very short time.

¼ lb mushroom stalks, 2 oz fresh butter, ½ a shallot, ½ a bay leaf, 1 oz plain flour, 1 pint of good creamy milk, a squeeze of lemon juice (or, if available, 1 tablespoonful of dry white wine), black pepper, and salt. Fried *croûtons*.

Slice the mushroom stalks thinly into rounds. Melt the butter in a thick saucepan. Put in a piece of shallot and bay leaf, coat them with the melted butter, and add the sliced mushroom stalks, sautéing them until they are almost cooked. If wine is being used it should be poured into the pan at this point, and the heat raised for a moment to disperse the alcohol. Then the flour should be sprinkled on and stirred with a wooden spoon, being allowed to cook for a few minutes without browning.

Heat the milk in another pan, and when it is just boiling pour it onto the mushroom mixture. Stir continuously until it is all well amalgamated, adjust the heat, and simmer for fifteen minutes. Put in the salt, ground black pepper, and a squeeze of lemon juice if wine is not being used. After another five minutes it is ready to serve, preferably with some small squares of dry bread, fried crisp in fresh butter, to provide a textural contrast to the smooth soup.

POTAGE À L'ANDALOUSE

1 lb potatoes, 1 small tin of tomato *purée*, salt, 1 large onion, 2 oz butter, 1 cube of beef concentrate, 2 oz grated *gruyère* (Cheshire or Wensleydale could be used), a *bouquet garni* (thyme, parsley, and bay leaf tied together for easy removal), 3 pints of hot water; fried *croûtons*.

Slice and chop the onion on a board with a sharp chopping knife, and sauté it for a few minutes in a saucepan in which the butter has been melted. Peel and slice the potatoes, put them in the pan with the onion, together with the tomato *purée*, the *bouquet garni*, and 3 pints of hot water. Simmer the soup for 1 hour with the lid on, and then pass it through a sieve. Put the *purée* back on the stove, add the grated cheese and the meat cube, and reheat without allowing it to boil, which would curdle the cheese. When the meat cube has dissolved, the soup is ready to serve, accompanied by fried *croûtons* or hot French bread.

POSTNAYA LAPSHA

The soup should be of a not very thick consistency with pieces of mushroom and the noodles well disposed in it. This is a Russian recipe;

they would probably use sunflower oil for the initial frying. Sunflower oil has its own particular flavour and if available should be used instead of butter.

If *Boletus edulis* are used the caps should be taken off the stems and sliced. The thick stems should be scraped, and chopped up quite small, as they are tougher than the fleshy caps.

12 mushrooms or 8 *Boletus edulis* (cèpes), 2 shallots, 1 clove of garlic, 2 tablespoonfuls of plain flour, 2 ounces of fresh butter, 4 ounces of noodles, 4 pints of water, salt and black pepper, ½ a bay leaf.

Peel and cut up the mushrooms and the onions. Crush the garlic with a little salt. Fry the onions and mushrooms together in melted butter in the bottom of an earthenware pot, and add the garlic. When these are soft, sprinkle on the flour, and stir well to prevent burning. Add salt and pepper. Meanwhile heat the water, and when it is just on the boil, pour it onto the mushroom, onion, and flour mixture, stirring until a smooth consistency is obtained. Adjust the heat and simmer for 15 minutes. Then throw in the noodles and continue to simmer until they are cooked (12–15 minutes if they are dry, 8 minutes if they are freshly made).

SOUPA AVGO LEMONO

This is an excellent Greek soup to make when plenty of chicken stock is left over after boiling a fowl. Rice and a *liaison* of eggs with some lemon juice are added to the stock. But before doing anything else, skim the fat from the top of the stock.

2 pints of skimmed chicken stock, 1 small onion, 2 ounces of Patna rice, 3 eggs, 1 large lemon, salt and cayenne pepper.

Heat the chicken stock in a pan, with the finely chopped onion. Then add the rice and simmer for 12–15 minutes. Break the eggs into a bowl and beat them. Add the juice of the lemon to the beaten eggs, stirring them together.

When the rice is cooked take a spoonful of the strained hot stock and add it to the egg mixture, and go on spoonful by spoonful until about half a pint of stock has been used. Turn down the heat and pour the diluted eggs back into the rest of the stock in the pan. Stir the soup until it has a creamy consistency. The mixture must not boil or the eggs will curdle. When the soup is thick and smooth, add salt if necessary and a few grains of cayenne pepper, and pour into hot soup plates.

SOUPE À LA BONNE FEMME

Kettner maintained that *soupe à la bonne femme* was an attempt to paint the character of a good woman, a culinary portrait uniting two principal concepts of womanhood, symbolized in the malleability of cream and the acidity of sorrel.

(1) These are the essential ingredients for 8 servings. ½ lb butter, 1 lb sorrel (cut first into narrow ribbons and then slantwise into diamonds), 4 pints of chicken broth, 3 egg yolks, 1 tumbler of cream, a little salt.

Melt most of the butter in a pan, put in the cut-up sorrel, a little salt, and sauté for a few minutes on a low flame. Then pour on the chicken broth, which should be already heated, and simmer for a ½ hour. Break the egg yolks, stir them together and, taking the saucepan off the fire, pour a little broth onto the yolks, stirring quickly, before returning the mixture to the pan. Continue to stir the soup over a gentle heat, so that the *liaison* of eggs and broth is successfully brought about and a homogeneously smooth consistency is achieved. Pour in the cream, stir in what is left of the butter, and serve this suave soup with French bread which has been five minutes in a hot oven, or with toast Melba.

In the course of repeated reproductions of the good lady's portrait, *soupe à la bonne femme* has lost some of the clarity of the original.

(2) This is the soup in its better known, but adulterated, form. 4 medium sized leeks, 2–3 ounces of butter, 3 peeled and quartered potatoes, 1 pint of clear *consommé* (q.v.), salt, 1 pint of milk.

Chop as finely as possible the white part of the leeks, removing the outside skin. Put the minced leeks with 2 ounces of butter into a thick pan over a gentle heat. Stew the leeks in the butter for about a quarter of an hour. Then cut the quartered potatoes into thin slices and put them in the pan. Heat up the *consommé* and pour it over the leeks and potatoes. Add sufficient salt to flavour the soup, and simmer gently. When the potatoes are cooked and the leeks are dispersed throughout, boil the pint of milk and add it to the soup. Just before serving put in the remaining butter.

LA SOUPE AUX CHOUX

There are many regional variations of this excellent soup, with regard to both ingredients and method. Some French women would deplore the omission of potatoes and sausages in the recipe given here, and others would propose a reversal of the cooking process.

In this recipe the cabbage and root vegetables are given a preliminary sauté before the liquid is added, and the chopped bacon, garlic, and parsley are put in half an hour before serving for added flavour.

But it is also possible to adopt the reverse method, first boiling the vegetables, and towards the end adding a *fricassée* of chopped and sautéd vegetables and herbs.

1 good-sized cabbage, 4 carrots, 2 turnips, 1 leek, 1 slice of bacon (or a piece of pickled pork weighing 1 lb), 2 cloves of garlic, parsley (savoury and chervil if available), 1 clove, salt and black pepper, 1 quart of water.

Cut up the cabbage and wash it well. Slice it into pieces about 2 inches square. Slice the leek in rounds, removing the outside skin, peel the carrots and turnips and cut them into pieces. Cut the fat off the slice of bacon (or take a piece of fat from the pickled pork) and put it in the bottom of a large saucepan over a gentle heat to extract the fat. When there is sufficient fat in the pan, throw in the cabbage, the leek, the carrot and turnip pieces and sauté them until they are soft. Meanwhile, heat about 1 quart of water and pour it onto the vegetables. Simmer for $\frac{3}{4}$ hour and then add a little salt and the clove. Continue cooking, with the lid on, for a further 2 hours, and $\frac{1}{2}$ hour before serving chop the bacon, parsley, chervil, savoury, and the 2 garlic cloves, salt and pepper them, and throw the mixture into the boiling soup.

When pickled pork is used in *la soup aux choux* it must first be de-salted by steeping in cold water for a few hours, and according to its size must be added to the soup in good time.

A piece weighing 1 lb would need three-quarters of an hour. If more bulk is required, the soup can be poured over slices of fried bread. This is a French habit and not at all to the taste of some English people. Crisp warm French bread served with the soup is often more acceptable.

SOUPE À L'OIGNON

La soupe à l'oignon is a well-known pick-me-up in France for those who have drunk too well, and is an example of the miraculous powers of the onion. It should be served in earthenware soup bowls, and prepared in an earthenware *marmite*. Failing this, china-lined ironware is better for the cooking than aluminium.

1 lb finely sliced Spanish onions, 1 clove, 1 small bay leaf, salt, black pepper, a little sugar, 2 pints of beef stock, some dried slices of bread, grated cheese, and about 2 oz fresh butter or beef dripping.

Melt most of the butter (or dripping) in the bottom of the *marmite*, and fry the onion slices until they are transparent and golden. At the same time, put in the bay leaf, and crumble the knob of the clove over the frying mixture. Add salt, a pinch of brown sugar, and some ground black pepper. Then heat the beef stock, and pour it onto the onion and butter mixture in the casserole. Simmer the soup for at least half an hour, and about 10 minutes before it is to be served fry the dry slices of bread in the rest of the butter in a separate pan. When they are golden, sprinkle grated cheese over each side of them and place one in the bottom of each hot soup bowl. Pour in the soup, and serve more grated cheese separately. This should properly be *gruyère*.

Alternatively, the soup can be poured into earthenware bowls, the fried bread sprinkled with cheese being floated on the top and the bowls placed under the grill for a few minutes to brown the cheese.

SOUPE À LA PAYSANNE

The peasant's soup is a clear broth with winter vegetables and a little pickled pork.

The vegetables required are 1 onion, 1 leek, 2 carrots, 2 turnips, 1 small cabbage, 4 potatoes, and a handful of French beans when available (frozen French beans can be used). Also ½ lb pickled pork which has been soaked for a few hours (the same quantity of mild bacon can be substituted), 1 tablespoonful of lard, salt, 1 garlic clove and *bouquet garni*, 4 pints of hot water.

Chop the onion and leek very finely and put them in a heavy aluminium saucepan with the lard and the pickled pork, cut up into small cubes, and cook them on a low flame without browning. Add the carrots and turnips, cut into four and sliced, and the sliced cabbage. String the French beans and break them into ½ inch pieces, put them in the pan, and stir the gently cooking vegetables with a wooden spoon to distribute cooking fat and heat. Then put in the potatoes sliced, add 4 pints of hot water, a pinch of kitchen salt, 1 crushed clove of garlic, and simmer gently for 3 hours. Enough for six.

SOUPE AUX POIREAUX ET AUX HARICOTS

This standby of French and Flemish households contains sorrel which is hardly used here either for soups or salads. The kind used by French people is not hedgerow sorrel, which has rather narrow leaves, but the broad-leaved variety called *Rumex acetosa*. It is easily grown, perennial, and can be obtained in seed form from Thompson & Morgan of Ipswich.

4 leeks, 4 ounces of haricot beans, 1 handful of sorrel, 4 potatoes, 2 ounces of butter, salt, pepper, 1 tablespoonful of cream, 2½ pints of water.

Soak the haricots overnight. Next day cook them for not less than 1 hour. When they are ready, melt the butter in the bottom of a heavy pan, and put in the sorrel, which has been well washed and then chopped. Clean the leeks, discarding the coarse outer leaves, chop them up, and put them into the pan. Peel the potatoes, slice them into rounds, and add them to the other vegetables. Cover with 2 pints of hot water and simmer for half an hour, before putting in the cooked haricots. Add salt and pepper and finally the cream. Take the soup off the heat and it is ready, rather thick with vegetables.

SOUPE AUX POISSONS

This recipe is particularly relevant on a seaside holiday, when the family have caught a fresh assortment of fish. But the saffron and garlic which it uses will not be readily available, and it is a good idea to take them with you. This applies even more to olive oil, which is usually only obtainable in extravagant small bottles in seaside grocers' shops.

1 mackerel, 1 herring, 1 whiting, 3 sprats or pilchards, 1 small fresh haddock, 1 piece of cod or pollack, 1 small crab, 3 table-spoonfuls of olive oil, 1 bay leaf, 1 sprig of thyme, parsley, 2 cloves, 3 tomatoes, 2 leeks, salt, pepper, 1 clove of garlic, ½ a gill of dry white wine, 3 pints of hot water, a pinch of saffron, and 2 tablespoonfuls of *vermicelli*.

Clean the fish and boil the crab for a few minutes. Put the oil in a fireproof casserole, add all the vegetables, cleaned and finely chopped, and simmer them in the oil over a moderate heat. Stir until they are slightly brown, pour in the wine and then add the water, little by little. Put in the fish (not the crab), raise the heat until the broth is simmering, put the lid on the casserole, and cook for about 20 minutes.

When the fish are cooked, take them out, remove the fish-bones, and pass fish and broth through a sieve. Return the *purée* to the casserole, re-heat, and add the flesh of the crab, the pinch of saffron, and the two tablespoonfuls of *vermicelli*. Simmer the soup for 10 more minutes and serve it with some finely grated cheese – not too strongly flavoured – sprinkled on the top.

ZUPPA COL BRODO DI MUGGINE

One of the best fishes to provide a delicious broth is the grey mullet. The fish does not perish in the process, but is served cold with a dress-ing of oil, lemon juice, and herbs. It is gently poached, and the resulting broth is combined with a *soffritto* of herbs and vegetables, simmered for a little while, passed through a sieve, and poured over already toasted bread in large soup plates. Grated parmesan, mixed with finely chopped parsley, savoury, chervil, is served separately. Sometimes dried fungi, which have been soaked for half an hour, cut up finely, and cooked for ten minutes in the sieved broth, are used for added flavour.

Grey mullet (weighing 2 lb), half a small stick of celery, 1 carrot, 1 onion, 2 garlic cloves, 1 sprig of parsley, 2 tablespoonfuls of oil, salt and pepper, 1 small tin of tomato *purée*, grated parmesan, 3 pints water.

Wipe the scales from the mullet, remove its gut, lay it in a large casserole with sufficient water to cover it, and bring it to the boil. Lower the flame and poach gently for about 20 minutes. Take out the fish, lay it on a dish, and when it is cold pour over it a dressing of oil, lemon juice, and chopped herbs.

Meanwhile prepare the herbs and vegetables which should be chopped and sautéd in olive oil. When these have acquired a little colour, add the tomato *purée*, the fish broth, and seasoning, and simmer altogether for half an hour. Pass the broth through a sieve, and, if you are adding dried fungi, return the broth to the saucepan, put in the fungi which have been soaked beforehand, and cook for 10 more minutes.

The soup should be served in large soup plates in which you have placed some slices of toasted French bread. Allow two tablespoonfuls of parmesan cheese for four people, combined with some chopped parsley.

This is a very simple way of preparing a fish soup, and can be used when other kinds of fish are available, whiting, for instance, or mackerel.

ZUPPA DI CANTARELLE

Although *chanterelles* can seldom be bought in shops, they are a common type of edible fungi which are so easily distinguished from all others that no risk attaches to cooking them (see page 270).

This soup requires 1 lb *chanterelles*, 2 oz butter, 5 or 6 shallots, 4 rashers of bacon, 1 tablespoonful of flour, parsley and basil, kitchen salt, 1 pint of milk, 1 pint of water, and 2 tablespoonfuls of cream. Also some fried bread.

The fungi should be quickly washed in cold running water to remove the sand or leaf mould that may attach to them, their stems should be trimmed at the base, and they should be dried with a clean cloth.

Slice the shallots finely, cut up the bacon into small pieces, and cook them both in the melted butter in a heavy pan. Slice up the *chanterelles*, put them in the pan, sprinkle them with a little chopped parsley and basil, and toss them over a moderate flame till they begin to produce their own liquor. Add salt, and sprinkle with the flour, stirring about with a wooden spoon to prevent the flour burning. Add the pint of milk which has been brought to the boil and the pint of hot water, and simmer the soup gently for half an hour. It will be a golden colour, and two tablespoonfuls of cream should be stirred into it just before serving it with an accompaniment of small squares of fried bread.

ZUPPA DI FAGIUOLI

Beans are the 'meat of the poor' in many European countries. The price of meat here makes it worthwhile to find more uses for such a valuable source of protein. It is not always realized that the merit of haricot beans is their ability to absorb flavours. To make them capable of absorbing, they must soak overnight and be subjected to at least an hour's preliminary cooking.

This Genoese recipe gives flavour to the beans by means of finely chopped herbs and aromatic vegetables, which are sautéd in olive oil, and this *soffritto* is used as the basis of the soup in which the beans are to finish cooking. The thick bean soup is completed by a few slices of bread cut up and fried in beef dripping.

Ingredients: 1 lb haricot beans (medium sized, soaked overnight, and simmered for 1 hour in 3 pints of water). For the *soffritto* you need 1 clove of garlic, 1 Spanish onion, a small bunch of basil and parsley, the peeled white part of a leek, 1 small carrot, and enough oil to cover the bottom of the frying pan. Salt and pepper. A small tin of tomato *purée* and some small squares of dry bread fried in beef dripping.

Put the soaked haricots on to cook 2 hours before you need to serve the soup, adding a little more water to that in which they have been steeped. An hour before the meal, prepare the *soffritto* by chopping finely the garlic clove, the onion, the herbs, the leek, and the carrot, and sauté them in olive oil for a few minutes. Add the tomato *purée*, salt and pepper, a few spoonfuls of the bean water, and raise the heat to boiling. Then pour the contents of the frying pan into the bean saucepan and continue the cooking until the beans are soft – about 1 hour, but it will be longer if small haricot beans have been used. Serve the soup in earthenware bowls or in a tureen, and the fried bread separately.

Pasta

7

PASTA, RISOTTO, PAELLA, GNOCCHI, POTATO DISHES, PIZZA, AND QUICHES

THE dishes in this section are based on a single theme. The theme is starch – in the form of *pasta*, rice, semolina, pastry, and potatoes.

Pasta dishes are an example of the Italian genius for elaboration from simple means. *Risotto* and *Paella* are two very different approaches to the same commodity – rice. The Italian *risotto* has a classical simplicity in which one flavour or ingredient tends to dominate. It has a delicacy in its many forms, to which the Spanish *paella*, incorporating a great variety of ingredients and in which no single one predominates, does not aspire.

In everyday terms *pasta*, *risotto*, and *paella* each provide the basis of a substantial meal. They take from thirty to forty minutes to prepare, are economical in the use of meat, poultry, and fish, employ oil or butter, which is more digestible than lard, and once the methods of their preparation have been established are capable of variation according to the means at one's disposal. They can in fact stand alone, with the addition of a green salad, cheese, and fruit, as a satisfying meal, particularly when accompanied by a glass of wine.

Neapolitan in origin, *pizza* is a dish made with leavened bread. Sold in quayside shops on the Genoese and Ligurian coast, it stills mid-morning pangs of hunger and appetites whetted by sea air. But as it often contains a top dressing of salt anchovies, it is again a stimulus to further eating and drinking. *Pizza* should be regarded as a dish for a convivial occasion, thirst provoking and served with wine.

The French *quiches* and *tartes* have rather less pretension to being a meal in themselves. They should be preceded by a soup, particularly as delicious food of this kind stimulates the appetite if it is not partly assuaged beforehand.

Pasta

In many parts of Italy, *pasta* is synonymous with food. A fragrant steaming dish of *pasta* is what the Latin stomach craves to fill the void created by a morning's fasting in the dry heat of summer and the windswept cold of winter.

As a rule *past'asciutta* * is eaten at midday, and *minestra in brodo* † at night. These are the prelude to a meal in bourgeois homes, when not preceded by *antipasto* (*hors d'œuvre*), and are followed by a dish of meat or fish, a salad, cheese, and fruit.

The Italians, who have not yet separated art from daily life, cannot resist using a material as plastic as flour and water in a multitude of ways; hence the shapes in the form of stars, melon seeds, rings, and snail shells among the *pasta* for *minestra in brodo*, and the strings, ribbons, conch shells, coxcombs, wheels, and butterflies for *past'asciutta*.

The kinds of *pasta* considered here are limited to those suitable for *past'asciutta*. They should have enough body to be worth eating served *al burro* (with cheese and butter), or *al sugo* (with sauce and cheese), or, after preliminary boiling, baked with sauce and cheese in the oven.

All *pasta* is cooked in a great deal of boiling water before being subjected to its various treatments. The finer *pasta* are sometimes cooked in chicken or veal stock, when available, *tagliatelle* and *lasagne* for instance.

Herbs are used both in the stuffings and in the sauce, and combine with parmesan cheese to give these *pasta* dishes a particular aromatic fragrance. This is rather different from French cooking where the *bouquet garni* consisting of parsley, thyme, and bay is used with more reserve. In the Italian kitchen, the parsley, basil, marjoram, and thyme are finely chopped, and with the garlic are the first to go into the pan to be gently cooked in olive oil. This is the starting off point of an Italian sauce or *risotto* before the introduction of tomato, mushrooms, chicken livers, chopped meats, or other ingredients.

Pasta is often served with fish in Italian coastal districts, with

* *past'asciutta*, literally translated, is dry *pasta*.
† *minestra in brodo* is soup *pasta* in broth.

SPAGHETTINI

VERMICELLI

SPAGHETTI

SPAGHETTONI

BUCATINI

MACCHERONI

MEZZA ZITE

ZITE

FETTUCCIE

FRANCESINE

MEZZA LASAGNE

LASAGNE

MEZZA LASAGNE MATASSA

CONCHIGLIE

CAPPE

RUOTE

FARFALLONI

MANICHE

MILLERIGHE

SCOLETTONI

mussels, fresh pilchards, fresh anchovies, or tunny; in Tuscany it is eaten with the sauce in which hare, duck, or pigeon has been braised. But there are two sauces for *past'asciutta* which are, with different accents of flavour, most often encountered. They are, *sugo di pomodoro* (tomato sauce) and *sugo alla bolognese*. The *pasta* is treated to a preliminary boiling in water for fifteen to twenty minutes, put into an earthenware dish in which a little olive oil is heating, and is then dressed with one of these sauces, and served very hot with additional grated parmesan.

SUGO DI POMODORO (1)

Put a sliced clove of garlic, a small handful of chopped parsley and basil into an aluminium pan with two tablespoonfuls of olive oil, and cook for a few minutes on a low heat. When the garlic begins to colour, add 7 or 8 tomatoes sliced up and salted, and cook them until soft for about thirty minutes. Pass the sauce through a sieve, return it to the pan, and add half a cup of grated parmesan cheese before pouring it onto the *pasta*.

As this sauce is served with farinaceous food, it is of a more liquid consistency than many sauces based on flour and butter combinations. All the same, it must not be watery, and if, after sieving, this is the case, it should be further simmered and reduced before adding the cheese.

Italian tomatoes are most often the small globe variety, harvested as a rule in August. There is a large industry for tinning tomatoes and *purée*, both of which are used a great deal for cooking. The flavour of these tomatoes is sharper and at the same time sweeter than that of English tomatoes, and to obtain the really characteristic flavour of this sauce, tinned Italian *estratto di pomodoro* can be used. (A small tin will make enough sauce for four people.)

SUGO DI POMODORO (2)

Cook a sliced clove of garlic, a small chopped onion, the white part of a leek, a small handful of parsley and basil, and a sprig of rosemary in 2 tablespoonfuls of olive oil. Empty the contents of a tin of Italian tomato *purée* into the simmering pan and add a small wineglass of red wine, a dessertspoonful of wine vinegar, 2 lumps of sugar, and a pinch of kitchen salt. Pour on a cupful of hot vegetable stock or beef *bouillon*.

Stir the *purée* and let it simmer until the sauce is of a proper consistency.

Besides having a sharper flavour, it has the advantage of requiring half the time to prepare, and, at a pinch, can be made while the *spaghetti* or *tagliatelle* is cooking.

Variations can be made on this basis by adding, for instance, 6–8 ounces of sliced mushrooms or a few pounded anchovies to simmer in the oil before introducing the tomato *purée*.

SUGO ALLA BOLOGNESE (1)

Chop 2 ounces of raw veal very finely with a chopping knife or *mezzaluna*. Slice 2 rashers of bacon, chop an onion, carrot, and 2 sticks of white celery, and put these together with a table-spoonful of oil (or 2 ounces of butter), ground pepper, and grated nutmeg into a pan.

Cook them together on a moderate flame in a heavy aluminium pan for a few minutes until the meat begins to brown, sprinkle with a little flour, pour on half a pint of good stock and simmer until the sauce has thickened and the meat is tender. Half a cup of cream can be added to improve this sauce a few minutes before taking the pan off the fire.

SUGO ALLA BOLOGNESE (2)

A more elaborate Bolognese sauce contains 2 ounces of raw lean beef finely chopped, a dozen sliced mushrooms, a few stoned black olives, 2 rashers of bacon or a slice of ham or smoked pork (Italian *Coppa* which has a smoky flavour) chopped, two anchovies pounded, a chopped onion, a garlic clove, basil, and sprig of rosemary; a glass of red wine (or less wine vinegar), a small tin of tomato *purée*, and ½ pint of beef broth.

Put the chopped beef, bacon, mushrooms, stoned olives, and pounded anchovies in a pan in which the onion, garlic, and herbs have begun cooking in a tablespoonful of oil. Cook them gently until the oil and the fat from the ham or bacon have been absorbed, and then add the wine. Let this sizzle for a few moments and reduce a little, when it is time to add the *purée* and half a pint of stock. This concoction should simmer gently on top of the stove for at least half an hour to allow the flavour of the meat to penetrate the sauce, and for longer if possible.

SPAGHETTI

This method of cooking *spaghetti* applies to other forms of *pasta*, but the length of time varies with their size and texture.
Spaghetti should be bought by the pound freshly made where this is possible, and otherwise in packets of Italian make. It should be long and not too thick. One pound is enough for four people.

Cook the *spaghetti* in a large saucepan of fast boiling salted water for 15 to 20 minutes. Hold the sticks upright in the saucepan for a few moments, and they will begin to bend from the bottom in the boiling water, and the complete lengths will curl into the pan. It is important that it should not be over-cooked, it must still have some bite in it, and this can only be ascertained by testing it after 15 minutes. Have a *terracotta* or fireproof dish warming in the oven, into which you have poured a tablespoonful of oil. When the *spaghetti* is cooked, drain it well, and turn it over in the warmed dish so that it is lightly oiled. While it is cooking prepare a tomato sauce, but if you wish to serve it *alla bolognese* you need to start preparing the ingredients for the sauce at least 20 minutes before boiling the spaghetti.

Don't try to break up the sticks before cooking, or to cut them afterwards in the thought that their length will embarrass your guests. Anyone who has ever seen an Italian eating *past'asciutta* in a *trattoria*, or a gentleman from Bologna surrounded by waiters in a Florentine restaurant, knows that even the most accomplished performers have no scruples about appearances. Let your guests drown their scruples in a glass of wine. Don't forget to serve grated parmesan with the *spaghetti*. It not only improves the taste, but improves the texture.

TAGLIATELLE ALL'UOVO

Tagliatelle can be bought freshly made in Soho shops, or made by reputable Italian firms in cellophane packets. When fresh and soft it takes about five minutes to cook. When dry and hard it requires boiling for fifteen to twenty minutes. Being a paste of egg and flour it is richer than *vermicelli* and *spaghetti*, both made from flour and water.

PASTE FOR TAGLIATELLE ALL'UOVO

2 eggs and a white of egg to ½ lb plain flour, for 4 people.

Make a mound of ½ lb flour with a hole in the middle on a clean board or piece of marble. Drop 2 eggs and a white into the hole and whisk them round a few times with your finger-tips and then begin to introduce the flour by a circular movement of the fingers. Work in sufficient flour to produce a firm but elastic dough, which should no longer stick to your fingers or the board. Divide the dough in half, as it is easier to roll out a small quantity. Then, allowing yourself plenty of table-top, roll out the paste with an even pressure away from you into a long oblong. The paste must be thin and even, thinner than a halfpenny's depth. If you are used to mixing pastry dough you will find that this egg and flour paste is much more resilient and easy to handle.

Leave the sheets of paste for a bit so that the egg dries a little. Then take a pastry cutter and divide it into long thin ribbons ¼ inch wide. This needs a steady hand and eye, and long even strands of *tagliatelle* should be the result.

If you prefer, lightly flour the sheet of paste, fold it in half, and roll it up like a swiss roll. Then with less art but more easily you can cut the roll into ¼-inch strips, unwind them, and hang them up in a warm place. *Tagliatelle* which is not for immediate use should be properly dried in this way.

FETTUCCINE and LASAGNE can be made in the same way as *tagliatelle*. But *fettuccine* must be cut in ⅛-inch strips which is rather exacting. *Lasagne* is easier, the strips being ½ inch in width.

All these ribbon pastes can be served *al sugo* (see page 94).

D

TAGLIATELLE COL PROSCIUTTO

Cut a quarter-inch thick slice of Italian *prosciutto* (raw smoked ham) into small pieces, chop an onion and a carrot finely, and cook these together in a pan with a tablespoonful of oil. Add the contents of a tin of tomato *purée* and a little stock to make a sauce.

Cook the *tagliatelle* for 15 minutes, drain it, dress it with the sauce, and sprinkle the dish with grated parmesan.

TAGLIATELLE VERDI

½ lb flour, 2 eggs, ½ lb raw spinach.

This is *tagliatelle* coloured with fresh boiled spinach. Cook the spinach, drain, and chop it finely. Pile ½ lb flour onto a pastry board, make a hole in the middle of it, into which you put 2 eggs and a handful of finely chopped cooked spinach, the cooked equivalent of ½ lb raw spinach. Make a paste by introducing sufficient flour to make an elastic dough and work it well. Draw out a fine sheet of paste with a rolling-pin, lightly flouring it to prevent it sticking. Roll this sheet of paste in a clean kitchen cloth and leave it to dry before cutting it into ¼-inch ribbons. *Tagliatelle* should be as long as possible, a sign of skilful manufacture.

This is considered to be more digestible than white *tagliatelle*. It needs more care, because the water in the spinach gives the paste a tendency to stick. If not for immediate use, the strands should be hung on a string in a warm place to dry. Serve *al sugo* or simply with a quantity of grated cheese and butter (parmesan or hard *pecorino*).

Green *lasagne* and *fettuccine* can be made in the same way.

MACCHERONI AL FORNO

The more substantial kinds of *pasta*, *maccheroni*, *bucatini*, *ʒite* (long varieties) and *scolettone*, *millerighi*, *fusille grande*, and *conchiglie* (short varieties) are often treated to a preliminary cooking in boiling water, and then are further cooked in a *balsamella* sauce and lightly browned under the grill, or are placed in an oven dish in a tomato or *bolognese* sauce with layers of cheese, and further baked in the oven.

MACCHERONI COLLA BALSAMELLA

1 pound of *maccheroni*, 3 ounces of butter, 2 dessertspoonfuls flour, and a pint of milk; 2 cupfuls of grated parmesan, an egg yolk.

Partly cook the *maccheroni* in boiling salted water, and then drain it, returning it to a pan with a little butter. Allow the *maccheroni* to absorb the butter, and then add sufficient milk for it to finish cooking. Meanwhile, make a *balsamella*, which is the Italian version of *sauce Béchamel*. It is made by combining 2 ounces of butter and 2 dessertspoonfuls of flour in a pan over a low flame, stirring the two together to obtain a smooth paste, when a pint of hot milk is added a little at a time, and the sauce is gently simmered till it is smooth. Take it off the fire and stir in the yolk of an egg. Put the *maccheroni*, which should now be tender but not flabby, in a fireproof dish, and pour the sauce over it together with a cupful of grated parmesan. Sprinkle the remaining cupful onto the top of the dish, and bake in a Regulo 7 oven for 10 minutes, or brown it under the grill.

MACCHERONI COL PANGRATTATO

This dish requires 1½ lb long *maccheroni*, 5 oz *gruyère* cheese, and 3 oz grated parmesan, 3 oz butter and 1½ pints milk, as well as a cupful of finely grated breadcrumbs, and a little flour.

Half cook the *maccheroni* (10 minutes) and remove it from the boiling water to drain. Mix half the butter with a dessertspoonful of flour over a low flame in a fairly large saucepan, and when it begins to brown pour in the hot milk, a little at a time, stirring the while. Allow this thin *balsamella* to simmer for 10 minutes. Put in the *maccheroni* and the grated *gruyère*, little by little, and let it simmer on a low heat (with asbestos mat) while it absorbs the liquid. Add the grated parmesan and the rest of the butter. Put the *maccheroni* in a fireproof dish, cover it with the breadcrumbs, which should be more like fine dust than crumbs, and brown in the oven, or under the grill.

RAVIOLI

Ravioli are now known to us as little envelopes of paste containing spinach and cheese, or forcemeat. They took this form in the kitchens of the Genoese.

But according to a very distinguished Italian sage, Signor Pellegrino Artusi, these are not *i veri ravioli* which are neither folded in a paste nor contain meat. The true *ravioli* consist of a mixture of *ricotta* (a milk curd cheese), a little parmesan, eggs, spinach, and nutmeg, rolled into balls and cooked in rapidly boiling water, and served with tomato sauce, or cheese and butter.

Ravioli alla Genovese

Ravioli can of course be bought in Italian grocery shops. But it can be a far better dish made at home, because the stuffing is freshly made and the paste contains a known quantity of eggs. *Ravioli* is sometimes falsely coloured with saffron or turmeric to simulate the eggs.

There are four pre-occupations: 1. The paste itself, which it is a simple operation to make, and can be made in twenty minutes. 2. The stuffing. 3. Cooking the completed *ravioli*. 4. Combining the *ravioli* with the sauce.

The stuffing should be made beforehand as it must be cold before laying on the paste. We give the stuffings first, for this reason.

Stuffings for Ravioli

1. This is a very delicate stuffing which contains half a breast of chicken, the brains of a lamb, 2 lambs' sweetbreads, a chicken's liver, a slice of fat ham, ¼ lb cooked spinach, some grated parmesan, and 2 egg yolks.

   Blanch the chicken, brains, and sweetbreads, and remove the membrane from brains and sweetbreads. Put them and the chicken liver in a pan with a nut of butter, and when they begin to brown pour on a little meat stock. Remove them from the stock after a few minutes' cooking, and chop them finely with a small slice of fat ham, add some boiled and sieved spinach, grated parmesan, nutmeg, and 2 egg yolks. Pound these all together in a mortar, add salt if necessary, and the stuffing, which should not be too damp, is ready to lay on the paste when it is cool.

2. This stuffing needs 6 ounces of veal, cut small, 4 ounces of bacon, a chopped onion, a bay leaf, thyme. A glass of white wine, ¼ pound of cooked spinach, and 2 egg yolks.

Put the veal, bacon, onion, and herbs in a pan with a little butter, and add after a few minutes the glass of white wine. Let these simmer together with the lid on, until the meat is cooked, when the lid should be removed, and the juice be allowed to reduce. Turn out onto a plate to cool, and then pound the mixture with a handful of cooked spinach (½ lb of spinach reduces to a cooked handful). Add the 2 egg yolks, season, and pass the mixture through a sieve.

3. 4 ounces of ham, 4 ounces of *Mortadella*, 2 ounces of beef marrow, 2 ounces of grated parmesan, 1 egg, and nutmeg.

4. ¾ lb cooked spinach, 4 oz grated parmesan, 1 egg yolk.

Take the cooked spinach and chop it finely, having carefully pressed out the surplus water. Add the grated parmesan and the yolk of an egg, and mix it into a smooth preparation.

Each of these stuffings should provide sufficient filling for about 70 *ravioli* cases.

Paste for Ravioli

½ lb flour and 2 eggs plus 1 egg white should produce a thin layer of paste roughly 1 foot 6 inches long and 9 inches wide, and make 72 *ravioli* 1½ inches square, enough for 5 or 6 people. If not so many are needed, it is still worth making this amount and keeping them for a day or two in a closed container in the refrigerator.

Make a mound of the flour on a clean board, press a hole in the centre, and drop in the eggs. Whisk them round with your finger-tips and with a continuous circular movement of the fingers begin to introduce the flour into the eggs; work sufficient flour in to produce a firm and elastic dough. It must be dry enough not to stick to your fingers or the board, and if this is not the case, work in more flour.

Divide the dough in half, and roll it out evenly into two equal very thin shapes. (Not so thin as to produce a weakness in the paste, which might tear in the cooking.)

Trim the sheets of paste into even oblongs and lightly dent one of them with the edge of a ruler at 1½-inch intervals across and down, so that you have the ghost of a chequer board, and in the centre of each square lay a teaspoonful of stuffing. Then, with a paintbrush wet the lines across and down, and lay the second sheet of paste very gently on top, and press down the lines between the stuffing both ways, so that the two pastes stick well together.

Divide the *ravioli* evenly with a fluted edged pastry cutter, or failing this, a knife. If by some misfortune some of the resulting envelopes remain unsealed, apply water with a finger and press together.

If this seems too perilous an operation, there is another way. Divide the paste into two as before, as it is always easier to roll out a smaller quantity evenly. Then with a 2-inch diameter tin top or round pastry cutter, cut a series of circles in the paste with as little waste as possible; fill the centres of each circle with stuffing, wet the edge all round, and fold over in a half circle, pressing the edges together, to make little stuffed half-moons. These are perfectly legitimate *ravioli* shapes, although they are more commonly the form used for *tortellini*, a Bolognese creation for soups.

Cooking and serving Ravioli

Prepare some tomato sauce (page 94) and 2 cupfuls of grated parmesan, or hard *pecorino* cheese. Cook the *ravioli* about 14 at a time in a large pan of boiling water. If you do more at once, they will bombard each other and perhaps break. They take five minutes to cook. When they rise to the surface, remove them with a draining spoon, and have ready a warmed earthenware dish in the oven containing a little hot tomato sauce. Lay the *ravioli* in the bottom of the dish, sprinkle with cheese, add a little more hot sauce, and repeat this operation in layers as the freshly cooked *ravioli* are ready. This will take about 25 minutes altogether (five batches), by then you will have a steaming dish of *pasta*. This method of combining the *ravioli* and the sauce is recommended to avoid turning the delicate envelopes in a saucepan with sauce, when they may break.

NOUILLES

These are a French variant of the Italian ribbon *pasta* and differ from them only in that more egg yolks are used in relation to the proportion of flour. Because of this, the *nouilles* need to be well floured when the paste has been made so that it does not stick while it is resting before being cut into strips.

To make enough *nouilles* for 4 to 5 people you will need: 10 ounces of plain flour, 1 whole egg and 6 yolks of egg, and a pinch of salt.

Put the flour onto a wooden board and make a hole in the middle of it. Into this hole put the salt. Beat the whole egg with the egg yolks and when they are well mixed pour them into the hole in the flour. With the tips of the fingers, work the flour into the eggs until it is all a lively, springy mass. Take the flour into the eggs from the sides of the hole little by little, until it is all well amalgamated. Then put it aside to rest in a cool place for 1 hour, covered with a cloth.

At the end of that time, if your board is small, divide the paste and either roll or pull it out until it is less than the thickness of a worn sixpenny piece. Trim it to a rectangular shape and, with a pastry cutter or sharp thin knife which has been dipped in flour, cut the paste into strips of not more than ¼ inch in width.

The *nouilles* can then be cooked in boiling salted water for about 5 minutes and served with a sauce such as *sugo di pomodoro* or more simply with fresh butter and freshly grated parmesan cheese. (In the latter form they are excellent served with veal or cutlets or with *Bœuf en daube* instead of the more usual *purée* of potatoes.)

Nouilles à la vénitienne

Having either made or bought the *nouilles*, cook them in plenty of water with some salt. The water should boil gently. If the *nouilles* are freshly made they will only take about 5 minutes to cook but if they are bought they will take from 12 to 15 minutes.

While this is happening, the sauce should be made from: 2 ounces of butter, 2 dessertspoonfuls of plain flour, 1 pint of milk, 2 ounces of ham, 8 mushrooms, 2 ounces of chicken meat, 2 ounces of freshly grated parmesan cheese, and a further 2 ounces of butter.

Melt the butter in a good sized pan and when it is frothing add the flour to it to make a *roux*. Let this cook, without getting coloured, for about 3 minutes. Heat the milk and when it is on the boil pour it onto the *roux*, little by little, while stirring well. Let this thin sauce cook gently. Meanwhile, chop the ham, wipe the mushrooms, and slice the chicken meat finely. Add all these to the sauce, which should be cooked for 15 minutes after the milk has been added.

By this time the *nouilles* should be ready. Drain them well and sprinkle them with half of the parmesan cheese. Then add them to the sauce, as carefully as possible so that they don't break, and pour them into a shallow fireproof dish. Sprinkle the rest of the grated parmesan cheese on top of the mixture and pour over it the 2 ounces of melted butter. Put the dish in a hot oven and let the top brown.

Risotto

There must be in Italy and the south of France as many ways of flavouring a dish of rice as there are fish or fowl.

Risotto – with frogs' legs, fish broth, fungi, with crayfish, inkfish, tuna, with truffles and tomatoes, with chicken livers, scallops, and *frutta di mare*.

In an Italian dish of rice the rice is flavoured in two ways: initially by sautéing the principal ingredient in the pan before frying the rice, and secondly by the addition of boiling and well-flavoured stock. The first process determines the flavour, and the second improves it. This is why a genuine veal, beef, or chicken stock should be used, or in the case of a fish *risotto*, a fish stock.

Always use Italian rice for *risotto* dishes. This method of cooking rice would not have been invented had not a rice with particularly absorbent qualities been grown in the Lombard plain: *riso arborio*.

When wine is used, it should be added when the rice has fried for a few minutes and acquired a transparent look. The wine should be allowed to bubble and reduce a little before adding the stock, to volatilize the alcohol.

The stock should be kept simmering in a pan, and should be added in small quantities at first, to ensure even expansion of the rice.

The proportion of liquid to rice is exactly two to one, so that if half a cupful of rice is allowed for each person, a cupful of stock will be needed to cook it.

The simmering of the rice should be lively. If the gas is too low the centre of the rice grains tend to remain hard, and the outside to become pulpy.

Because the rice must cook until the liquid is perfectly absorbed, the last few minutes of cooking are critical. Many people prefer, therefore, to start the *risotto* off in a heavy pan on top of the stove, and to complete the cooking when all the stock has been added in an earthenware lidded casserole in the oven. If the whole operation is done on top of the stove, an asbestos mat should be placed on the flame to spread the heat when frying has given place to simmering.

When the rice is cooked, it is a good thing to stretch a clean cloth over the casserole, leaving it for 5 minutes in a warm oven. Just before serving, mix a little fresh butter with the rice.

RISOTTO WITH CHICKEN LIVERS

For four people buy 12 ounces of chicken livers and use a pound of Italian rice. A small glass of white wine, an onion, chopped parsley and basil, a slice of bacon, a pint of chicken stock, olive oil, and a tablespoonful of parmesan are also needed.

Chop an onion, a small handful of fresh parsley and basil, and put them in a heavy pan with 2 tablespoonfuls of oil and the chopped slice of rather fat bacon. Cook these together on a low flame, and then add the chicken livers, which should have been washed and salted. (Be very careful that they are fresh, discard any that look diseased.) Let the chicken livers cook gently for a few minutes only, and remove them. Put in the rice, stir it until it has absorbed the remaining oil, add the white wine and then (little by little) the heated chicken stock, and, increasing the flame a little while putting an asbestos mat on it to distribute the heat, let the rice cook for 20 minutes. By this time most of the moisture will have been absorbed, but if the rice is not entirely cooked add a little more stock. Cut up the livers and put them back into the pan with the rice for a few minutes. Sprinkle the chopped parsley and basil, stir in a tablespoonful of grated parmesan, and the dish is ready to serve.

(Don't on any account leave the livers in the pan while the rice is cooking or they will have the texture of little pieces of leather.)

A RISOTTO FOR LEAN DAYS

For this dish you need only buy 2 scallops and 4 ounces of mushrooms. The rest of the ingredients should be already in your own kitchen. A pound of Italian rice, a few anchovies, a small tin of tomato *purée*, a leek, a stick of celery, a carrot, a small spoonful of basil, an onion and a garlic clove, olive oil, and 2 slices of lean bacon. Enough for four people.

Slice the garlic clove and cook it in 2 tablespoonfuls of oil. Then add the onion, the leek (only the white part, peel off the outside skin), the carrot, and a white celery stick, all of which should be finely chopped, the bacon diced, and cook them all together, without browning, on a low flame. Slice up the mushrooms and put them into the pan as well. Meanwhile scoop the scallops from their shells, wash them carefully, separate the orange tongue-like portion from the rest, and cut the white part into squares and put them into the pan. The orange part requires very little cooking and is put in later. Now stir the rice into this mixture. After a few minutes it will have become transparent and this is the time to add the tomato *purée* and 4 cups of boiling water. Increase the speed of the cooking and make quite sure that nothing is sticking to the bottom of the pan when you start simmering. This part of the cooking should be lively. The rice will take about 30 minutes to cook, by which time it should have absorbed the liquid. The orange part of the scallops should be put in about five minutes before the rice is ready. (Any white shellfish has a tendency to stick to the bottom of the pan, so it is wise to stir now and then.)

RISOTTO ALLA MILANESE

This recipe is for a dish of rice which is served at the beginning of a meal in northern Italy, and it is doubtful whether it can fairly rate as a main dish. But as it is a delicious way of cooking rice, we put it in with the suggestion that it might be followed by veal cutlets and a green salad.

For five people: 2½ cups of rice, 3 ounces of butter, 2 ounces of beef marrow, an onion, ½ a cup of parmesan, a pinch of saffron, a wineglassful of red wine, and 5 cups of hot beef *bouillon*.

Chop the onion finely and cook it in a heavy pan with the beef marrow and half the butter. When onion and marrow are browned, add the rice, moving it about the pan until it has absorbed the rest of the butter. Pour on the wine, let it fizzle up and reduce a little, and then add 5 cups of hot beef *bouillon*, and the saffron. Leave it to cook for at least twenty minutes, and before removing it from the fire add the rest of the butter and the parmesan, and serve more grated parmesan in a separate dish.

The quality of the *bouillon* or stock is very important in the Italian rice dishes as the system of cooking the rice – the gentle frying followed by lively simmering – is designed to make the rice absorb the flavour both of the *battuto* – in this case the onion, marrow, and butter – and the *bouillon*.

Saffron in Italian cooking is used in two ways. When in powdered form it is usually thrown into the rice at the end of the cooking. Powdered saffron may be adulterated. When bought in stamen form, it is pounded and infused into a cup of hot stock, and added to the rice after frying. Both methods produce a fragrant yellow rice, and the saffron has the added virtue of stimulating the appetite.

RISOTTO WITH MUSSELS

Mussel beds are to be found on rocky coasts where a fresh-water stream drains into the sea. Fishermen will sometimes divulge their whereabouts, when nothing is easier than to gather them in a bucket on an ebbing tide, keeping enough sea-water to cover them. A reliable fishmonger is the next best resort.

4 dozen mussels are needed for this dish. 1½ lb rice, a handful of dried fungi (preferably *cèpes*), a glass of white wine, a clove of garlic, onion, celery, fresh parsley, and grated parmesan.

If the mussels come straight out of the sea, they need vigorous scrubbing, the beards must be removed, any that are open should be rejected, and the rest should be left in a bucket of sea-water, with an upturned plate on the bottom, for the sand particles to sink to the bottom. If they come from the fishmonger, scrub and beard them, and leave in a pail of salt water.

There are several ways of opening mussels (see page 150), depending on how they are to be used. In the case of this *risotto* where a quantity of stock is needed, pour 4 cupfuls of water into a saucepan, throw in the mussels, and bring them to the boil, when the shells should open. Remove the mussels from their shells, and decant the stock.

In a heavy aluminium pan on a low heat, put 2 tablespoonfuls of olive oil, an onion finely chopped, a sliced garlic clove, with parsley and celery cut very finely with a chopping knife. When these begin to change colour, throw in the shelled mussels and a handful of dried fungi which have been re-animated in warm water. Stir in the rice, and when it becomes transparent add a wineglassful of white wine. Let this simmer for a few minutes, and then add the mussel stock. The rice should be simmered rather briskly for five minutes and then finish cooking in an already heated earthenware casserole in the oven (Regulo 6) for fifteen to twenty minutes. When all the liquid is absorbed and the rice cooked but not mushy, stir in a handful of freshly chopped parsley and grated parmesan, and serve.

RISOTTO AUX FRUITS DE MER

The expression *fruits de mer* means little unless one has lived for a time on the shores of the Mediterranean, where the *fruits de mer* or *frutta di mare* are brought up from the beach every day, to appear for the midday meal. Clams, eaten uncooked as salty *apéritifs*, little crabs which have a milky sweetness, small octopi fried in batter with fresh anchovies and fresh sardines, and *scampi*, grilled with a dressing of herbs, oil, and piquant tomato sauce. They all have the sweet-salt freshness of sea fruit.

This is a more elaborate way of preparing *risotto* with shellfish, requiring 2 dozen mussels, 1 dozen clams, a small lobster, and 2 dozen prawns, 2 lb rice (8 cupfuls), and a small tin of tomato *purée*; this should be ample for 6 to 7 people.

Scrub the mussels, tweak off the black beards which attach at the shell-joint, and put them into a saucepan with the clams, a finely cut onion, carrot, and a sprig of parsley, thyme, and bay, a glass of water and 3 or 4 peppercorns, on a brisk flame.

Cover the saucepan, and after a few moments the mussels and clams will open. Drain the liquid into a vessel to allow any sand to sink to the bottom, and decant it for later use. Remove the mussels and clams from their shells.

Cut the white meat of an already boiled lobster into small pieces and remove the shells from the prawns. Then make a *roux* of a walnut of butter and a spoonful of flour on a low flame, without allowing it to brown and add a glassful of the mussel liquor to make a thick sauce. Incorporate 2 egg yolks mixed with the juice of a lemon into the sauce, removing the pan from the fire to do this, and return it for a few moments to blend the sauce, without on any account allowing it to boil.

Half of this sauce should be used for dressing the shellfish, which should be ready in a casserole. The other half should be thinned with a few spoonfuls of the remaining mussel water, to pour over the rice before serving.

Preparation of the rice: Heat a large walnut of butter in a saucepan and put in a finely chopped onion, with 4 cupfuls of Italian rice. When the rice becomes slightly transparent pour on a glass of white wine which should be slightly reduced, upon which you can add the contents of a tin of tomato *purée*, the remaining mussel water, and if this is insufficient, add enough water to double the amount of liquid in relation to rice. (Better still, boil up the shells of the prawns and the lobster shell, and use this liquid.) Cook the *risotto* on a medium flame with an asbestos mat to spread the heat all over the bottom of the pan, until the liquid is absorbed.

Gently heat the mussels, lobster, and prawns in the sauce that has been reserved, and just before the rice is ready, add the clams, which tend to harden if cooked for more than a few minutes. Then pile the rice round a large oval or circular dish, make a hole in the middle and fill this with the shellfish embalmed in their sauce. Pour the sauce which has been thinned over the rice itself, and serve with a flourish.

A sophisticated way of serving this dish of rice is to take as many pudding basins of ½ pound size as you have guests, oil them inside, and when the rice is ready, half fill the basins with rice. Then, making a hole in the centre of each, fill them with the shellfish enveloped in its sauce. This filling must be done firmly, or there will be a *débâcle* when the dish is served. In Florence, the waiter actually brings the plate covered with its upturned pudding bowl to the table, and then neatly removes the bowl, leaving a mound of *risotto* on the plate, over which a little more sauce is poured.

This method of serving rice can be applied to most *risotti*, but as it is essential to serve it hot, the dressing for the rice must be warming in a casserole or *bain-marie*, the moulds must be hot and oiled, and the actual operation of embalming the rice in the moulds quickly done.

Paella

We have included the Spanish dish *paella* in this section because its basic ingredient is rice although it also contains as large a variety of poultry, shellfish, sausages, and vegetables as are available. Butter is expensive in Spain so that most of the cooking is done in oil, but, ideally, some of the ingredients of a *paella* should be cooked in butter.

As can be seen from the list of ingredients, a *paella* is a dish which is made in a large quantity and for this reason we have not given detailed proportions for it. The result should be a mound of yellow rice with many differing morsels well and freely dispersed in it.

For eight people, use, say: 2 pounds of rice, some uncooked frying chicken, prawns, mussels, scallops, crayfish, a little ham, some sausages, onions, tomatoes, red peppers, green olives, peas, mushrooms, saffron, oil, butter, salt, pepper, and 1 pint of chicken stock.

Cut the chicken into small pieces, shell the prawns and cray-fish, prepare and open the mussels over a good heat and con-serve their liquid. Skin and seed the tomatoes, wipe the mush-rooms, slice the onions very finely, skin the sausages if necessary, and cut the scallops.

Heat about 2 ounces of butter in a *cocotte* and fry the chicken in it until it is golden brown. Fry the sliced onions in another pan in some olive oil. Cut the ham in cubes of about 1 inch square and fry them in butter. Fry, rather lightly, the sausages. Fry the tomatoes and mushrooms.

Throw the rice into a pan of boiling salted water and let it boil regularly until half-cooked (10 minutes) then drain it well. Put the half-cooked rice into the pan where the chicken is cook-ing and fry it, adding more butter if it seems to be needed. When the rice is shining, add the tomatoes and the onions and the saffron diluted in a little stock. Then pour on about ¾ pint of hot chicken stock. Let the stock and rice mixture simmer until the stock is almost absorbed.

At this point add, very gently so that nothing breaks, the prawns, the ham, the sausage, the mushrooms, the peas, and the mussels, and scallops which must also have been cooked in a little butter. Taste the *paella* and add any seasoning you think it needs, then put it in a very low oven – with a dry cloth over it – and leave it there until the stock is completely absorbed and the rice is dry, but not overcooked.

The *paella* can then be turned onto a flat, hot dish or served direct from the *cocotte*. It can be decorated with strips of red peppers which have been gently cooked in a little butter or oil.

Once the method of making a *paella* has been grasped, it is capable of adaptation to whatever ingredients are to hand. It does in fact require less strenuous attention than a *risotto*.

Tinned tunny fish, anchovies, black or green olives, salt cod (see page 130), rock lobster, chicken livers, fungi, French garlic sausage, can go into the *paella*, as well as the diced meat of one or two mutton chops. The best rice to use is Patna rice. Chopped walnuts or hazel nuts, a few capers, some small pickled onions or sliced gherkins, grated lemon peel, can be used at will.

Paella can in fact be treated as a vehicle for divers condiments, but there should always be a balance between the fish and meat elements and a piquant taste best communicated by Spanish pimentoes, fresh or tinned, olives, saffron, and anchovies.

Gnocchi

In Italy, *gnocchi* are made either from a mixture of cooked potato and flour or from semolina cooked in milk. In most recipes both of these mixtures are bound with egg. Some recipes for the potato and flour version omit the egg, but its inclusion adds to the nutritive value of the dish as well as acting as a binding agent for the other ingredients.

SEMOLINA GNOCCHI

1 pint of milk, 4 ounces of semolina, 2 fresh eggs, salt, pepper, a little grated nutmeg, and 3 ounces of freshly grated parmesan cheese, with about a dessertspoonful of olive oil, and 1 ounce of butter.

Put the milk into a thick saucepan and bring it to the boil. Sprinkle the semolina into the milk while it is boiling and stir well until it is smooth and free from any lumps. Let the mixture cook evenly, stirring all the time, for 7 minutes. Take the pan off the fire and season the semolina with salt, black pepper, and a little nutmeg. Let the mixture cool. When it is no longer hot, beat up the eggs and incorporate them with the semolina and milk.

Pour the semolina into a well-oiled flat tin to obtain an overall thickness of ½ an inch. Then leave it to cool.

About 30 minutes before you wish to serve the *gnocchi*, cut the cold semolina into 1-inch squares (or circles, if you like) and lay them in a shallow, well-buttered earthenware dish. Dust the *gnocchi* liberally with the grated parmesan and put small knobs of butter over the top. Put the dish in a hot oven until the *gnocchi* are brown on top and then serve them with more parmesan, handed separately, and a home-made tomato sauce (*sugo di pomodoro*).

GNOCCHI

SUGO DI POMODORO FOR GNOCCHI

1 pound of tomatoes, 1 chopped onion, 1 carrot, 1 stick of celery, a little thyme, ½ a bay leaf, some chopped basil (either fresh or dried), about 6 fat bacon rinds with pepper and salt, 1 teaspoonful of brown sugar, and a dessertspoonful of lemon juice.

Skin the tomatoes and chop them. Chop the other vegetables. Put the bacon rinds in a pan over a gentle heat to extract the fat. Remove the bacon rinds, throw in the chopped vegetables and the tomatoes. When they are simmering add the sugar, the herbs, and the lemon juice. Let this cook in the pan, well covered, for an hour over a very gentle heat. Then pass it through a sieve and taste it. If necessary adjust the seasoning. Return the sauce to the pan, heat it, and serve with the *gnocchi*. (See also page 94.)

POTATO GNOCCHI

This recipe does not include an egg but is made from: 2 pounds of potatoes, boiled and sieved, ¾ pound of plain flour, salt, black pepper, and a little nutmeg, with 2 ounces of freshly grated parmesan cheese, 1 dessertspoonful of olive oil.

Have the flour ready, with the salt, pepper, and nutmeg added to it, and mix it into the potato until a smooth dough is obtained.

Form this dough into a strip or roll about 1 inch in diameter and cut it into little cubes of dough each about 1 inch square; these cubes can be put aside until needed if kept in a cool place.

To cook the *gnocchi* heat a large panful of salted water and when it is boiling drop the cubes in small numbers into the water. Press each of them in the middle with your finger and thumb as you do this. Cook each batch of *gnocchi* for about 5 minutes or until they rise to the surface, when they are done.

Lift them out with a perforated spoon and put them into a warmed, well-oiled, earthenware dish. Put the dish into the oven and keep them hot while the rest are cooking. When all the *gnocchi* are cooked and in the dish, sprinkle them well with the parmesan and serve with more parmesan, handed separately, and a tomato sauce.

POTATO GNOCCHI WITH EGG

Use the same ingredients and method as in the previous recipe, but when the flour has been well mixed into the potatoes add 2 well-beaten egg yolks and blend them in with the flour and potato dough. Then continue as before.

TUROSCSUSZA (HUNGARIAN)

For the dough the ingredients are: 1 pound of plain flour, 2 fresh eggs, some salt, and for the accompaniment to the dough, the ingredients are: ½ pound of white curd cheese, 2 cups of sour cream, ½ pound of bacon, some salt.

To make the dough, mix sufficient salt with the flour, and then mix in the 2 eggs with the tips of the fingers. Knead well, roll out the dough, not too thinly, and don't let it get dry. Then, with the fingers, tear off small squares of about 1½ inches until it is all used. This dough should not be cut with a knife.

Boil the squares in salted water, and meanwhile cut the bacon into dice and fry them in a pan until they are crisp. Keep the bacon hot. When the dough squares are cooked, drain them and put them in the hot bacon fat left in the other pan. Stir them about carefully so that they are coated with the bacon fat, and then put them in a heated shallow earthenware dish. Pour the cold sour cream over the squares, rub the curd cheese through a sieve over the sour cream, and, finally, sprinkle the crisp pieces of diced bacon over all. The dough squares and diced bacon should be as hot as possible and the sour cream and cheese should be cold.

Potato Dishes

LE GRATIN SAVOYARD

2 lb of Dutch, or waxy, potatoes, 1½ pints of *bouillon*, 4 oz fresh grated *gruyère* cheese, 2 oz butter, salt, pepper, a little grated nutmeg.

Slice the potatoes thinly and evenly and put them in a basin. Add to them the freshly ground black pepper and salt and

the grated nutmeg. Pour over the cold *bouillon*. Mix it all well
together. Using some of the butter, grease a shallow earthenware dish and put the contents of the basin into this dish. Press
the potatoes down so that the slices lie flat. Dispose the grated
gruyère cheese over the top of the potatoes and put the rest of
the butter, in little pieces, over the cheese. Put the dish into a
moderate oven and cook for 45 minutes to 1 hour.

LE GRATIN SAVOYARD AUX BOLETS

This is made in the same way as *le gratin savoyard*, only the
ingredients are equal quantities of potatoes and *cèpes* (see page
266) thinly sliced, sprinkled with *bouillon*, and laid in a shallow
earthenware dish which has been rubbed over with butter and
a little garlic. Salt and pepper are added and the top is sprinkled
with some dry breadcrumbs over which are placed some pieces
of butter. The dish is baked in a moderate oven for about
45 minutes.

POMMES DE TERRE DAUPHINOISES

This is an ideal accompaniment to a veal and mushroom casserole,
when prepared in its simplest form. But with slight elaboration it can
stand alone.

2 lb potatoes, a clove of garlic, chopped thyme and parsley, 1½
pints of milk, salt, 3 oz butter, and a very large shallow fireproof
dish are needed, and a teaspoonful of olive oil to oil the dish.

Oil the bottom of the dish. Peel the potatoes and slice them
very thinly. Lay them on the bottom of the dish, slice the garlic
and distribute it over the potatoes with some herbs and salt.
Put another layer of potatoes down, then some more garlic and
some more herbs and salt, and go on with this until the dish is
full. Sprinkle on the rest of the herbs, put small knobs of butter
all over the top, and pour on the milk.

Bake in a Regulo 7 oven for 45 minutes, by which time the
potato slices should be tender and the top of the dish a crisp
golden colour.

Served on its own it can be roofed over with pared slices of bacon. About 8 rashers will be needed, and if they are sufficiently fat, the butter used can be reduced.

Alternatively a lid of sliced tomatoes can be laid on the potatoes, interspersed with black stoned olives, and sprinkled with grated cheese and a top dressing of herbs. The combination of the tomatoes, cheese, olives, and herbs achieved in the baking is particularly delicious.

TORTA DI PATATE

You will need: 2 pounds of raw peeled potatoes of the dry, floury kind, 2 ounces of raw ham or lean bacon, 1 yolk of egg and 2 egg whites, ½ gill of top of the milk, ½ clove of garlic, 3 ounces of *mozzarella* or *pecorino* cheese (or soft curd cheese), a pinch of salt, black pepper, grated nutmeg 2 ounces of butter, and about 4 ounces of very fine dry breadcrumbs.

Cook and drain the potatoes. Beat them well until they are free from lumps and beat in the hot top of the milk.

Fry the ham or bacon lightly, cut it into cubes and add them to the potatoes. Put in the crushed clove of garlic. Beat the yolk of egg into the mixture. Taste, and if necessary add a very little salt and some black pepper. Then fold in the cheese, which should have been previously cut into ½-inch cubes. Beat up the 2 egg whites very stiffly and fold them into the potato mixture.

Have a buttered cake tin ready which is coated with most of the breadcrumbs fried in the butter. Pour the potato mixture into the tin, make the top level and cover it with the rest of the breadcrumbs which have also been fried in butter. Put the tin in the middle of a hot oven and bake it for about 20 minutes. When it is cooked, turn the potato cake onto a hot, flat dish and serve it by cutting it in wedges as if cutting a cake, which is exactly what it should look like.

Pizza

Pizza bought piping hot in the quayside shops of Santa Margherita or Rapallo is a very far cry from a Welsh rarebit ordered in a café at Aberystwyth, although the idea of melted cheese informs them both. *Pizza* originally consisted of a foundation of *polenta*, boiled maize flour, a kind of solid maize porridge poured out onto a wooden slab with a covering of tomato sauce, a hunger killer universally consumed by peasants in northern Italy. What was left of this dish was allowed to get cold, was sprinkled with cheese, cut into squares, and toasted before the fire. It resembles *mammaliga*, an equally solid confection, and one of the main supports of the Rumanian peasant.

It has since been transformed by the Neapolitans into a more delicate and appetizing dish, a layer of risen bread dough being pulled out to a quarter-inch thickness and put on a well-oiled baking sheet, covered with a variety of dressings, in which *mozzarella*, black olives, tomatoes, anchovies, basil, and marjoram play their part. Onions, chopped and slowly cooked in oil till they are transparent are sometimes laid on the dough before the melting cheese or tomato are put on. The dish has become not a hunger killer but a very piquant appetizer.

PIZZA

The ingredients are: ½ pound of proved bread dough – which some bakers will let one buy – ¾ teacup of olive oil, 1 pound of tomatoes, 12 anchovies, 12 black olives, 2 teacupfuls of freshly grated parmesan cheese, or the equivalent in sliced *mozzarella* or soft curd cheese, 1 clove of garlic, some black pepper, chopped basil, and marjoram.

Note: If you wish you can use a small tin of Italian tomato *purée*, instead of the fresh tomatoes. If you do this the tomato *purée* will need to be diluted a little with either vegetable stock or water.

First, get the oven really hot. Then take an ordinary metal baking dish or sheet and pour in half the olive oil. Put the dish aside in a warm place. Next, pull out the proven bread dough until it is less than ¼ inch thick all over. Put this thin layer of dough in the baking dish, cover it with a cloth, and put it aside in a draught-free, warm place for 15 to 20 minutes so that the dough may rise.

While this is happening, plunge the tomatoes in boiling water and skin them, or dilute the tomato *purée*. Chop the anchovies, stone the olives and cut each of them into 4 or 5 pieces. Grate the cheese, and crush the garlic.

Put the cheese evenly over the top of the dough and distribute the tomatoes (or tomato *purée*) over the cheese. Sprinkle the garlic, basil, and marjoram over the tomatoes and grind on some black pepper. Put the anchovy pieces and the olives on the top. Pour over the rest of the oil so that the top is coated with it.

Put the baking dish in the middle of the oven, and reduce the heat by half. Let the *pizza* bake for 20 to 30 minutes, depending on its size.

When ready it will be very crisp and brown at the bottom and sides, and the top will be covered with a wonderful amalgam of tomatoes, herbs, anchovies, and olives while some of the cheese will have soaked through to the dough underneath.

SOFT CURD CHEESE

Let about 4 pints of milk go sour by pouring the milk into a shallow bowl and leaving it in a warm part of the kitchen. When making the curd cheese in very cold weather, warm the milk a little and mix a spoonful of sour cream, yoghourt, or sour milk with it.

Whichever method is used, leave the milk in the bowl until it is set like a junket. Then put it into a very low oven for 2 to 3 hours so that the curd may separate from the whey. Strain off the whey and put the curd into a muslin or fine linen bag, hang it over a bowl to drain during the next 12 hours.

Wrap the drained curd in a clean piece of fine cloth and put it on a sieve. Put a flat plate on top of it and put a weight on the plate. Leave to drain for another 12 hours when it will be ready to use.

Quiches

Tartes and *quiches* are both French contributions to the art of combining light pastries with a great variety of fillings. In fact the *tartes* more often contain sweet fillings, for instance, *la tarte alsacienne* filled with fresh cream, *la tarte aux pruneaux* a puff paste baked with dried stoned plums and apricot jam from the district of Morvan, *la tarte aux raisins* a speciality of Lorraine filled with white grapes on a layer of apple slices, *la tarte au fromage* from the Pays de Gex, which is a remarkable combination of a light sweet pastry, with a filling of fresh cream cheese, melted with cream, yolks of egg, vanilla, castor sugar, and whipped whites of egg.

But there are others with savoury fillings, typically *la tarte à la flamme* made in Lorraine, an oblong pastry filled with narrow strips of bacon, eggs, and cream, and *la tarte à l'oignon* for which a recipe is given here.

More often when the *tarte* has a substantial filling its name changes to *tourte* – for instance *la tourte aux épinards*, a flat tart of crisp paste with a mixture laid upon it, consisting of spinach sautéd with butter to which egg yolks and thick cream are added, *la tourte aux poissons*, *à la viande*, etc.

Quiches are equally variable in their content and are usually served as an *hors d'œuvre*. Originally made with bread dough and baked with a mixture of eggs, cheese, and perhaps cream on top, they are as indigenous to Lorraine as *pizza* is to the Ligurian coast. The invention of *pâte feuilletée* (attributed to Claude Lorraine long after he had abandoned his apprenticeship to a pastry cook to become a painter) has refined this confection into a very rich and melting dish.

PÂTE FEUILLETÉE FOR TARTES AND QUICHES

The fat and the flour must be of equal weight, using plain flour and fresh unsalted butter. The amount of water may vary to a small extent as flour differs in its capacity for absorption. This pastry must always be rolled out in the same direction.

The ingredients are: 4 ounces of plain flour, 4 ounces of butter, a pinch of salt, and about a ¼ gill of cold water. If the butter is salted, leave out the pinch of salt.

Put the flour in a heap on a pastry board and make a hole in the mound of flour. Put in this hole, a ¼ ounce of the butter – cut into small pieces – and the salt. Then add the water, a little at a time, and work it in with the flour and butter, both quickly and lightly, with the tips of the fingers. When an elastic and springy consistency is achieved, and the flour, water, and butter are well amalgamated, make the paste into a ball with your hands. Sprinkle a little flour over it and make a few cuts on its top surface with a knife. Cover it with a cloth and put it aside to rest, in a cool place, for 15 minutes.

At the end of that time, roll out the ball of paste and put the rest of the butter (3¾ ounces) in a lump on the middle of it and fold the paste evenly over the lump of butter. The butter should be at room temperature and not chilled. Roll out the paste lightly, don't press down on it, until you have made a strip which is about twice as long as its breadth. Fold the two long sides to meet in the centre of the strip and fold the two short ends towards each other so that they meet in the centre. Fold the centre of the paste over, so that the two new short ends touch each other. (If this seems very difficult to understand, try the folding process out with a sheet of paper first.) Put the packet of paste to rest for 15 minutes in a cool place.

Repeat this rolling and folding process twice more allowing 15 minutes resting time after each operation.

At the end of the last 15 minutes' rest, the paste is ready, and may be rolled out and put in a buttered, shallow, metal case. Bake the pastry blind in a hot oven, say Regulo 7, for about 20 minutes, with some grains of rice on the bottom of the tart to prevent it puffing.

The time needed to make this *pâte feuilletée* is approximately 20 minutes for the mixing, rolling, and folding process and the resting time for the pastry is 60 minutes. If you wish, it is perfectly satisfactory to leave the pastry unbaked overnight in a cool place.

TARTE À L'OIGNON

Have the *pâte feuilletée* already cooked in its case.

The filling is made from: 4 large onions, 4 ounces of butter, 3 rashers of bacon, 3 fresh eggs, and 4 tablespoonfuls of cream.

Cut the onions into thin slices. Put them into a pan with some cold salted water, bring it quickly to the boil, cook briskly for 3 minutes and then drain them. Melt the butter in a shallow pan, cook the onion slices in it until they are golden in colour. In another pan fry the bacon until it is crisp and cut it into dice. Mix onions and bacon together and let them cool. Beat the eggs, blend in the cream, combine the eggs and cream with bacon and onions and pour the mixture into the pastry case. Bake it in a moderate oven until it is set and golden. Serve and eat while it is still very hot.

QUICHE (i)

Having made and baked a case of *pâte feuilletée* (page 119), take just under 4 ounces of grated *gruyère* cheese, 1 well-beaten egg, and ½ pint of fresh cream.

Mix the cheese with the egg and add the cream to it. Pour the mixture into the pastry case and bake it in a moderate oven for about 20 minutes or until it is set and golden on top.

QUICHE (ii)

The pastry case can either have been baked beforehand or it can be cooked with the filling which is made from: 3½ ounces of grated cheese, 1 well-beaten egg, just under ½ pint of evaporated milk, and ½ gill of fresh milk, with a pinch of paprika pepper and a scrape of nutmeg.

Note: the Swedish full cream hard cheese is very good for this dish.

The cheese, which must be finely grated, is mixed with the beaten egg, a pinch of paprika pepper, and a scrape of nutmeg. The evaporated milk is made up to ½ pint of liquid by adding fresh milk to it. Pour this onto the egg and cheese and blend it until it is smooth and even. Then pour the mixture into the pastry case and bake it in a moderate oven for 25 minutes, or until well set.

QUICHE LORRAINE

This is the veritable *quiche lorraine*. A number of recipes for it include small pieces of *gruyère* placed on the bottom of the pastry with the bacon. But the simplicity of the cream and bacon mixture on its own is very good indeed.

In this dish the pastry and its contents are baked together in the first instance.

Line a shallow metal dish with *pâte feuilletée* which can have been made with: 8 ounces of plain flour, 6 ounces of butter, 2 ounces of beef dripping, and about ½ gill of cold water. A pinch of salt if necessary.

For the filling: 4 rashers of bacon (green bacon is very good for this), 1 good sized fresh egg, ½ pint of fresh cream, some black pepper (a very small pinch of salt if the bacon is not highly salted), and about ½ ounce of butter.

Cut the bacon into dice, fry them until they are crisp, and let them cool. Beat up the egg with salt, if you think it necessary, and some freshly ground black pepper, and then add the cream and mix it well. Put the fried bacon at the bottom of the pastry case and pour on the egg and cream mixture. Put very thin pieces of the butter over the top of the filling and bake the *quiche* in a low oven for about 25 minutes or until it is set and golden on top.

Note: None of those mixtures of egg and cream or milk should be cooked in too hot an oven as, if the mixture boils, it spoils.

ITALIAN SHORT PASTRY

There are Italian flans which are the equivalent of the French *tourtes*, but the pastry is short, not flaky. This short pastry is made with half the amount of fat (which is butter) to the amount of flour, bound with yolk of egg and a little very cold water. The case is baked blind and the filling cooked in it afterwards.

It is made with: 8 ounces of plain flour, 4 ounces of butter and 2 yolks of egg with about 2 dessertspoonfuls of very cold water, and a pinch of salt.

Put the flour into a bowl with the salt and cut the butter into it with a flexible bladed knife helped with the tips of the fingers until the mixture is dry, crumbly, and very fine. Then make a hole in the centre of it and drop in the egg yolks. Mix them into the flour and butter with a wooden spoon until a smooth, firm paste is obtained. Add a very little cold water. Ideally, this paste should then be wrapped in a cloth and put aside to rest in a cold place until the next day, but if you want to use it at once, roll it out and line a flan case with it and then bake it in a moderate oven for roughly 20 minutes. Put some dry beans in the bottom to prevent the pastry rising. This is a very good short pastry and with the addition of a little sugar would be admirable for a sweet filling of fresh fruit or mixture of honey and almonds or walnuts.

A SPINACH FILLING FOR A PASTRY FLAN

A savoury filling is made with spinach which is prepared in a similar way to a spinach *soufflé*.

2 pounds of spinach, 1 finely chopped onion, 2 ounces of grated parmesan cheese, 2 ounces of butter, 2 ounces of flour, ½ pint of cream (or top of the milk), 2 fresh eggs, salt, black pepper, and a little grated nutmeg.

Having prepared the spinach, half cook it in the minimum of water, drain it well and chop it up, or put it through a *mouli-légumes*. Warm the butter in a pan and cook the chopped onion in it until it is melted and golden. Sprinkle the flour onto the butter and onion and cook all together for, say, 3 minutes, stirring all the time to prevent the flour from colouring or burning. At the same time heat the cream or top of the milk and when it is almost boiling pour it onto the flour in the other pan, stirring until the sauce is smooth and bland. Adjust the heat and let this sauce cook gently for 10 minutes. Add the chopped spinach to the sauce and cook until the spinach is soft. Take the pan off the fire and let its contents cool.

Beat the eggs, add the grated cheese to them and when the

sauce is cool add them to it. Taste for seasoning and put in as much salt, black pepper, and grated nutmeg as it requires. Pour the mixture into the pastry case and bake it in a moderate oven for 20 to 25 minutes. Serve as soon as it is cooked or the spinach filling will fall and become flabby.

Fish

8

FISH

ONE of the most pervading aromas of the English kitchen is that of boiling fish. The function of seasoning in cooking is not only to develop the taste of what is being cooked and impart delicate flavours to food, but to remove any unpleasant odours that may be unleashed in the cooking. The French practice of poaching fish in a spiced and seasoned *court-bouillon* embraces these three objectives. Unless the fish is straight out of the sea, when nothing can really spoil its flavour, it is advisable to adopt the French habit. A *court-bouillon in its simplest form* can consist of the amount of water which will properly immerse the fish, a tablespoonful of wine vinegar, a bay leaf, a sprig of thyme, a little parsley, an onion pierced with a clove, and a carrot sliced in two. These ingredients are simmered together for half an hour, and the liquid is allowed to cool before use. When the moment for poaching the fish has arrived, the liquid is strained, brought to the boil, the fish is put in, and when the boiling has reasserted itself, the heat is lowered, and the fish gently poached, with an occasional bubble rising, and the lid on, for the time required. If it is to be served cold, it is then allowed to cool in its liquor. The *court-bouillon* neutralizes the unpleasant smell of cooking fish, the poaching achieves the cooking without desiccating the firmness of the flesh, and what taste the fish has is contained by its immersion in the first place in the boiling liquor. In addition some of the liquid can be used for the preparation of the sauce.

This method is all the more relevant to those whose source of fish supply is the urban fishmonger. Very little fish which has survived the delays of packing, transport, and marketing, is in any real sense fresh. If one examines the eye of any fish exposed on the marble slab, it is next to impossible to detect that vivacity which M. Reboul, the celebrated author of *La Cuisine Provençale*, insists is the true indication of freshness. A vivacious eye and flesh that is firm to the touch are really the characteristics of last night's catch. More usually the eye has glazed and sunk deep into its socket. The firmness of the flesh has a rather longer duration, and by this we must judge. Colour is to some extent an indication, particularly in such fish as mackerel which should have a brilliant iridescence.

In respect of freshness there is a theory that those fish like salmon, mackerel, and herrings which frequent the surface areas of water are those which decay most rapidly when exposed to the air, while the fish which lurk in the depths keep fresh longer when out of the water. This certainly is true of the carp, which lies dormant in the mud for great lengths of time in winter, and which is not impaired by several days of travel or delayed purchase after death.

We have included a number of unfamiliar recipes for cooking fish, some of which are rather highly seasoned. When fish is perfectly fresh there can be no better way of dealing with it than by baking with butter, or poaching in an aromatic *court-bouillon* and serving with a delicious sauce, a mayonnaise, a *sauce tartare*, or *sauce rémoulade*.

ALOSE À LA PIQUERETTE   *Shad, perch, pike, bream*

Any river fish can be subjected to this form of preparation, not only the shad which, though found in quantity and of superior quality in the Severn, is not very often on sale in the fishmonger's. The characteristic of the dish is the use of white Anjou wine – from the Coteaux de Saumur, the Coteaux de la Loire, or the Coteaux du Layon – in the cooking, with fine breadcrumbs and butter to thicken the sauce.

Cut the shad, or whichever river fish, such as perch, pike, or bream, is in question, into slices about 1 inch thick, and put them into a casserole with an onion hashed, a little crushed garlic, salt, and a bouquet of herbs. Cover the slices with dry white wine, and cook in the oven for twenty minutes per pound of fish, or a little less. (The cooking time varies with the texture of the fish.) About a quarter of an hour before the cooking is completed put in a quantity of very fine baked breadcrumbs. When the fish is ready, dish it up on a hot plate, remove the herbs, and add a good lump of butter to the sauce and pour it over the fish. Serve an Anjou wine with this dish.

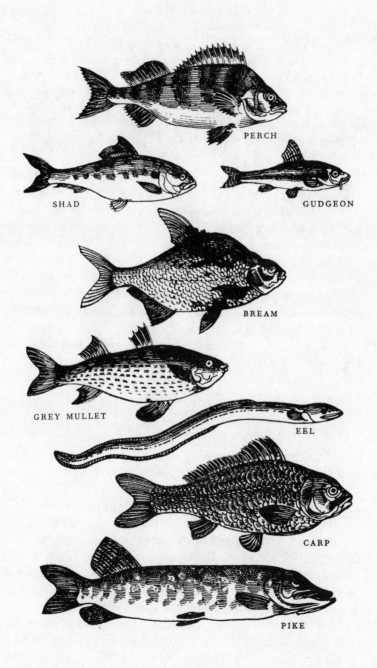

PERCH

SHAD

GUDGEON

BREAM

GREY MULLET

EEL

CARP

PIKE

BACALAO (MORUE) *Salt cod*

A predilection for salt cod is really an acquired taste for English
people. The recipes for preparing it are mostly Spanish, French, Greek,
and Creole. In Victorian times it was sometimes served here garnished
with parsnips and dressed with an egg sauce, not a very attractive
proposition. If not at the fishmongers, it can usually be obtained from
continental stores or delicatessen shops. If there is a choice, Icelandic
and Newfoundland salt cod is better than English.

The fillets should be rather thick and white; if thin and yellow,
the fish, when brought back to life by cooking, will be stringy.
The fish should be put to soak for at least twelve hours before
use, and preferably overnight, and the water should be changed
from time to time.

Normally, the fish is trimmed of fins after soaking, cut up, and
put into a pan of cold water, with a *bouquet garni* and a slice or
two of lemon, and slowly brought to the boil. As soon as boiling
point is reached the heat must be lowered, as boiling toughens
it, and it should poach until it flakes easily. Then it should be
drained, skinned, and the bones removed, and it is ready to incorporate in a dish. Allow six or seven ounces of prepared fish
for each person.

BACALAO CON PATATAS *Salt cod*

1 lb dry salt cod, 2 lb potatoes, 1 lb onions, 2 tomatoes, 1 clove
of garlic, 1 tablespoonful of chopped parsley, saffron, ¼ pint of
olive oil, freshly ground white pepper, flour.

Soak the cod for at least 12 hours and change the water it is
soaking in four times. Then put it in a saucepan with sufficient
cold water to cover it and bring the water to the boil. When it
boils, take the cod out. Remove the bones and divide it into
pieces suitable for serving. Roll each piece in flour. Heat the oil
in a frying pan, fry the pieces to a golden colour, and keep them
warm in the oven while the vegetables are cooking.

Slice the potatoes, chop the onions, and put them in a saucepan
with the parsley and the clove of garlic, which should be crushed
to a pulp. Pour over a little of the oil in which the cod was

frying, add sufficient boiling water to cover the vegetables, and simmer. About 10 minutes before the vegetables are cooked, add the saffron and the white pepper with the tomatoes – which should have their skins removed. Simmer until most of the liquid is absorbed. Taste for seasoning, then turn the vegetables onto a hot, flat dish, put the fried pieces of cod on top, and it is ready to serve.

BARBUE BONNE FEMME   *Brill*

Escoffier said that brill, if served whole, may be looked upon as the understudy of the chicken turbot, but even though it may receive precisely the same treatment as turbot, it cannot hope to raise the same expectations.

1 brill weighing 2½–3 lb, 3 or 4 shallots, parsley, 4 oz mushrooms, 5 oz butter, ⅔ to ¾ pint of liquid made up of half fish stock and half dry white wine, 2 tablespoonfuls of cream (or top of the milk).

Take a large flat earthenware or fireproof china dish and grease it with 2 ounces of butter. Chop the shallots very finely indeed, and sprinkle them on the bottom of the dish, with the parsley, which has been chopped and pounded. Put the mushrooms in, cut into small pieces.

Raise the fillets a little from each side of the backbone of the brill with a sharp pointed knife, but don't remove them from the bone altogether. Lay the fish on the bed of shallots, parsley, and mushrooms, and pour on the fish stock and white wine.

Put the dish in a moderate oven and let the fish cook gently. Baste it from time to time, and when the fish is ready, in about 35 to 40 minutes, keep it warm and transfer the liquid to a saucepan. Reduce this over a strong flame to half its quantity, then add the cream and the remaining 3 ounces of butter. Cover the brill with this sauce and serve it in the dish in which it has cooked.

BRANDADE DE MORUE   *Salt cod*

Grimod de la Reynière was the first man to write down a recipe for a *brandade*. This is what he said: 'Among the provincial *ragoûts* in

131

most distinguished favour in Paris are the *brandades* of salt fish. A *restaurateur* of the Palais Royal is well known to have made his fortune by his method of preparing them. We give the recipe as it was communicated to us in a village of Languedoc which enjoys a reputation at once brilliant and merited for this very article. The singular name of *brandade*, though not found in any dictionary, is derived doubtless from the old French verb *brandir*, which means to shake; and this action, almost continual, is in fact indispensable to render the *ragoût* what it ought to be. Soak for 24 hours a fine piece of salt fish. Put it on the fire in sufficient water, carefully taking it off when it begins to boil. Put butter, oil, parsley and garlic into a stewpan upon a gentle fire. In the meantime skin the fish and divide it into small bits. Put the pieces in the stewpan, and add from time to time more oil, butter, or milk, as the whole is seen to thicken. Shake the stewpan for a long time over the fire, so as to reduce the salt fish to a kind of cream. The recipe is very simple but we do not cease to repeat that the success of the *brandade* depends on shaking the stewpan for a very long time. This alone can effect the extreme division or disunion of all the parts of the naturally tough fish and metamorphose it into a sort of cream.'

We give this description in full for its own sake, and to make clear that the *brandade* is nothing short of a transformation – a very tough fish is turned into a sort of cream – which explains why there are different methods of bringing it about. In the first, the shaking method is hastened forward by the use of a wooden spoon. In the second, the partly cooked and boned fish is pounded in a mortar. We advocate the energetic use of a wooden spoon.

Ingredients: 1½ lb of salt cod, nearly 1 pint of olive oil, ¼ pint of creamy milk, juice of 1 lemon, a pinch of ground white pepper, 1 crushed clove of garlic, grated nutmeg, chopped parsley, and a garnish of fried bread.

Soak the cod overnight. Put it in a heavy aluminium pan, cover with water, and bring slowly to the boil. At the moment when it reaches boiling point, take it out, drain it, and remove the bones carefully, but not the skin. Put the broken up fish in a casserole on a very low heat. It is wise to use an asbestos mat. Have ready a little pan containing nearly a pint of olive oil. Keep it warm but not hot, likewise a little pan of warm creamy milk.

Begin by putting a spoonful of oil with the cod, and work it with a wooden spoon, crushing the pieces of fish against the sides

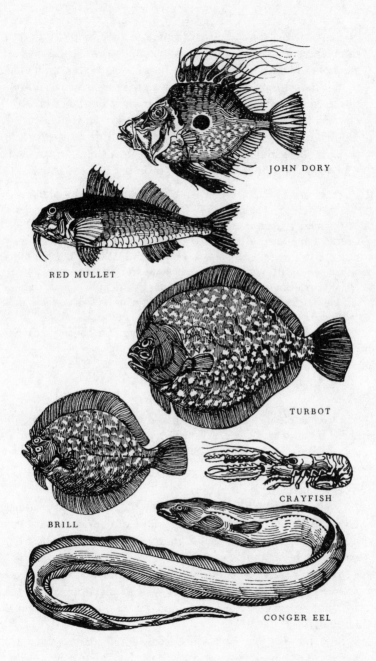

JOHN DORY

RED MULLET

TURBOT

BRILL

CRAYFISH

CONGER EEL

of the pan. Go on adding from time to time, and a little at a time, alternate spoonfuls of oil and milk, working the mixture energetically with the spoon. The transformation brought about by this industrious effort together with the very gradual addition of the oil and milk should result in a creamy substance in which there is not one flake of fish apparent. Seasoning is then added: a pinch of pepper, the juice of a lemon, a little crushed garlic, parsley, some grated nutmeg. Serve the *brandade* on a dish surrounded by neatly cut fried bread, or in hot *vol-au-vent* cases.

It is sometimes maintained that the dish is ruined by the addition of garlic. We have the testimony of M. Austin de Croze, M. Reboul, and the *Encyclopédie Gastronomique* for its inclusion.

Considerable energy is required to prepare a *brandade*, and great care. If the fish preparation gets too hot, or if by misfortune the oil or milk are overheated, the oil will separate from the mixture. A low temperature during the process, the crushing of the fish against the side of the pan in the first place, and vigorous stirring as fresh oil and milk are added are essential.

A *brandade* is a *plat du jour* only in the sense of a culinary achievement. It is very rich and is to be eaten with restraint.

CABILLAUD À LA SAINTE MÉNÉHOULD *Cod*

The cod is cleaned and stuffed, baked and served in a dish surrounded by an oyster sauce. As this is rather an expensive dish on account of the oysters, it should be reserved for an occasion when there are a number of guests.

This recipe is for eight people:

1 cod weighing 4 lb, and for its stuffing: ¼ lb shredded veal suet, ¼ lb fine breadcrumbs, 1 tablespoonful of chopped parsley, a little thyme, 1 chopped shallot, nutmeg, pepper and salt, 2 egg yolks, 2 tablespoonfuls of milk.

2 dozen oysters, 6 oz butter, 1 pint of fish stock – made from fishbones and root vegetables – 2 wineglassfuls of white wine, 1 oz butter kneaded with 1 oz flour, the juice of 1 lemon, bread raspings.

Stuff the fish, having pounded the ingredients together in a mortar to a smooth paste, and sew it up. Lay it entire in a baking dish and score the thick shoulders with deep incisions made with a pointed chef's knife. Melt the 6 ounces of butter, pour it over the fish, add the liquor from a dozen of the oysters – freshly opened – and put the dish in the centre of a moderate oven. It will take at least an hour to cook and should be basted from time to time with the butter and oyster liquor. After three-quarters of an hour, sprinkle the fish with finely grated breadcrumbs, baste again, and do this again after some minutes, so that the fish has a golden crust.

Heat the fish stock in a shallow pan, add the wine and the kneaded butter, stirring while it reduces and thickens. Five minutes before the fish is ready to serve, put in the 2 dozen oysters and their remaining liquor with the lemon juice, but do not overheat the sauce or the oysters will be tough. Pour some of this sauce round the fish and serve the rest in a sauceboat.

If you should be daunted by the prospect of opening twenty-four oysters in your own kitchen and have no expert at hand, the fishmonger would oblige, but you must take a receptacle into which their juice can be poured. In such a case, not many hours should elapse before incorporating them in the sauce.

To open oysters, hold the flat top upwards so as not to lose a drop of the juice, insert a short pointed knife in the joint of the oyster shell and, with some conviction and a horizontal movement of the knife, cut the muscle connecting it with the upper shell.

CARPE À LA CHAMBORD *Carp*

Freshwater fish are regarded with suspicion by English cooks, particularly those members of the carp family, 'coarse' fish like the common carp, bream, and tench, which lurk in the depths of still and muddy waters. Coarse and insipid is the usual verdict, with the added reflection that they feed on mud and garbage. As a rule the muddy accusation is forestalled by transferring the fish alive into a freshwater tank with running water.

If you ask the fishmonger to scale and clean your carp, be sure to insist on taking home the roes and the head. The former make an *hors d'œuvre*, the latter contains a delicacy in the form of the palate, sometimes called the carp's tongue. If the carp is being cooked *en matelote* the head should be simmered slowly in a spiced *court-bouillon* and allowed to cool in its liquor. The palate can then be removed and served as an *hors d'œuvre* with a little oil and lemon juice.

It is quite true that it is useless to boil, fry, or grill this fish; it should be stewed or braised. But the real discovery of how to treat it was made by one of the cooks at Chambord, where the great lake was full of enormous carp. The skin with its heavy scales was removed, leaving only the skin along the belly for the preservation of the stuffing, the fish being stuffed with *quenelles* of whiting or veal stuffing, and larded with strips of fat bacon and cooked truffles, or, on lean days, with strips of eel and truffles. (In the latter case the fish was barded with bacon in the braising pan, as the whole point of the treatment is to introduce the bacon fat into the body of the fish to combat its natural dryness.) The fish was then laid on its stomach in a capacious braising pan, more than half immersed in a *mirepoix* of white wine and covered with a buttered paper. The fish was served in its own sauce and garnished with truffles, crayfish, *quenelles* of whiting, and soft carp's roes.

If you are sufficiently enterprising to attempt the real thing, clean the carp, save the roes, and stuff it with the following mixture: equal quantities of butter and fine breadcrumbs – say 6 ounces of each combined together in a mortar with a handful of chopped parsley, thyme, a minced shallot, grated nutmeg, pepper and salt. Work in 2 egg yolks, a spoonful of milk and pound smooth.

Remove the skin along the back on both sides and lard the fish symmetrically with strips of fat bacon which have lain in a little salt and chopped herbs. A few little mushrooms, sliced, can be substituted for the truffles.

Prepare a *mirepoix* of white wine: mince the following vegetables very finely – 2 carrots, 2 onions, 2 shallots, 1 bay leaf, 1 garlic clove, a sprig of thyme, with $\frac{1}{4}$ lb fat bacon and a little raw ham. Set this preparation on the fire with a little olive oil to simmer gently, then pour over it a pint of white wine.

Lay the stuffed carp stomach down on the drainer of a fish kettle, and surround it with the *mirepoix*, which should reach about half way up its sides. Cover the fish with a buttered paper or aluminium foil, and braise for an hour in a moderate oven.

It is customary to serve this noble object surrounded by crayfish cooked in a *court-bouillon* of white wine, with its roes, sliced and sautéd in butter, with *quenelles* of whiting, and its own sauce passed through a sieve and enriched with a little butter.

CARPE BRAISÉE AU VIN ROUGE *Carp*

A carp of 3 or 4 lb, 6 oz fat bacon, 3 or 4 medium onions, 4 carrots, 2 garlic cloves, a bunch of herbs, salt and ground pepper, just over a pint of red wine, 1 pint of boiling water, 3 or 4 anchovies.

Prepare a carp of 3 or 4 lb in weight by removing its scales and entrails, washing it well, and leave it for a few hours in salt water to which a tablespoonful of wine vinegar has been added.

Place some strips of fat bacon on the bottom of your fish kettle together with some onions and carrots sliced in rounds, 2 garlic cloves, a bunch of herbs, and 3 or 4 anchovies cut up. Lay the fish on this vegetable bed. Season with salt and ground pepper; set the kettle on a low flame and put on the lid so that the vegetables begin to sweat. After ten minutes or so they will begin to brown, when a glass of red wine should be poured over the fish and allowed to evaporate. Then pour a pint of boiling water and a pint of red wine onto the fish, leaving it to cook gently with the lid on for about an hour. As the fish will not be entirely covered by the liquid it should be basted from time to time.

When the fish is cooked lift it out and keep it in a warm oven while you prepare the sauce. Pass the juice and vegetables through a sieve and reduce the liquor by rapid boiling. Then in a small saucepan, melt a dessertspoonful of butter, stir in the same quantity of flour, cook it on a low fire, add the juice of the fish, and bring this sauce to the boil. Let it cook, while stirring, for some minutes, and before serving add a lump of butter and the juice of a lemon. Pike responds very well to the same treatment.

COLD TROUT

For a dish of cold trout one should allow 1 trout for each person if the fish are about $\frac{1}{2}$ lb in weight.

For 4 such trout prepare a *court-bouillon* consisting of $1\frac{1}{2}$ pints of water, $\frac{1}{2}$ oz coarse salt, $1\frac{1}{2}$ tablespoonfuls of wine vinegar, $\frac{1}{2}$ a carrot, a slice of onion, and a *bouquet garni* composed of parsley, thyme, and $\frac{1}{2}$ a bay leaf. Boil these together for half an hour. The *court-bouillon* will have more flavour if allowed to cool before use.

Boil it up again and put in the fish, which have been cleaned. Lower the heat, cook for a few minutes, and take the pan off the stove, allowing the liquid to cool a little before extracting the fish and laying them on a shallow dish.

Then dissolve ¾ ounce of gelatine in the liquid, and when the gelatine is completely absorbed, strain most of the *court-bouillon* through a fine sieve over the trout in the dish, and put it in a cool place so that the jelly sets. Pour the rest off into a basin to set. Then decorate the trout with chervil and tarragon and chopped hard-boiled eggs. Chop the remaining jellied *court-bouillon* and pile it round the dish. Serve very cold with some thin slices of lemon.

DORADE AU CIDRE   *Red bream, John Dory*

Prepare a stuffing for your cleaned fish consisting of 2 hard-boiled eggs, some fine breadcrumbs, 4 ounces of mushrooms and an onion which have been sautéd beforehand, some basil, parsley, chervil, chives, and salt. All the ingredients should be chopped very finely before combining them.

Stuff the fish and lay it in a large oval fireproof dish, which has been buttered beforehand. Cover it with knobs of butter and pour over it some vintage cider. Put it in a moderate oven and leave it to cook for about 1 hour.

FILETS DE SOLE À LA NORMANDE

This is a classic dish. It is the *matelote* brought to perfection. Fillets of sole are cooked in cider or white wine, a relish of mussels, oysters, and mushrooms is separately prepared, and sole and relish are presented bathed in a rich sauce with a garnish of heart-shaped *croûtons*, sometimes crayfish which have been stewed in white wine, and little gudgeon dressed with breadcrumbs and fried in butter. *Calvados*, the rather fierce apple brandy, is sometimes added at the last moment to the sauce after being set alight in a spoon, or sprinkled on the fillets before their immersion in the sauce.

The crux of the matter is the preparation of the sauce. The relish and garnish for the dish is capable of variation and we propose here the dish in its simplest form, having regard both to excellence and expense. As the preparation takes time it is worth making for six people.

Ingredients: 12 fillets of sole, ¾ pint medium dry white wine, or vintage cider, salt, pepper, and butter for the dish. For the stock: a small whiting, the bones of the sole, ½ pint white wine, 1 pint of water, an onion, 2 carrots, sprig of thyme, bay leaf, basil, a clove of garlic, salt and pepper. For the sauce: a tablespoonful of plain flour, a tablespoonful of butter, 1 pint of creamy milk, 3 gills of single cream. The relish: 20 button mushrooms, 20 little onions, ¼ lb white grapes, 3–4 ounces of butter. For the garnish: 12 heart-shaped *croûtons* fried in butter, 12 Dublin Bay prawns.

Most of the preparations should be carried out well in advance, for peace of mind. Begin by putting the ingredients for the stock in a pan, slicing onion and carrots, cover, and simmer for at least an hour, skimming now and then. In the meantime cook the fillets either in a large fireproof dish in the oven, or in a large frying-pan, four at a time, on top of the stove. This is perhaps simpler and more economical as the same wine will serve the three relays, and there is less risk of overcooking. Butter the bottom of dish or pan, sprinkle the fillets with salt and pepper, and just cover with wine. Simmer for a few minutes until the fish is white. Remove the cooked fish onto a large buttered dish deep enough to contain all ingredients. Prepare the relish by quickly washing, wiping, and sautéing the mushrooms in butter, letting them simmer for ten minutes. Peel the grapes. Peel six of the prawns and put the shells into the fish stock. Peel the little onions, and boil them in salted water for five minutes, strain, and simmer in butter for 15 minutes. Taste the fish stock, strain it, add the wine in which the fillets have cooked, and reduce the liquor over a fierce heat. This may take 20 minutes, but keep an eye on it as towards the end of the reduction there is a chance of burning. The stock reduced to a *fumet* or essence has the appearance and consistency of treacle. It is this essence which will impart the real flavour to the sauce without impairing its creamy white colour. Two dessertspoonfuls of essence will be the entire result of this operation. Cut some bread in heart shapes – a special heart pastry cutter does this best – and fry till golden in butter. About 20 minutes before you wish to serve the dish, prepare the sauce. Heat the tablespoonful of butter, sprinkle with flour, cook while stirring for a few minutes, and pour on a heated pint of milk slowly stirring all the time. Warm the dish of sole in the oven. When the sauce begins to thicken, add the cream and essence from the fish stock, stir over a gentle heat until the sauce has by slight evaporation achieved a rich creamy consistency. Put in the mushrooms, shelled prawns, grapes, and little onions, allow a few minutes for them to be heated through, and pour the sauce over the fillets. Turn up the oven for a few moments so that the sauce acquires a glazed appearance, and at the last minute decorate the dish with the *croûtons* and remaining unpealed prawns. Each item in this dish must be perfectly cooked and nothing overcooked. The sauce can be thickened with egg yolks and lemon juice, if preferred. But cream, provided it is used in the correct proportions, produces an admirable result. If oysters and mussels are employed in the relish, they should be only sufficiently heated to open them, and incorporated at the last moment. Their juice should be added to the sauce.

GOUJONS FRITS   *Gudgeon*

These small fish, members of the carp family, but more resembling smelts, seldom appear at the fishmonger's, in spite of being common in most of our rivers.

Roll the little fish in seasoned plain flour, and fry them quickly in fresh butter, shaking the pan so that they cook evenly. Serve them on hot plates with a slice of lemon.

If you like they can be fried with *fines herbes*, chopped parsley, chervil, chives, and tarragon.

A more elaborate method is to dip the fish in beaten egg, then in dry breadcrumbs, and again in beaten egg, after which they can be fried in deep fat. They should be served with lemon slices to counteract the richness of the cooking medium.

GIUVECHI   *Pike, carp, red mullet, cod*

Giuvechi is a Rumanian way of preparing fish which can be applied to freshwater pike and carp as well as to the common cod.

Pike should be cooked as soon as possible after it has come out of the water. It has a rather glutinous exterior, and many people make the mistake of overwashing it to remove the glue. This makes dryer an already dry fish. The pike should be simply gutted by slitting it up the belly, and wiped with a cloth. The scales should not be removed. Carp is well suited to this mode of preparation as it is by nature of indifferent taste. If cod is used, the most suitable part is a cut from the shoulder.

2–3 lb of one of the above fish. The same quantity of mixed vegetables (carrots, turnips, French beans, peas), and little onions or shallots. 2 tablespoonfuls of olive oil, 2 garlic cloves, a few coriander seeds and wholespice ground to a powder, a small tin of tomato *purée*, the juice of a lemon, a handful of raisins, thyme and parsley, salt, a tumbler of water.

Make a fine hash of the vegetables, with the exception of the peas, and sauté them in olive oil on a low flame, adding the chopped thyme and parsley, garlic, and spices, for about five minutes. Put in the tomato *purée*, a pinch of sugar, salt, and a little water, bring this to the boil, throw in the peas and raisins and simmer for ten minutes. A wineglass of white wine poured onto the vegetables just before the addition of the tomato *purée* will improve this dish. Lay the cleaned fish in a greased fire-proof dish. They should be left whole if small, and sliced up otherwise. Pour the juice of a lemon over the vegetable pre-paration and cover the fish with it. Cover with a buttered paper and bake in the oven until the fish is tender, basting from time to time. Fish prepared in this way is intended to be served cold.

HARENGS SAURS À LA ROUMAINE *Herrings*

Before Rumania disappeared behind the Iron Curtain it was pos-sible for travellers to enjoy in Bucharest several gastronomic pleasures, the chief being an unlimited supply of caviare, and sturgeon fresh from the Black Sea. But the Rumanians also have a taste for highly seasoned dishes, and this one is a typical example:

Half a dozen pickled herrings; a large tin of tomato *purée*; water; 3 tablespoonfuls of white wine vinegar; sugar; tarragon, basil, chervil, a dozen stoned black olives, 2 teaspoonfuls of capers, and 2 tablespoonfuls of olive oil.

Leave the pickled herrings in cold water for about three hours to remove excess of salt.

Make a thick sauce with the tomato *purée* diluted with a little water, adding a pinch of sugar, and pour it over the herrings which have been drained and laid in a serving dish.

Make a fine hash of the herbs, olives, and capers and boil all together in the vinegar for a few moments. Leave the preparation to cool, stir in the olive oil, and pour it over the herrings in their tomato sauce. Serve this dish very cold, accompanied only by crisp French bread and a green salad.

HERRING SALAD

4 fresh herrings with their roes, ¼ pint of dry white wine, 2 table-spoonfuls of sour cream or, failing that, yoghourt, 2 tablespoon-fuls of mild vinegar, 1 onion, 1 clove of garlic, 1 teaspoonful of French mustard, the yolks of 2 hard-boiled eggs, a pinch of paprika, 4 peppercorns, salt, and 1 tablespoonful of fresh herbs, consisting of chopped parsley, chives, a small piece of bay leaf, dill, and chervil, ½ to ¾ of a pint milk, ½ pint water.

Clean the herrings, scale them and put them to soak in a basin with the milk covering them, for about 1 hour. Then put the wine and vinegar with a little water in a saucepan of sufficient size to take the herrings, with the peppercorns, the bay leaf, the chopped herbs, the onion, and the chopped garlic. Put the herrings into this liquid, raise the heat, and poach them for about 3 to 4 minutes. Remove them carefully and put them on the serving dish. When they are cold, drain the liquid in which they have been cooked through a sieve and mix a little of it with the sour cream, the mustard, paprika, and salt. Then add this to the 2 pounded yolks of egg so that a sauce is obtained. Pour this sauce when it is well amalgamated over the herrings. Serve with rye bread and butter as an *hors d'œuvre* – or after *soupe à la bonne femme*.

HOUT MECHOUI   *Red mullet, conger eel, mackerel, halibut*

This is simply the English phonetical equivalent for the Arabic 'grilled fish'. A Tunisian grill usually done on a charcoal brazier, it depends for its success on a controlled heat, which must be gentle at

first and only brown the fish at the last moment. A variety of fish can
be used, red mullet, slices of conger eel, mackerel, halibut, and rock
salmon.

2 lb of one of the above fish; salt, pepper, and powdered cumin.
For basting: 4 tablespoonfuls of olive oil, the same amount of
lemon juice, 2 pounded cloves of garlic.

Make several incisions in the fish on both sides about an inch
long and in each put a pinch of salt, pepper, and cumin, which
have been mixed together.

Grill the fish on both sides very gently, basting it with the
dressing of oil, lemon, and garlic, for 10 minutes to a quarter of
an hour. Then increase the heat which should be sufficient to
brown it before serving. Put the fish on a heated dish, pour over
it the basting juice, and serve with a long French loaf which has
been heated five minutes in the oven. A dish of French beans,
blanched in boiling water and allowed to simmer in a little
butter, could follow.

Cumin is very like caraway in its fruit form, but it has a stranger flavour
which defies analysis. If cumin is distrusted, ground coriander seeds,
which have a less exotic flavour, can be used.

LOBSTER

Lobster is even an expensive dish in quite humble inns round the
coast of Brittany where it is caught in considerable numbers. The question whether it should be prepared simply or in an elaborate way is all
the more tantalizing when the choice is presented on such rare occasions.

The answer probably is that if the lobster is still alive it should be
cooked in salted water, and served cold with mayonnaise, and if it is
already cooked by the fishmonger, and therefore not absolutely fresh,
it can be prepared à la bretonne and served with saffron, rice, or more
elaborately à l'armoricaine.

HOMARD À LA BRETONNE   *Lobster*

1 lobster weighing 2 pounds, 1 pint of prawns, 1 pint of shrimps,
4 ounces of mushrooms, 2 onions, 1 gill dry white wine, ½ pint
of cream, 3 tablespoonfuls of mild dry grated cheese (*gruyère*),

½ a bay leaf, 3 ounces of butter, and a little pepper. (3 pints of salted water, if the lobster is still alive.)

(A lobster is cooked by putting it into boiling salted water, simmering it for 20–30 minutes, and letting it cool in its own liquid.)

Peel the shrimps and prawns, and save the shells of both. Chop the onions finely. Melt 2 ounces of butter in a saucepan and sauté the onions without letting them colour. Heat the wine, pour it onto the onions, and let it reduce a little. Put in the bay leaf and the shrimp and prawn shells, and cook for 15 minutes. Pass the liquid through a fine sieve. Taste it and add salt if necessary, and before incorporating the cream into the sauce prepare the mushrooms, which should be sliced and sautéd in the remaining ounce of butter.

Remove the lobster from its liquid, take the meat from the shell and claws and cut into neat pieces about one inch square, and put them into an earthenware or china fireproof dish, with the prawns, shrimps, and mushrooms. Put the cream into a small pan, and warm it over a gentle heat, stirring it until it begins to thicken. Pour on the wine from which the onion and prawn shells have been filtered, and when the sauce is smooth, pour it over the lobster. Sprinkle with grated cheese and put the dish in a hot oven to brown the top. Serve with plainly boiled rice flavoured with saffron.

MAQUEREAUX À L'HONGROISE — *Mackerel*

4 fresh mackerel, salt, 1 teaspoonful of paprika pepper, ¼ lb thinly sliced bacon, 2 green paprikas, ½ lb tomatoes, 1 onion, 3 large potatoes, 1 cup of sour cream (yoghourt will do), 1 tablespoonful of lard.

Use a shallow fireproof baking dish from which the fish may be served.

Clean the fish, scale them, and with a sharp knife make incisions in each of them on each side at intervals of about 1 inch. Rub each fish with a little salt and the paprika pepper. Cut the bacon, green paprikas, tomatoes, and onion into slices of about the width of ¼ inch and put them alternately into the cuts made in the fish. The seeds and coarse core of the green paprikas must, of course, be removed before they are sliced. Slice the potatoes thinly.

Grease the baking dish with the lard and cover the bottom of it with the thin slices of raw potato. Put the fish on the potatoes and pour over a little of the sour cream or yoghourt. Put the dish into a hot oven and let the fish cook for about 25 minutes, basting it well with the rest of the sour cream until the pieces of bacon become brown.

MAQUEREAUX AU VIN BLANC *Mackerel*

Maquereaux au vin blanc is usually prepared on top of the stove, but if you don't wish to risk cracking a fireproof dish, this can be done in an enamelled-iron *cocotte* over a flame, or alternatively in earthenware or fireproof china in the oven.

Butter a fireproof dish and lay in it as many mackerel as you need, cleaned, with heads and tails removed, and with the skins removed, if you can manage it.

Allow ¼ pint of dry white wine, 2 shallots, and a few small sliced mushrooms for each fish, with an ounce of butter, salt and black pepper.

Chop the shallots very finely, lay them on the mackerel, and put the sliced mushrooms round the fish. Sprinkle a little salt and freshly ground black pepper over, and pour on the wine.

Raise the heat until the wine is simmering – or put the dish in the oven to the same end – and after a minute or two carefully turn the fish over and cook for a further few minutes till tender. Remove the dish from the heat, and let the mackerel cool in the liquid. If there is too much, pour it off into a saucepan, and reduce it over a good heat before pouring it over the fish.

This is to be eaten cold. If a hot dish is preferred, the sauce must be reduced, thickened with a brown *roux*, poured over the fish with the addition of a little butter, and sprinkled with baked crumbs before being put in the oven for a few minutes to amalgamate the sauce.

An ideal dish in which to cook this is a rather long narrow one made by a Swedish firm in enamelled iron, which is now on the market, and is suitable for braising and baking all kinds of fish.

MATELOTE

The *matelote* of river fish stewed with herbs and red or white wine seems to be almost unknown in this country, except by those who have idled on the banks of Seine or Saône.

Whether a simple *matelote* of river fish or a more elaborate and splendid *matelote normande* – fillets of sole or turbot bathed in a marvellous and creamy sauce in which delectable mushrooms, little onions, mussels, prawns, and sometimes grapes form part of a submerged archipelago whose surface is embellished by crayfish tails, heart-shaped *croûtons*, and sometimes gudgeon fried in butter – this *plat* is one of the prides and pleasures of the French table.

The method of preparation is normally that given in the recipe for *matelote à la canotière*, but the ingredients, the type of wine and brandy used, vary with the district, and the garnishes vary likewise, but the *matelote* usually includes a garnish of mushrooms sauté and little onions braised in butter and incorporated in the sauce.

Only the Normandy *matelote* uses sea fish such as sole, turbot, and brill, and cider and *calvados* instead of wine and cognac. See *sole à la normande* (page 138).

MATELOTE À LA CANOTIÈRE   *Carp, eels*

As this is not a cheap dish in terms of wine it is best to make it for a special occasion and, for this reason, the recipe is given for 6 or 7 people.

2 lb carp, 1 lb eel, 4 garlic cloves, ¼ lb onions, 2 oz butter, a *bouquet garni*, 1½ pints of dry white wine, a liqueur glass of brandy, ½ lb button mushrooms, 18 little onions, flour and butter for the sauce, chopped parsley.

Slice a small carp (large ones weigh from 4 to 5 pounds) and 1 lb of eel and sauté the pieces in a casserole in which 4 crushed garlic cloves and ¼ pound of hashed onions have already been sautéd in butter. Then pour half a wineglass of brandy over the fish and set light to it. Heat the wine in a separate pan and pour it over the fish, add the *bouquet garni*, put on the lid, and cook for about 20 minutes, very briskly.

During this time, prepare ½ pound of mushrooms by frying them in a little butter and, after blanching the little onions for 5 minutes in boiling water, put them in a pan with some butter and cook them with the lid on over a low heat. When all are cooked, put the onions, mushrooms, and the fish into another casserole to keep warm. Reduce the liquid in which the fish has cooked by $\frac{1}{3}$, add a little more butter and pour the sauce over the carp and eel slices in the casserole, and sprinkle with parsley. Serve in deep plates in which toasted French bread rubbed with garlic has been laid. If the *matelote* is prepared for a special occasion it can be dressed with fried gudgeon and river crayfish cooked in a *court-bouillon* of white wine.

Eels are fairly plentiful in the winter months in the south of England and can be bought alive at many fishmongers and in street markets.

The *matelote* of river fish usually includes slices of eel, pike, carp, or bream, sometimes perch, barbel, and tench. Eels are normally an ingredient of this dish, and provide a special suavity to the sauce. The practice of flaring the fish with brandy before pouring on the wine is to remove any trace of oiliness, and is not a mere extravagance.

For the sake of interest, some of the regional variations are outlined here. In the *matelote de Seine, Marne, et Oise*, these fish are stewed in red wine and *bouillon*, with a flavouring of vegetables and herbs, the liquor in which they have cooked being sieved and reduced, thickened with a little flour and butter, and poured over slices of fish which are served in a deep china dish garnished with *croûtons*, slices of hard-boiled eggs, and crayfish which have been cooked separately in a *court-bouillon* of white wine.

In Champagne the *matelote* is prepared by sautéing shallots and garlic in butter with thyme, bay, spices, and chopped herbs, laying the fish slices on this prepared bed, flaring with brandy and moistening with champagne. The sauce is passed through a sieve before serving the fish on toasted bread.

Sometimes the sauce is thickened with yolk of egg and cream rather than with kneaded butter as in the *matelote lorraine* which incorporates small onions braised, and mushrooms sautéd in the sauce, the fish being served in their sauce on toast.

In Burgundy the *matelote de Saône* consists of carp, tench, pike, and barbel, eel, and perch, cooked in red wine with onions, garlic, herbs, and little onions and mushrooms are included in the sauce.

In the *matelote lyonnaise*, thick slices of eel, carp, tench, perch, and pike are stewed with onions, carrots, parsley, thyme, bay leaf, and garlic, red *Beaujolais* wine, and a little brandy. It is served on fried *croûtons* rubbed with garlic and the sauce is thickened with butter. The dish is dressed with fried eggs, sautéd mushrooms, and crayfish cooked in dry white wine.

We have only mentioned a few of the *matelotes* to illustrate the diverse gastronomic combinations resulting from a gentle pastime, the invention of the French, and the resources of a countryside threaded with rivers and staked with vines.

MERLANS BERCY   *Whiting*

Fishmongers sometimes palm off a pollack, haddock, or codling on an unsuspecting customer in place of silver whiting. Whiting usually do not exceed 1½ lb in weight, and are distinguished from the haddock by having no barbule under the chin and from the pollack and codling by being underhung, and they have a more delicate flavour than their impersonators.

4 whiting weighing not less than ½ lb each, 1 chopped shallot, 1 dessertspoonful of finely chopped and pounded parsley, ¼ pint of dry white wine, salt and pepper, 3 to 4 ounces of fresh butter.

Use 1 ounce of the butter to grease a flat earthenware baking dish and then sprinkle on it the chopped shallot and parsley. Lay the whiting on this mixture and put a little salt and ground black pepper on each. Moisten the fish with the white wine and then put the dish in a gentle oven.

Let the fish cook for 30 minutes and baste them with the liquid in which they are cooking at least three times during the cooking period. Then pour off the liquid from the baking dish into another saucepan and let it reduce by half. Add the remainder of the butter to the reduced liquor and pour the resultant sauce over the whiting.

Put the baking dish under a red-hot grill and let the surface brown before serving the fish. The browning process should be done as quickly as possible to avoid overcooking the fish.

MERLANS EN TRANCHES AUX MOULES   *Whiting, cod*

3 pints of mussels, ⅓ pint white wine, 4 silver whiting, 1 onion, carrot, thyme, bay leaf, 1 garlic clove. For the sauce: 1 ounce of butter, 1 ounce of flour, 2 egg yolks, the juice of ½ a lemon.

Scrub the mussels in advance with a stiff brush, wash them in running water, and leave them in a bucket of fresh water. Throw away any that are already open. When once you start, the dish will not take more than half an hour to prepare.

Put the mussels in a saucepan with the wine, put on the lid, and shake them briskly over a strong flame. The shaking allows the mussels to change places and ensures that they will open at more or less the same time.

In four or five minutes they should have opened. Drain off the liquor into a bowl and allow any sediment to fall to the bottom. Remove the mussels from their shells. Cut the whiting into slices about one inch thick and put them in a pan with the onion and carrot hashed very finely indeed, and the sprig of thyme, bay leaf, and garlic.

Pour the mussel liquor onto the fish, making sure that the sediment remains behind. Cover the pan and simmer for ten minutes.

While the fish is cooking, make a sauce by melting the butter in another pan, sprinkle with flour and cook gently for a few minutes without browning. When the fish is cooked, pour the juice through a strainer onto the *roux* and stir till the sauce is smooth. Remove the sauce from the heat, add a little of it to the egg yolks and lemon juice before returning these to the pan. Heat the sauce again on a low flame (or in a *bain-marie*), without letting it boil, and put in the mussels when it has thickened. To serve, place the fish slices round a large oval dish and pour the mussels in the sauce into the centre.

This treatment could be applied to slices of cod, if you think they are worthy of it.

MERLUZA AL HORNO   *Haddock*

Either fresh or dried haddock is used for this dish which can be prepared and cooked in a very short space of time.

    1 haddock, 4 tablespoonfuls of dry white wine, 1 clove of garlic crushed to a pulp, 2 tablespoonfuls of olive oil, 1 tablespoonful

of tomato *purée*, 1 tablespoonful of finely chopped parsley, 3 tablespoonfuls of dried breadcrumbs, and salt and black pepper.

Cut the fish into pieces of the right size for serving and put them in a fireproof dish into which 1 tablespoonful of olive oil has been poured. Then sprinkle the 4 tablespoonfuls of white wine over the fish, put the tomato *purée* over it next, then the garlic which has been crushed to a pulp with some salt, then some freshly ground black pepper, and, finally, the finely chopped parsley and the dried breadcrumbs distributed evenly over all.

Have the oven ready at a moderate heat, put the dish into it and let the fish cook for 20 to 25 minutes depending on the size of the pieces. When the fish is ready, serve it from the fireproof dish with some crusty bread and fresh butter.

MOULES À LA BORDELAISE   *Mussels*

The amounts given are for one person only: 1 quart of fresh mussels, 1 wineglass of white wine, 2 ounces of butter, 3 finely chopped shallots, 1 dessertspoonful of chopped parsley, 2 table-spoonfuls of dry breadcrumbs, and ¼ pint of diluted tomato *purée* (or the equivalent in fresh tomatoes simmered, sieved, and made into a *purée*), black pepper and salt.

Melt the butter in a shallow pan, when it is foaming put in the chopped shallots and sauté them until they have slightly coloured. Sprinkle on the dried breadcrumbs which will absorb the butter, and then add the tomato *purée*. If the *purée* is very thick it should be diluted with a small quantity of water. Simmer the sauce and let it reduce.

Clean the mussels in several waters and open them by heating the wine in a small saucepan, putting the mussels into a shallow pan over a good heat, shaking them well, and pouring over them the hot wine. In two minutes all the mussels should have opened. Take the pan off the fire, extract the mussels from their shells and put them on one side. Throw the shells away and pour the liquid through a very fine sieve leaving the sediment behind.

Add the strained liquid from the mussels to the sauce and cook for another five minutes when it should attain the right con-sistency, taste for seasoning, and add salt and pepper if necessary.

Take the pan off the fire, put in the mussels and some finely chopped parsley, and serve with crisp French bread and butter.

The whole art of preparing mussels is to apply a fierce heat to open them as quickly as possible, and remove them from their shells. Cooking toughens them, so once they have been incorporated in the sauce they should not wait to be served.

MOULES FRITES   *Mussels*

Mussels can be coated with batter and fried in deep fat or they can be coated with egg and dry breadcrumbs and fried in butter. This latter method is the best.

The amounts given are for one person only: 1 quart of fresh mussels, 4 ounces of butter, 1 egg yolk beaten with a little of the white, 2 ounces of fine dry home-made breadcrumbs, 2 quarters of lemon with pips removed.

Clean and beard the mussels and open them by shaking them over a good heat in a shallow pan with the lid on. When all the shells are open, extract the mussels and dry them on a piece of butter muslin.

Dip each one into the beaten egg, then into the dry breadcrumbs and again into the egg. Put 4 ounces of butter into a large shallow pan over a good heat, and when the butter is past the foaming stage put the mussels in.

Shake the pan over the fire until each coated mussel is golden brown. Serve at once on a very hot plate with the quarters of lemon.

Moules frites are not a *plat du jour* in the substantial sense. In Normandy or Holland one is more likely to order them as a mid-morning snack or make a late-evening expedition to some unpretentious inn which specializes in marine food. All the same, a dish of fried mussels, a glass of draught cider, French bread, and *Camembert* cheese makes a very acceptable lunch.

MOULES À LA PROVENÇALE   *Mussels*

1 quart of mussels, 2 ounces of butter, 1 minced shallot, 1 clove of garlic crushed with salt, 1 dessertspoonful of chopped parsley,

ground pepper, a pinch of mixed spice, 1 ounce of dry fine breadcrumbs. The amounts given are for 1 person only.

Pound the minced shallot, crushed garlic, and parsley with pepper and spice in a mortar, and combine this mixture with the butter into a smooth paste.

Clean the mussels in several waters and open them by shaking them over a hot flame in a shallow pan with the lid on. After about three minutes the shells will open. Remove the mussels from their shells and put them in a shallow baking dish. Strain their liquid over them, being careful to leave all sandy sediment behind.

Put little pieces of the butter mixture over the mussels, and sprinkle the dish with the breadcrumbs.

Put the dish in a hot oven only sufficiently long enough for the garlic and parsley butter to impregnate the mussels and for the breadcrumbs to brown, four to five minutes. Put a long French loaf in the oven at the same time, and use the hot bread to mop up the delicious sauce.

MOULES MARINIÈRES   *Mussels*

Use a quart of mussels for each person. Wash them in running water, brush and beard them, and leave them for a time in a pail of water. Discard any that are already open.

Take a large saucepan and put in the mussels together with a carrot and an onion chopped up small, a piece of chopped celery, a bay leaf, and a sprig of parsley. Pour on a little white wine and cook the mussels with the lid on, shaking the pan. In four or five minutes they should have opened.

Pour off the liquor into a bowl to allow any sediment to fall to the bottom, and meanwhile remove the upper shell from the mussels and put the half shells containing them into a covered pan to keep warm.

Chop one or two shallots and put them in a pan with a glass of white wine, simmer and reduce, and pour in the liquor in which the mussels have cooked. Let this reduce by about half, and thicken the sauce by adding a little lump of kneaded butter, the size of a walnut; season the sauce, add the juice of a lemon, some chopped parsley. Put the mussels into fairly capacious soup plates, and pour the sauce, which is fairly thin in consistency, over them.

MORUE À LA CRÉOLE   *Salt cod*

This is a dish of poached salt cod with sauté tomatoes and peppers. The ingredients: 2 pounds of *morue*, 2 onions, 6 tomatoes, 4 red peppers, lemon juice, 2 ounces of butter, 1 clove of garlic, a tablespoonful of baked breadcrumbs, salt and black pepper, a little finely chopped parsley, and 2 tablespoonfuls of olive oil.

Poach the *morue* in the manner described above (page 130). At the same time, put a tablespoonful of olive oil in a sauté-pan to heat. Cut the tomatoes in half, remove the seeds, and season with salt and fresh ground pepper. Fry the tomatoes, cut side down, in the olive oil, turn them over, sprinkle the uppermost side with parsley, a little crushed garlic, and finally the dried bread-crumbs, and put them in a moderate oven to finish cooking. Boil the red peppers for at least ten minutes, when they should be peeled, slit open, and the core and seeds removed. Put them in the oven with a little olive oil and covered with a buttered paper while you fry the onions, which should be chopped small and sautéd in 2 ounces of butter. When these are golden, spread them on the bottom of an earthenware dish, lay the tomatoes on top. Then flake the *morue*, remove all the bones and skin, and lay it on top of the onion and tomato bed. Put the sweet peppers and their oil on top of the fish. Sprinkle the dish with lemon juice, and put it in the oven for a few minutes so that it is really hot. Serve with plain boiled floury potatoes.

PERCH

Perch are beautiful and bold river fish which do not often find their way to the fishmongers. They are more prized by the French and are often served in the little riverside restaurants along the Seine as one of the ingredients of a *matelote*.

They are not large, two or three pounds being quite a fine sized fish.

They are a rich greenish brown above fading into golden white below. On the sides are a row of dark bands of colour, the tail and some of the fins are bright red. The first dorsal fin is armed with eight or nine very sharp spikes, and these must be removed before preparing the fish for cooking, or they may cause an unpleasant wound. The scales of this fish are very strong, and need to be removed by brushing it from tail to head with a stiff-bristled brush. If there is no brush available another method is to plunge the fish into boiling water for three minutes, when the scales soften and can be removed without damaging the skin underneath.

FRIED PERCH

Allow ½ lb fish per person, or more if necessary. Having scaled and cleaned the fish, roll them in a little plain flour which has been seasoned with salt and ground black pepper.

Allow an ounce of butter per fish, and melt this in a sauté-pan. When it is foaming put in the perch, and fry them first on one side, then on the other, about 4 minutes on each side. Serve at once with a little melted butter and a squeeze of lemon juice.

PERCHES À LA HOLLANDAISE *Perch*

4 perch weighing ½ lb each. A *court-bouillon* composed of 1¾ pints salted water, a dessertspoonful of wine vinegar, a bouquet of parsley, thyme, and bay. 2 lb floury potatoes, 4 oz slightly salted butter, ½ a lemon, 1 dessertspoonful of finely chopped parsley.

Cook the potatoes in boiling water, and meanwhile put the ingredients for the *court-bouillon* into a thick saucepan or fish kettle and boil for 8 minutes. Put in the fish, readjust the heat and let the perch poach in the liquid for 12 minutes, with only an occasional bubble plopping on the surface.

Take out the fish, drain them, and keep them hot over a pan of boiling water. Drain the potatoes and put them round the fish. Melt some butter, add the juice of the lemon, and the chopped parsley, and pour over the dish.

Perch can of course be served *à la meunière*, *au gratin*, grilled, or *en matelote* (q.v.). In each case take care to remove the dorsal fin and the scales before preparing the fish.

PESCADO À L'ASTURIANA *Sole, halibut, brill, rock salmon*

Fillets of sole or any white fish of firm flesh such as halibut, brill, or rock salmon are poached in a wine and mushroom sauce quite unexceptionally but for the addition of a little grated chocolate which suggests affinities with the Italian *salsa agro-dolce*.

2 pounds of firm white fish, a wineglassful of dry white wine, 5 ounces of butter, 2 finely hashed onions, 1 teaspoonful of grated chocolate, 12 mushrooms, a tumbler of water, 1 tablespoonful of plain flour, salt and ground pepper.

Put 3 ounces of butter into an earthenware casserole on an asbestos mat on a moderate heat, and when it is foaming add the onion hash and cook gently till tender. Sprinkle on the flour and stir about till the butter has absorbed it and it is golden. Heat the water and pour it into the pan, stirring till a smooth sauce is obtained, add the glass of wine, the grated chocolate, and salt and pepper. Poach the fillets of fish either on top of the stove, or in a moderate oven, in the sauce, but in either case the cooking must be gentle. While this is going on, take the 2 remaining ounces of butter and sauté the mushrooms. The fish will not take more than 20 minutes to cook, and the mushrooms should be added to the sauce about 10 minutes before serving.

PESCI ARROSTITI E FREDDI *Red mullet, mackerel, grey mullet*

One of the Venetian ways of preparing fish is by baking them with herbs and oil in earthenware in the oven, applying a little more oil when they have cooled, and serving them with slices of lemon and fresh herbs, very cold. Red mullet, mackerel, or grey mullet are suitable fish for such treatment.

4 fish, ¼ pint olive oil, 2 bay leaves shredded, 1 dessertspoonful each of finely chopped parsley, chives, chervil, a little thyme and fennel, cayenne pepper, salt, a lemon.

Clean the fish, dry them, and sprinkle them with a little cayenne pepper. Lay them in an earthenware shallow baking dish and pour half the oil on them. Make a few long incisions in the uppermost sides of the fish, and lay the different herbs in the cuts with a little salt. Squeeze half the lemon over the fish, put the dish in a hot oven near the top so that they brown.

Cook them for 25–30 minutes according to their size. Take out the dish and leave it to cool. Before the fish are cold pour the rest of the olive oil over them and squeeze over the rest of the lemon juice. Serve the fish really cold with a little potato salad.

PESCI IN UMIDO E FREDDI   *Sea perch, red mullet*

This is a method of cooking fish of size and substance, for instance the sea perch or red mullet, which is practised by Neapolitan cooks in the small village inns on the Sorrento promontory. The fish are prepared in a *court-bouillon* of water, herbs, and lemon juice or wine vinegar, and allowed to cool in the resulting liquid. They are then removed and olive oil, freshly chopped herbs, and lemon juice are sprinkled over them. The fish is served very cold with boiled new potatoes.

Basil is the herb employed. A fish weighing 2½ or 3 lb will take 20–30 minutes gentle poaching depending on its substance. It should receive its oil, lemon, and herb treatment some hours before being served, and the oil and lemon juice should be spooned over it from time to time.

PSARI PLAKI   *Bream, chicken turbot, halibut, brill*

Bream looks handsome, lacks consistency, and is rather bony. It is therefore a disappointment when cooked in a *court-bouillon* and served straight with a sauce. But it improves by baking with olive oil and vegetable accompaniments, a typical Greek treatment for fish of considerable size which can be applied to chicken turbot, halibut, and brill.

1 big bream weighing 3–4 lb, 2 onions, 1 lb potatoes, 2 carrots, 2 sticks of celery, ½ lb tomatoes, 4 tablespoonfuls of olive oil, salt and pepper, some finely chopped parsley, half a lemon.

Prepare the vegetables and slice them all into pieces of the same size. Put the oil into a frying pan, and sauté the vegetables, beginning with the onions and ending with the tomatoes.

Clean the fish and lay it in a large shallow baking dish which has been greased beforehand. Sprinkle the fish with salt and pepper and squeeze a little lemon juice over it. Put the vegetables round the fish together with the oil from the frying pan, pouring a little oil over the fish.

Cover with greaseproof paper and bake in a moderate oven for about 30 minutes, or a little longer if necessary, basting from time to time. Before serving, sprinkle some finely chopped parsley over the dish.

RAIE AUX OIGNONS ET AU FROMAGE   *Skate*

Usually prepared by simple poaching and served with *beurre noire* or caper sauce, skate is improved by the following treatment:

You will need 2 lb of skate, a dozen small onions, a ¼ lb of grated *gruyère* and some slices of bread cut into heart shapes and fried in butter or olive oil, together with 1 ounce of butter, 2 shallots, 1 tablespoonful of flour, 2 cloves, a bay leaf, thyme, salt and pepper, and a tumbler of milk for the sauce.

Melt the butter in a pan, mince the shallots and sauté them for a few minutes, sprinkle with flour, stir about, add the tumbler of milk which has been heated to boiling point, allow the sauce to thicken and put in the cloves, herbs, and seasoning.

Poach the skate in this sauce for 15 to 20 minutes and meanwhile prepare the little onions, which should be blanched for 5 minutes and then allowed to cook gently in butter with the lid on.

When the skate is sufficiently poached, remove it from the sauce and lay it in a baking dish which has been oiled and sprinkled with half the grated *gruyère*. Dispose the onions in the dish, strain the sauce over the fish, sprinkle with the remainder of the cheese, and bake for 15 minutes in the oven, by which time it should present a golden surface.

Fry heart-shaped *croûtons* in butter while the fish is baking and dress the dish.

ROUGETS À LA NIÇOISE   *Red mullet, John Dory,*
                                        grey mullet, brill, halibut

The *pays Niçois* conjures in English minds the promise of exotic pleasures. Not the least of these is the spectacle of the fish markets in Cagnes and Mentone, where the midnight catch is displayed, a gleaming haul of marine crustacean splendour. There the gilded John Dory and the rosy mullet are held in great esteem and are both subjected to a typical method of preparation to enhance their naturally delicious flavour.

This consists of two culinary operations: a preliminary grilling of the fish after dressing it with olive oil, usually done over a charcoal brazier, and after this, the fish is baked with a finely chopped dressing of herbs, mushrooms, garlic, onion, and breadcrumbs, sprinkled with white wine.

This method of cooking is of course only suitable for fish with firm flesh, but it can be used to advantage with fish less excellent in themselves, grey mullet, brill, and halibut. Where the grill is not reliable – many gas grills fail in this respect – it is as well to heat a little olive oil in a sauté-pan and sauté the fish instead of grilling it.

2 lb red mullet, 2 tablespoonfuls of olive oil, 4 oz mushrooms, an onion, 2 shallots, basil or parsley, a handful of fine breadcrumbs, ¼ pint of white wine.

Wipe the mullets, gut them carefully and replace the liver inside the fish. Dress them with olive oil and put them under the grill for 3 minutes on each side. (Or dust them with seasoned flour to prevent sticking and sauté them in a pan.) Make a very fine hash of the herbs, onion, shallots, mushrooms, and garlic, and sauté this preparation in olive oil before laying it on the fish in a greased ovenproof dish. Sprinkle with breadcrumbs and pour on the wine. Bake in a hot oven for 15 minutes. The fish can be served cold with stoned black olives and a crisp French loaf. A good *vin rosé* should be served with it, for instance a *Coteaux de Vence* or a *Tavel*.

SALMON

Salmon is the best of freshwater fish, the most expensive, the rare occasion fish. It is quite natural that one should be seized with anxiety at the thought of doing it justice, both in cooking it, and providing it with the right accompaniments.

There is a great difference in flavour between a salmon cooked soon after it is caught and one that has languished for a day or two on a marble slab, so the first essential is to go to a first-class fishmonger whose high-quality trade ensures that it is fresh.

If as sometimes happens, one is tempted by salmon in a street market at a remarkably low price, that price is usually a reflection on its freshness. In such a case it is a good thing to lay the fish for an hour or two in a marinade of white vinegar and herbs before submitting it to the *court-bouillon*.

We give here a recipe for a *court-bouillon* in which the salmon is to be cooked whole. The quantities can be proportionately reduced if smaller portions are in question.

5 quarts of water, $\frac{1}{2}$ pint of wine vinegar, 2 ounces of coarse salt, $\frac{1}{2}$ ounce of peppercorns, $\frac{3}{4}$ lb carrots, 1 lb of onions, a sprig of thyme and bay leaf, 2 ounces of parsley stalks.

Put all the ingredients – except the peppercorns – into a saucepan and bring to the boil. Allow the liquid to simmer for 40 minutes, then add the peppercorns. Simmer the *court-bouillon* for a further 10 minutes, strain off the liquid through a tammy and put it aside until it is needed. If the peppercorns were stewed too long in the *court-bouillon* it would give a bitterness to the preparation.

Before poaching, the fish is to be cleaned, washed, and trimmed, and laid on the drainer of a fish kettle. When the whole fish is to be cooked the *court-bouillon* is prepared in advance and allowed to cool. It is poured over the fish in the appropriate vessel and brought quickly to the boil, the heat is then moderated and the fish is allowed to poach without actually boiling, with the lid on. This method prevents the flesh from shrinking too rapidly and allows the skin to remain intact, thus preserving its appearance. (The same instructions apply to whole fish poached in salted water, the proportions being $\frac{1}{4}$ ounce of coarse salt to each quart of water.)

If the salmon – or any other fish for that matter – is to be sliced before cooking, the procedure is different. The fish is cut into slices not less than $\frac{3}{4}$ inch thick, weighing about 8 ounces, and these are placed in a boiling *court-bouillon* which has the effect of sealing the exposed surfaces and confining the juices, which would escape with consequent loss of flavour if the slices were slowly brought to the boil. The sealing of the fish takes place instantly, and the heat should then be reduced while the cooking process is completed.

In either case, if the salmon is to be served cold, the flavour is improved by allowing it to cool in the liquid in which it has cooked.

Cold salmon, which many people prefer to hot, should be served with an accompaniment of stuffed hard boiled eggs, shrimps or prawns, cucumber salad, tomato salad, a salad of lettuce, chicory, or endive, and plenty of freshly made mayonnaise.

SAUCE MAYONNAISE

There is no definitive mayonnaise sauce. It is always a union of egg yolks and oil, but with a variety of accent provided by wine vinegar, lemon juice, mustard, etc. The quality of the oil matters for this sauce, and the egg yolks must be fresh. The recipe given here can bear the substitution of wine vinegar for lemon juice, and the addition of mustard for greater piquancy. A clove of garlic can be pounded in the mortar – ideal utensil for making mayonnaise – before beginning the sauce.

To make the sauce, separate carefully the yolks from the whites of 2 eggs, and put them in a bowl with a pinch of salt, a little pepper, and the juice of $\frac{1}{2}$ a lemon. Stir together with a wooden spoon and begin adding drop by drop some olive oil, stirring continuously in the same direction. To make enough sauce to serve with salmon or turbot for four people at least half a pint of oil is needed, and the juice of a lemon. As the stirring proceeds the oil may be added in a thin thread rather than drop by drop, but to prevent the sauce from becoming too thick a teaspoonful of water should be added from time to time, and a few drops of lemon juice. Continuous stirring in one direction and the sparse application of the oil is the basis of success with this sauce.

If, by some misfortune, the sauce separates it can be restored by beginning again with a fresh yolk of egg in another basin, and transferring the separated mixture little by little into it. The separation occurs for several reasons. Sometimes the oil is too cold. In winter one should keep it near the stove where it can maintain a moderate temperature. Sometimes the sauce is allowed to get too thick too quickly; an occasional flick of water or lemon juice prevents this. The egg yolks must be fresh. Equally in summer the oil may not be cool enough. In hot weather one should cool the basin before starting. In spite of an occasional failure, this is a simple sauce to make.

SAUCE TARTARE

This sauce is an elaboration of mayonnaise, using a little mustard which goes into the mortar with the egg yolks, and usually wine vinegar instead of lemon juice. When the sauce has thickened a fine hash of shallot, gherkin, capers, *fines herbes*, and sometimes a few sorrel leaves (stripped, blanched, and chopped), are added. This is a particularly delicious cold sauce for all firm fish.

GRILLED SALMON

If you wish to grill or broil salmon, it should be cut into slices from 1 to 1½ inches thick. Each slice should be sprinkled lightly with some table salt and then painted with melted butter or olive oil. The slices should be grilled under a brisk fire for the earlier part of the operation and then the heat should be adjusted for the later cooking-through stage. It will take about 25 minutes to grill a slice of salmon 1½ inches thick, as it should be well done.

SAUMON À LA MEUNIÈRE   *Salmon*

Salmon slices can also be cooked successfully *à la meunière* in the same way as trout. The salmon should be cut into slices and each should be about ½ an inch thick. Season these slices with salt and pepper mixed with very little plain flour, and then cook them in hot clarified butter in a thick frying-pan, so that the outside of the slice sets and its inside juices are sealed. The whole cooking process should be rapid. Clarified butter is made by cooking the butter very slowly until all the water has evaporated from it, and then allowing it to cool and solidify.

SOLE AU VIN BLANC   *Sole*

Remove the skins from 4 soles and cut off and clean their heads.
Prepare a little fish stock with the fish heads, a sliced carrot,
onion, sprig of parsley and bay leaf, to which should be added
¼ pint of white wine and the same quantity of water. Simmer for
half an hour and pass the stock through a sieve. Put the soles
into a buttered fireproof dish on a bed of very finely hashed
carrot and onion. Pour on a glass of white wine, cover with a
buttered paper, and cook in the oven for not more than ten
minutes.

Melt a nut of butter in a saucepan, sprinkle with flour, cook
for a few minutes, and pour on the stock which should be
allowed to thicken before a *liaison* of 2 egg yolks, the juice of a
lemon, and a little butter is added to it. Add the juice in which
the soles have cooked to the sauce, and pour this sauce, which
should be thick and smooth, over the soles, and serve with a
garnish of lemon.

TRUITES À LA MEUNIÈRE   *Trout*

1 trout of about 8 ounces for each person, 2 tablespoonfuls of
plain flour to which salt and freshly ground pepper has been
added, 2 ounces of clarified butter (which is made by cooking
butter very slowly until all the water has evaporated from it, and
then allowing it to cool and solidify), 1 large teaspoonful of
finely chopped parsley, ½ a lemon, and 1 ounce of fresh butter.

Wipe the trout and roll each one in a little plain flour previously seasoned with salt and pepper. Put the clarified butter into
a thick frying-pan and heat it. Then add the trout and fry it,
first on one side and then on the other, until it is golden brown.
The whole cooking time should take about 7 minutes, that is
3½ minutes for each side.

Put the trout on a hot flat dish, sprinkle a little finely chopped
parsley over it, then a squeeze of lemon juice, and, finally, the
last ounce of butter which has been heated till it is lightly brown
and smells of nuts, and which is known as *beurre noisette*.

TURBOT

A large turbot weighing 4 lb presents a problem to most households if it is to be served whole. The *turbotière*, the specially shaped lidded pan which was a feature of Victorian kitchens, is now a rarity. No pan will be large enough to contain the turbot, unless a preserving pan can be found, for which a lid must be extemporized.

A turbot should be served whole and majestic and complete with fins. Do not add to the feeling of awe, which should inspire you in cooking this fish, a feeling of guilt by mutilating its natural shape. (At the worst, cut it across the middle, severing tail from head.)

The texture of the turbot is very firm, and when straight from the sea its flavour is reminiscent of lobster. A turbot which is dark skinned on both sides is often better than the usual ones which are dark on one side and white on the other.

There are divergent recommendations for the *court-bouillon* in which it should cook – for instance, plain salted water or one part milk to six parts water with herbs and slices of lemon.

We prefer a *court-bouillon* of ½ a pint of white wine, a pint of water, with 2 small carrots sliced lengthways, a sliced onion, a clove, lemon rind, thyme, parsley, a sprig of rosemary, and a bay leaf, simmered for at least half an hour, which should be just enough to cover a 4-lb fish lying in a preserving pan. If a preserving pan is being used, butter the bottom before laying in the fish, so that it will slide out more easily. Strain the *court-bouillon* over it, and bring it slowly to the boil, keeping the pan covered. Reduce the heat, and simmer for about a quarter of an hour, when a pointed knife should be inserted into the fleshy shoulder; if there is no resistance as the bone is approached, it should be ready.

If the turbot is to be served cold, let it cool in the *court-bouillon*, and then lay it on a large dish, garnish it with lemon slices, parsley, and nasturtium flowers, and serve with it a *sauce béarnaise*, a mayonnaise sauce, or *sauce rémoulade*.

SAUCE BÉARNAISE

For approximately five tablespoonfuls of sauce the following ingredients and quantities should be used: 8 tablespoonfuls of butter, 2 egg yolks, 4 tablespoonfuls of white wine, 4 table-spoonfuls of white wine vinegar, 1 teaspoonful of hashed shallots, 1 teaspoonful of chopped tarragon, 1 teaspoonful of chopped chervil, and separately a little tarragon and chervil chopped together.

Boil the wine, vinegar, chopped shallot, and the teaspoonfuls of tarragon and chervil. Let the liquid reduce until there are only $1\frac{1}{2}$ tablespoonfuls left, leave this to cool and strain it.

Using a small pan set in a *bain-marie* in which the water is hot but not boiling, put in the strained liquid, the two egg yolks, three tablespoonfuls of butter and a tablespoonful of cold water, a small pinch of salt. Beat the preparation lightly until the butter is melted and then add, beating all the time, the five remaining tablespoonfuls of butter, in little dabs. The sauce thickens to a consistency of a mayonnaise, and should be completed by the addition of the chopped tarragon and chervil.

SAUCE RÉMOULADE

This is produced in the same way as the *sauce mayonnaise* already described (see page 160) to which are added 2 blanched shallots, 2 fillets of anchovy, 1 tablespoonful of capers, and 4 or 5 little gherkins, all of which have been chopped up very finely indeed. It can be equally well made with pounded hard-boiled egg yolks as the point of departure.

Cuts and Joints

CUTS AND JOINTS

SINCE the disappearance of rationing of meat and the steep rise in its price, newspapers and magazines have returned to the Victorian practice of presenting graphically the different joints and cuts of meat with the appropriate animal drawn in outline and marked off in corresponding areas, paying particular attention to the cheaper cuts.

Every cook should become familiar with these joints, and save thereby the humiliation of being given a piece of topside instead of the silverside for which she asked, and finding she has paid for the more expensive cut. Butchers sometimes trade on ignorance, and the price of meat is so high that one needs to know the anatomy of the animal in question, and what proportion of fat and lean to expect in the various cuts.

In many of the dishes in this section the cheaper cuts can be used, because on the whole a long period of cooking is prescribed, during which the fibres of the meat are softened. This allows one to be extravagant when roasting or grilling and more economical in braising, stewing, and casseroling. But it is only fair to say that the quality of meat used in a *daube*, for instance, in spite of the very prolonged and slow cooking, is important. Where rump steak or silverside would emerge from the *daube* in a state almost as fibreless as cheese, shin of beef, whose texture is already spoiled by veins of gristle, would not repay the time and trouble. Where a lengthy preparation is involved, as in *veau saumoné*, for instance, when the meat must steep in pickle for a week beforehand, it would be silly to expend such care on anything less than a veal fillet. But these are exceptions.

English people have always excelled in roasting meat, so we have concentrated here on dishes which combine in the cooking a preparation of beef, mutton, veal, or pork with aromatic vegetables, herbs, and spices. Some of these are of very humble origin, sausages and lentils, bacon and red cabbage, and the Russian *Selianka* which combines pork and *sauerkraut*, dishes whose consistencies are rather unfamiliar here.

Beef

Since some thirty years ago Virginia Woolf embalmed the delicious *Bœuf en daube* in her novel *To the Lighthouse*, its aroma has been stealing into readers' minds with a poetic fragrance which has removed it far from the realm of everyday life. Here apparently was a dish which Mrs Dalloway's cook took three days to make and which at a critical moment was ripe for serving.

Bœuf en daube belongs to the ancient category of hermetic cookery, like the gipsies' hedgehog wrapped in clay. The *daubière*, its lid sealed with a paste of flour and water, lay all night in the smouldering ashes of a wood fire, with pieces of live charcoal on the lid.

Today not many people have a *daubière* whose lid will bear the application of burning charcoal, so the dish should be lidded earthenware or iron and put in the oven. There are of course regional variations for the *daube*; two are given here, one in which it should be served hot with a steaming dish of *Tagliatelle al burro*, and the other including a calf's foot which is served cold in its own jelly.

BŒUF EN DAUBE À LA PROVENÇALE

For five people: 2 lb of rump steak, 2 onions, 3 carrots, parsley, thyme, and bay, a sprig of celery, ½ teaspoonful of cinnamon, black pepper, 3 garlic cloves, a slice of orange peel, salt, ½ a bottle of *Médoc*, a wineglassful of wine vinegar, 3 oz bacon fat, a dozen black olives.

Cut the meat into substantial squares, beat the pieces and rub them in salt and sliced garlic. Put them in a *terrine* with 2 onions cut in halves, 2 or 3 sliced carrots, the *bouquet garni*, pepper, and cinnamon. Pour ½ a bottle of *Médoc* over the meat, the wineglassful of vinegar, and leave it to marinade for at least 6 hours, overnight if you like.

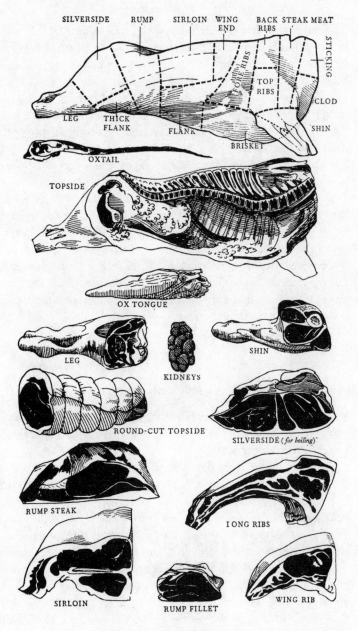

SILVERSIDE RUMP SIRLOIN WING END BACK RIBS STEAK MEAT

STICKING

FORE RIBS

TOP RIBS

CLOD

LEG THICK FLANK FLANK SHIN

BRISKET

OXTAIL

TOPSIDE

OX TONGUE

LEG KIDNEYS SHIN

ROUND-CUT TOPSIDE SILVERSIDE (*for boiling*)

RUMP STEAK LONG RIBS

SIRLOIN RUMP FILLET WING RIB

Beef

Next day melt the bacon fat in a frying-pan and brown 2 sliced onions. Drain the meat and wipe it with a cloth before sautéing it in the frying-pan with the vegetables which have been removed from the marinade and dried. Put the contents of the pan into a fireproof lidded casserole, add salt, 2 or 3 garlic cloves, a fresh bunch of herbs, a small slice of orange peel. Reduce the marinade by half by fast boiling and pour it over the meat. Add enough hot water to cover, put on the lid, and seal it with a flour and water paste. Put the dish in a very slow oven, and leave it for 5 or 6 hours.

Before serving, remove the fat, pass the sauce and vegetables through a sieve and return it to the dish. Blanch a dozen black olives, which have been stoned, and add them to the sauce. Serve the *daube* in the pot in which it was cooked, dressed with roasted red peppers, sliced and sautéd for a few minutes in butter, and an accompanying dish of *nouilles*. The meat and sauce, which should be almost of the consistency of jam, present a very dark appearance and the strips of pimento relieve the sombre tone.

BŒUF EN DAUBE D'APRÈS JEAN-JACQUES ROUSSEAU

3 lb of silverside, ¼-lb slice of rather fat ham, a calf's foot (split, blanched, and cut in 4), a large onion, a carrot, a bunch of herbs, ½ pint of dry white wine.

Trim off the fat from the meat. Chop the fat up with the ham, the onion, and the carrot into a very fine hash. Lay this on the bottom of an earthenware or iron casserole, put it on a lively heat while the fat melts, and then brown the piece of beef in it. Pour over about ½ a pint of dry white wine, and some of the strained water in which the calf's foot has been blanched, so that the meat is covered. Put in the pieces of calf's foot and the herbs, put on the lid, and cook in a slow oven for a long time. After about 3 hours, the beef must be turned over, and continue with the cooking for at least another 2 hours. Then let it cool. Skim the fat from the surface of the gravy, remove the calf's foot and the herbs, and serve cold in its own jelly.

This is a very simple dish. There is no doubt that an earthenware casserole is the best vehicle for slow cooking of this kind. As it is risky to put earthenware pots directly on gas jets or electric hotplates, even with an asbestos mat, the preliminary melting of fat and browning of meat can be done in a heavy frying-pan, and the meat and its aromatic base can then be transferred to an earthenware utensil.

BŒUF MODE À L'ANCIENNE

This is a classic dish, which exactly illustrates the difficult art of braising. As this subject has been treated at some length in the chapter on cooking methods, we recommend the reader to turn to page 50 before trying this recipe.

A piece of beef weighing 3 to 4 lb, preferably from the rump, 6 ounces of larding bacon. For the marinade: 2 onions, 1 garlic clove, a bouquet of herbs, salt, ground pepper, spices (coriander, clove, nutmeg, allspice, cinnamon), ½ bottle of white wine. Besides: about 1 pint of *bouillon*, 2 calves' feet (split, blanched, boned, and cut in 4 pieces), 2 dozen little onions and sufficient butter or olive oil in which to sauté them.

Cut some long strips from the larding bacon, season them with a crushed clove of garlic, chopped parsley, ground pepper, and salt, and thread them through the beef so that the ends emerge on both sides. Put the piece of larded beef in an earthenware crock, with the carrots and onions sliced into 4, the bunch of herbs, a clove of garlic, and the spices. Pour over it the white wine, and leave the meat in the marinade for 5 or 6 hours, turning it once or twice.

Slice up the remaining larding bacon, and lay the slices on the bottom of an enamelled-iron pan which will just contain the beef and accompanying vegetables and calves' feet. Take the meat, carrots, and onions from the marinade, wipe them with a cloth, put them into the pan over a moderate heat, and put on the lid. After some minutes, the lard will have rendered some of its fat, the heat should then be increased and the meat turned about in the fat to brown on all sides. This will take from 15 to 20 minutes, and when the browning process is accomplished, pour on the marinade, and let it reduce by about half, with the lid off the pan. Then put in the pieces of calves' feet, which have been previously blanched for 20 minutes in salted water and the bones removed, and pour on enough hot stock to bring the liquid in the pan up to the level of the top of the beef. Put on the lid, and cook very gently, either on top of the stove or in a slow oven for at least 4 hours.

The garnish of little onions and carrots is separately prepared. The carrots are trimmed, blanched for 5 minutes, and added to the onions, which have been peeled and sautéd in a little butter. A few spoonfuls of meat juice or good stock are added, and the pan is left to simmer for a while with the lid on, being shaken from time to time to prevent sticking and burning.

When the cooking of the beef is completed, the meat is taken out and laid on a dish, surrounded by the pieces of calves' feet, the little onions, and carrots. The sauce is strained, all fat is removed from its surface, it is slightly reduced if necessary, and poured over the meat.

If it is to be served cold the procedure is exactly the same, but the sauce must be considerably reduced to ensure that it sets in a jelly.

This dish is sometimes improved by the addition of a liqueur glass of brandy. The brandy is added when the beef has been browned on all sides, and is sprinkled over the meat and set alight before the wine is poured on.

BŒUF STROGANOFF

This is a simple preparation of tender beef fillet cut into strips, sautéd in butter, and embalmed with mushrooms in a sour cream sauce.

1½ lb fillet of beef, salt and ground pepper, an onion, ½ lb button mushrooms, 4 oz butter, a small glass of white wine, about 1 pint of sour cream, lemon juice.

Cut the fillet into ½-inch slices, salt and pepper them, beat them with the blunt edge of a chef's knife, and cut them into strips about 3 inches long and ¾ inch wide.

Hash the onion, slice the mushrooms and sauté them in 2 ounces of butter in a sauté-pan or aluminium frying-pan. In another pan, which should be made very hot, melt the remaining 2 ounces of butter, and fry the strips of beef in it very quickly. If the pan is hot enough the beef should brown in a very few minutes, when the strips should be removed and kept warm for a moment while the sauce is completed. Pour the glass of white wine over the mushroom and onion hash, raise the heat, and reduce the wine almost to nothing. Then pour in the thick sour cream, heating it gently without boiling. Transfer the fried beef strips into the mushroom and cream sauce. Taste the sauce which may still need a few drops of lemon juice. Serve very hot in a china or silver *entrée* dish, garnished with fresh parsley, with a white Burgundy.

To obtain sour cream, buy the cream a day or two before-hand, pour it into an earthenware bowl, and stand it in a warm place, or over the stove, covered with muslin.

CULOTTE DE BŒUF, SAUCE PEBRONATE

Crush 2 cloves of garlic and put them into a pan in which olive oil has been heated. Beat 2 pounds of rump steak, trim it, cut it into squares, and brown them in the olive oil. Soak the browned meat with white wine, put in a *bouquet garni* which includes a sprig of rosemary, season, put on the lid, and simmer gently on a low flame or in the oven for about 2 hours. Look at the meat from time to time to see that all the moisture has not evaporated. If it has, add a little more wine, or stock, but only a minimum to prevent the meat from drying.

Meanwhile prepare a *pebronate* sauce in the following manner: hash a large onion and fry till golden with 1 or 2 pounded garlic cloves in a little olive oil. Peel 1 lb tomatoes, halve them, and remove the pips. Blanch ½ lb of red pimentos for 10 minutes, slice them lengthways, remove the seeds and core, and skin them. Pound a handful of juniper berries and chop some thyme, parsley, and basil together.

Sprinkle the onion hash with the chopped herbs, add the sliced tomatoes, strips of pimento, and the pounded juniper berries, and simmer for a few minutes. Moisten with a glassful of red wine, which should be reduced on a lively heat, then simmer the sauce gently, with a lid on, for at least an hour. If the beef is cooking in the oven, the sauce can be put on the shelf below.

This *ragoût* should be served with *tagliatelli* or *lasagne al burro* (page 92) and accompanied by a Côte du Rhône wine.

ESTOUFFADE DE BŒUF À LA NIÇOISE

2 lb silverside or buttock steak, ¼ lb lean bacon, 1 lb onions, ½ pint white wine, a little stock (a cube of beef concentrate diluted with water will do), 3 oz fat pork, parsley and basil, 2 garlic cloves, 1 lb tomatoes, a *bouquet garni* including rosemary, 12 stoned black olives.

Trim the beef of all its fat, chop the fat, and melt it in a heavy casserole. Meanwhile cut the meat up into blocks about an inch square, and if the lean bacon is in one piece, cut it into ½-inch cubes. If it is already sliced, trim off the rind and cut into strips. Remove the débris from the melting fat, brown the beef and bacon, pour on the white wine, raising the heat so that the wine is reduced rather quickly. In another pan sauté strips of fat pork which have been cut about ¼ inch thick and 2 inches long, sprinkle them with finely chopped herbs and salt, and when they have rendered some of their fat, put in the tomatoes, peeled and sliced into 4. Crush 2 cloves of garlic and put them in, with a bunch of herbs including a bay leaf and a sprig of rosemary tied together for subsequent removal, and the stoned olives. Now transfer the contents of this pan to the casserole and add sufficient hot stock or diluted beef concentrate to cover the meat.

Cover closely and simmer this *ragoût* in a slow oven for 2 to 3 hours. Serve either with boiled Patna rice or ribbon *pasta*, boiled and dressed with olive oil or butter, with a *Tavel* wine.

FRICADELLES

In French *fricadelles*, in Italian *polpette*, these are nothing more nor less than forcemeat balls. But prepared with more delicate ingredients than the English rissole, and served with *nouilles* or *pasta*, and a rich mushroom or tomato sauce, they are not to be despised.

Using raw beef, lamb, or veal: 1 lb meat, ¼ lb salt pork (not obligatory, but it improves the flavour), ½ lb butter, 5 oz breadcrumbs (previously soaked in milk and squeezed dry), 2 eggs, 2 oz chopped onion sautéd in a little butter, a tablespoonful of chopped herbs (parsley, marjoram, and basil), black pepper, nutmeg, salt. Plain flour. Butter or clarified beef dripping for frying.

Trim the meat of fat and gristle, chop it finely, and mix it with the butter in a pudding bowl. Put in the breadcrumbs, salt, the onion hash, the chopped herbs, pepper and nutmeg, and then beat the eggs and bind the mixture. The mixture is improved by pounding in a mortar. Divide it into 8 or 10 equal portions, and form them into balls, dusting the outside with a little flour.

Heat some butter or beef dripping in a pan and fry the *fricadelles*, browning them on all sides, until they are crisp without, and cooked inside. This will take about 15 minutes, but the time varies with their size. Serve them with *spaghetti al sugo di pomodoro*, reserving some of the sauce to pour round the *fricadelles*.

Using cooked beef, lamb, or veal: 1 lb cooked meat, the pulp of 3 potatoes baked in their jackets, 3 oz chopped onion sautéd in a little butter, 1 egg, salt, pepper, nutmeg, a tablespoonful of finely chopped parsley and basil, 2 pounded leaves of rosemary, plain flour. Some clarified butter or beef dripping for frying. The method of preparing these *fricadelles* is the same as in the recipe for raw beef, but the cooking time is naturally less, not more than 10 minutes.

GULYAS

Gulyas should be a rich dish of beef or veal cooked with onions, paprika pepper, and herbs, to which sliced rounds of already partly boiled potatoes are added to absorb some of the sauce towards the end of the cooking.

Gulyas in its own country is as common as Irish stew in ours, and subject to as many misrepresentations. In clumsy hands it appears as a hot amorphous stew in which gristly meats are floating. But with proper materials the paprika pepper can be used to enhance the *ragoût* instead of acting as a disguise for unsavoury meat. For anyone who has eaten a well-prepared *gulyas* in one of the little restaurants on the Buda side of the Danube, overlooking the lantern-threaded bridges and the electric glitter of Pesth on a warm summer night before the war, this is a dish worth making.

2 lb rump steak, 1 lb onions, 3 oz lard, 1 oz paprika, 2 tablespoonfuls of flour, salt, 1 lb potatoes, 1 pint of stock, 1 lb tomatoes, a clove of garlic, a *bouquet garni*, a glass of red wine.

Melt the fat in an earthenware casserole or enamelled-iron pot, slice the onions and brown them. Make a small mound of seasoned flour and another of paprika. Cut the meat into 1-inch cubes and roll them first in the paprika and then in the flour. Brown the meat in the fat, and peel the tomatoes which should be sliced and added. After a few moments, pour on the wine, let it evaporate a little, sprinkle over the meat any flour that is left and the rest of the paprika. Add enough stock to cover and the *bouquet garni*, put on the lid, and cook in a slow oven for two hours. After an hour and a half, put in 1 lb of small potatoes which have been partially boiled already and proceed with the cooking until most of the sauce has been absorbed. *Tokay* would be an ideal wine to serve with this, and Lager a possibility.

Although this dish can stand alone, it can well be served with aubergines sautéd in butter, or with a dish of mushrooms or fungi.

Veal *gulyas* is prepared in the same way, except that white wine should be used instead of red and the dish is improved by adding at the same time as the sliced potatoes a few mushrooms already sautéd in butter and some stoned blanched black olives.

LE BOUILLI

In the section on Soup the theory and constituents of the *pot-au-feu* have already been discussed, and something has been said about the resulting boiled beef. Where the meat is intended for serving it should not be allowed to cook until it is deprived of all its juices, even if this results in a slightly less sapid stock. Boiled beef, if served hot, should be accompanied not only by the root vegetables with which it has cooked, but by a dish of *haricots verts* sautéd in a little butter, some freshly boiled potatoes, little onions blanched and sautéd in butter, and small gherkins. If it is served cold, it can be garnished quite simply with gherkins, and served with sea salt ground in a salt mill, and French mustard. The piquant Italian *salsa verde* is excellent with cold boiled beef, which in such a case could be served with hot baked potatoes and a salad of tomatoes.

SALSA VERDE

Reduce the following ingredients to a molecular state with a heavy chopping knife or *mezzaluna*: 1 dessertspoonful of capers, 2 anchovy fillets, 1 shallot, and 1 clove of garlic. Put this preparation into a sauceboat, and add to it a tablespoonful of very finely chopped parsley and basil. Dilute with 3 tablespoonfuls of good olive oil, and the juice of 1 lemon. This sauce is also excellent for cold boiled fowl, and as a dressing for fish poached in a *court-bouillon*.

LE BOUILLI AUX SALADE DE POMMES DE TERRE

Cut up the beef into neat little cubes, and prepare a potato salad by boiling 2 lb peeled potatoes, draining them, and placing them in an earthenware vessel. Slice the potatoes with a knife, instead of mashing them, and while they are still steaming pour in a thread of olive oil, at the same time turning the potatoes about with the knife. Chop very finely a shallot, 1 or 2 gherkins, and some fresh parsley, and sprinkle them into the potato. Season, add a little lemon juice, and incorporate the cubes of boiled beef.

MRS CULE'S PICKLED TONGUE

1 ox tongue, ¼ lb common salt, ¼ lb bay salt, ¼ lb Demerara sugar, ½ oz ground black pepper, 2 oz saltpetre, and about 12 juniper berries.

The butcher will remove most of the bones from the tongue which should then be put into an earthenware bowl. Mix the ingredients of the pickle together and rub them into the tongue on all its surfaces. Put the tongue in its bowl in a cool place. Leave it in the pickle for 3 weeks and each day turn it over and redistribute the pickle over the exposed area.

When the 3 weeks are up, put the tongue in a large pot with plenty of cold water. Put the pot over a moderate heat and bring the water to the boil. Then remove the scum, put a lid on and simmer the tongue for 25 minutes to each pound of its weight and 25 minutes over.

When it is cooked, remove the skin and any little bones that may have been left at the root. Trim the fat if there seems to be too much.

Put it into a mould or cake tin, just large enough to hold it, which has been rinsed out with some cold water. Then take a ¼ pint of the cooking liquor, remove any fat from it, and pour it over the tongue. Lay a flat plate on the exposed surface and weight it down. Put in a cool place for 24 hours to set, before turning out.

When tongues are priced reasonably, this makes an excellent basis for a cold meal. The tongue could also be smoked after being in the pickle, in which case it could be kept for future use in the same way as a smoked ham or bacon.

Saltpetre can be bought by the ounce at any chemist's. Bay salt, if not available, can be replaced by using rock salt and a dozen bay leaves.

MOUSSAKA

Moussaka is a Balkan version of shepherd's pie. Its particular flavour derives from aubergines which are either dispersed in layers between the very well spiced and seasoned minced beef or used as the lining and the lid of the earthenware vessel in which it is cooked. As a rule a rather light egg batter is poured over the dish about half an hour before the end of the cooking, which should form a golden crust. This is not always an improvement, particularly when the batter, not having been given time to stand, emerges in the form of a sodden pancake. Having experienced a diversity of preparations bearing this name in Split, Dubrovnik, and Bucharest as well as in Greek restaurants in London, we propound the following recipe:

2 lb lean minced beef, ¼ lb bacon rashers, 1 tablespoonful olive oil, 2 Spanish onions, 2 carrots, 1 leek, fresh basil and parsley, a little coriander, mace, and allspice pounded together, 2 cloves of garlic, a tin of tomato *purée*, a tablespoonful of red wine vinegar,

some stock or *bouillon*, ½ lb potatoes, 2 large shiny aubergines. (When the purple skin of the aubergine is dull, it has already deteriorated.)

The dish is prepared in a heavy frying-pan and transferred to a large open earthenware dish. Heat the olive oil, chop the onions, carrots, leek, and bacon together into a fine hash, and put them in the pan. Crush the garlic cloves and put them in. When the vegetables have cooked for some minutes, sprinkle the minced meat with salt, the powdered spice, and the chopped herbs, and sauté the meat, turning it about so that it all comes in contact with the heat, and slightly browns. Pour on the wine vinegar, some *bouillon*, and the tomato *purée* dissolved in a little stock. Simmer this gently while the aubergines are prepared. Slice them into rounds about ¼ inch thick, sprinkle them with salt, and put a large heavy plate over them for 10 minutes while they exude some of their moisture. Then wipe them with a cloth, and sauté them in fairly abundant olive oil. They have a great faculty for absorbing fat, which will prevent them from burning in the oven. Put a layer of aubergine slices round the earthenware dish, which has been oiled beforehand, and lay on top of this the preparation of minced beef with all the liquor and accompaniments. Put a layer of aubergines over the top, and peel and slice thinly the ½ lb potatoes, which in our recipe replaces the rather doubtful batter. Sprinkle with a little salt, see that the meat juice comes to the level of the potatoes, lay over the top a buttered paper and a lid, and cook slowly for 1½ hours. Towards the end the lid can be removed, so that the potatoes brown.

PAUPIETTES DE BŒUF

1 lb fillet of beef, ¼ lb streaky bacon slices or larding bacon, 2 oz salt belly of pork, a garlic clove, parsley, coriander and allspice, pepper, a carrot and an onion, a wineglassful of white wine, a cup of *bouillon*, a bay leaf and sprig of thyme.

Cut the fillet into 8 or 9 slender slices, trim them into a neat shape, and beat them out with the blunt edge of a chef's knife.

Prepare a very fine hash of the trimmings of the meat, the slice of salt pork, the pounded garlic clove and the powdered coriander, allspice, and black pepper, mix it with some chopped parsley, and spread it thinly on each slice of fillet. If you have pestle and mortar, the hash will be improved by pounding. Then roll up the fillets and tie them with tape.

Put the bacon slices, or thin strips of larding bacon, on the bottom of a casserole large enough to take the *paupiettes* with a hashed carrot and onion. Put in the little rolls of beef, put on the lid, and let the fat melt on a modest flame. After some minutes pour over the glass of white wine, reduce it, and add the cup of hot *bouillon*. Put in a bay leaf and a sprig of thyme, and put the casserole in a moderate oven

When the meat is tender, which can be ascertained by piercing one of the *paupiettes* with the point of a carving fork, remove the lid, put the casserole in the top of the oven, and baste the meat frequently with the juice to produce a fine glazed appearance.

Put the rolls of beef onto a serving platter, keeping them warm, and pass the juice through a strainer into a little pan. Remove the fat from the surface, reduce the sauce if it is not sufficiently concentrated, and pour it over the rolled fillets. Sprinkle the dish with a little chopped parsley, and serve it with a *purée* of potatoes well beaten with butter, hot milk, nutmeg, and an egg yolk, and a salad of red pimentoes or a dish of green peas, and a bottle of *Médoc*.

PIMENTO SALAD

Use 1 lb red and 1 lb green peppers. Halve them from stem to point, remove seeds and core, and sauté them in some olive oil to which a crushed garlic clove has been added. Shake the pan to prevent sticking, sprinkle with salt, add three or four tomatoes cut in halves, and a small amount of liquor, which can be red wine, *bouillon*, or a tablespoonful of wine vinegar and some water, sufficient only to prevent burning. This minimum liquid will be gradually increased by the pimentoes own juice. Simmer for about an hour, with the lid on the pan. Remove the peppers onto a large oval dish, red and green peppers being disposed alternately, remove the skins, which will be easily detachable, reduce the liquor in which they have cooked if this is necessary, strain and pour over the dish. This salad is served cold. It can be used as an *hors d'œuvre* with anchovies, French bread, and ground pepper.

TRIPE CATALANE

2 lb tripe, and seasoned stock to cook it in composed of 1 quart of water, a little white wine or cider, 2 onions, 2 carrots, 2 leeks, 4 sprigs of parsley, a sprig of thyme and a bay leaf.

Besides: 1 onion, 4 tomatoes, 1 clove of garlic, grated nutmeg, parsley, salt, pepper, 2 ounces of lard, 1 glass of dry white wine (or cider), a sprig of thyme, a leaf or two of basil, a little marjoram, ½ a bay leaf.

Wash the tripe well and put it in a large stewpot with the water, wine, vegetables, and herbs, and let it simmer for not less than 2 hours or until it is tender.

Take it out of the stock and cut it up into small pieces. Chop the onion finely and skin and cut up the tomatoes. Melt the lard in a shallow pan and when it is hot sauté the tripe, the chopped onion, and tomatoes in it. Add the herbs, the nutmeg, a little salt and pepper, some of the chopped parsley, and ½ the garlic clove crushed with some salt. Cook this over a moderate heat, pour on the glass of white wine, which should be allowed to reduce a little. Then cover the pan and put it in a slow oven for about 5 minutes. The dish will then be ready and can be served decorated with a little freshly chopped parsley and the remaining ½ clove of garlic finely chopped and sprinkled over it, to be eaten with rye bread and black olives. Drink with it a white Anjou wine.

Lamb and Mutton

ARROSTO D'AGNELLO ALL'ARETINA

Rub a leg of lamb with salt and ground peppercorns, lay it in an earthenware crock, and pour over it 3 tablespoonfuls of olive oil and a tablespoonful of red wine vinegar. Prick the fat on the leg here and there with the point of a knife and leave it, turning it about in the marinade from time to time, for several hours.

Then put it in the roasting pan with a branch of rosemary, a clove of garlic, and the marinade.

Roast in a not too hot oven for an hour and a half. The joint should be basted from time to time.

GIGOT AUX HARICOTS

This is a departure from normal treatment of the Sunday joint. Instead of a baking tin it calls for a large oval fireproof dish.

A small leg or shoulder of mutton weighing 4 lb, 2 tablespoonfuls of olive oil, 2 garlic cloves, a lemon, thyme and rosemary, 2 large Spanish onions, 2 oz ham or bacon fat, a small glass of red wine, a tablespoonful of flour, a tin of tomato *purée*, fine dry breadcrumbs, 1 lb haricot beans.

Soak the haricot beans the night before in twice their quantity of water. Rub the skin of the joint with kitchen salt, pour a little olive oil and the lemon juice over it, and leave it overnight.

On the following day, cook the soaked haricots for an hour and a half in fresh salted water in a covered pan. Put the meat in a large earthenware or fireproof china dish, pour over it the oil and lemon juice in which it has been lying, add a little more oil to cover the bottom of the dish, put 2 garlic cloves under the meat, and a bunch of thyme and rosemary. Set it to roast in the oven at about 365 deg. an hour and a half before the meal.

Meanwhile, to prepare the beans, cut the onions into halves, slice them and fry them in bacon fat until they begin to brown. Sprinkle the onions with a tablespoonful of flour, brown it, working with a spoon so that it doesn't catch the bottom of the pan and burn, add salt, a small glass of red wine which should bubble up and partially evaporate, and then stir in a little haricot bean stock. Add the tomato *purée*, allow the sauce to thicken, then add the haricot beans and simmer gently.

When the joint has roasted for an hour, the bean sauce should be poured into the dish in which it is roasting, distributed evenly round the joint, and covered with baked breadcrumbs.

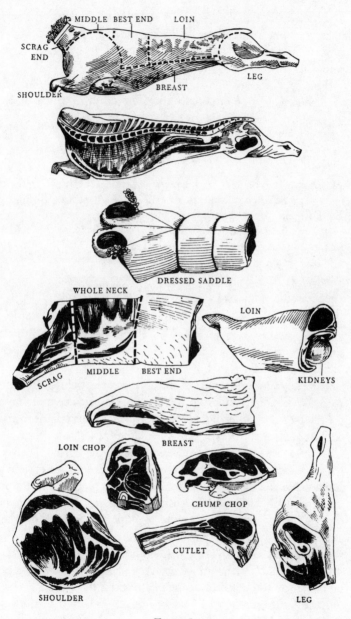

Lamb

The dish is then put back in the oven and allowed to continue cooking for a further half hour, when the breadcrumbs will form a golden crust. Sprinkle some fresh chopped parsley round the dish.

This cannot be done in a baking tin for the good reasons that the beans would be bound to burn, would taste of tin, and the tin could not be brought to table.

HARICOT OR HALICOT DE MOUTON

This is a *ragoût*, or stew, which some authorities derive from the old French verb *halicoter* meaning, 'to cut in small pieces'. Recipes for *halicot du mouton* existed before the haricot bean was generally known, and none of these recipes contained them. The garniture was made up of turnips, potatoes, and onions only. The dish is now usually called *haricot de mouton* and it is prepared in the same way as a *ragoût de mouton aux pommes de terre.*

2 lb stewing mutton, 2 level tablespoonfuls of plain flour, 1 clove of garlic crushed with some salt, 3 dessertspoonfuls of tomato *purée*, 1 *bouquet garni*, 1½ lb potatoes, 1 lb turnips, 24 small onions, 4 oz pork fat, 1¾ pints of *bouillon* or water, some salt, pepper, and a pinch of sugar.

Cut the mutton into pieces and slice 1 of the onions. Put about 1 ounce of the pork fat into the bottom of a thick saucepan and fry the pieces of mutton and onion. When the meat has browned, add a pinch of sugar and then sprinkle on the flour. Mix it well, stirring with a wooden spoon, and add the crushed clove of garlic. Moisten the whole with the hot *bouillon*, or water, add the tomato *purée* and the *bouquet garni*. Cover the pan, put it in a medium oven and let it cook there for about 1 hour. Then, take out the pieces of mutton, remove any skin and bones from them, and put the meat back in the pan. Add the potatoes, which should be peeled and quartered, the onions, and the turnips, which if large should be cut into quarters. Put in the rest of the pork fat cut into little pieces. Put the pan back in the oven with its lid on, and let it remain for a further hour by which time the vegetables should be cooked and the sauce of the right consistency. Remove the *bouquet garni* before serving.

RAGOÛT DE MOUTON BERBÈRE

Either half a leg or half a shoulder of mutton, ½ lb dried Tunisian apricots, ¼ pint of olive oil, 2 lb finely chopped onions, 2 small turnips, 3 carrots, 1 clove of garlic, some powdered paprika, curry powder, saffron, cinnamon, cumin, and cloves, salt, a branch of thyme, and 2 bay leaves. Hot water.

Soak the apricots overnight.

Cut the meat from the bone into cubes of about 1 inch square. Heat the oil in a large heavy pan and brown the mutton on all sides in the oil. Then add the finely chopped onions, browning them in the oil without burning them, and the chopped carrot and turnip. Sprinkle over all: salt, a small pinch of curry powder, and equally little cinnamon, powdered cloves or wholespice, powdered cumin, saffron, and the paprika. Put in the branch of thyme and the bay leaves. Have some hot water ready and pour enough over the meat and vegetables to cover them. Put the lid on the pan and let the mixture simmer gently for not less than 2 hours and preferably for longer. Half an hour before the dish is to be eaten, the previously soaked apricots should be added so that they are well cooked and assimilated when the dish is served. The *ragoût* should be accompanied by boiled rice.

CASSOULET

The ingredients of a *cassoulet*, a characteristic dish of Languedoc, vary according to its district of origin, but it is always an aromatic concoction of haricot beans cooked slowly and for a long time in a capacious earthen pot, with various meats – mutton, pork, goose, preserved or freshly roasted – in a sauce to which onions, tomatoes, and garlic usually contribute their flavours.

The *cassoulet de Carcassonne* consists of haricot beans stewed with bacon rinds, carrots, garlic, and the *saucisson de pays*, to which pieces of preserved goose are added, after being browned in goose fat, with cutlets of pork and pounded garlic. In the *cassoulet de Toulouse*, rather similar to the above, a small leg of mutton is used instead of pork, with Toulouse sausage and a *purée* of tomatoes added.

In the mountain villages of Bas-Languedoc, the *cassoulet* takes the form of pork, cut into cubes, with sausages and strips of seasoned lard, simmered with beans, and flavoured with herbs. The dish is sprinkled with grated crumbs and pounded juniper berries, and slowly baked in the oven. The Gascon *cassoulet* combines a preserved goose leg, sliced and browned in its own fat, with slices of pork and garlic chopped with parsley. In this dish white wine and mashed potatoes are added to beans and meat, and the dish is completed with slices of bacon and fried sausage, the whole being sprinkled with crumbs and melted goose dripping before being left to combine for some hours in a slow oven.

In the face of this diversity it is clear that a certain latitude is permissible in the choice of meats, and owing to the fact that substantial pieces of meat are partially roasted beforehand it is hardly worthwhile preparing a *cassoulet* for less than six people.

Ingredients could include: 1½ lb haricot beans, 2 lb knuckle end of leg of lamb or mutton, ¾ lb loin of pork, a ¼ lb slice of streaky bacon, ¼ lb French garlic sausage *en bloc*, 2 onions, 4 cloves of garlic, a bunch of parsley, thyme, a tin of tomato *purée*, ¼ pint red wine, 1½ pints stock or vegetable *bouillon*.

The haricot beans should soak overnight, and be subjected to a preliminary cooking for 1½ hours in about 4 pints of water with a sprig of thyme and a little salt, before they are ready for use.

While the beans are simmering, the knuckle of lamb (or mutton) should be partially roasted in a moderate oven for ¾ of an hour. Remove the skin, with a ¼ inch of fat adhering to it, from the loin of pork and slice it into inch-wide strips. The rest of the fat should be trimmed off, cut up, and used to brown the pork meat which is cut into ½-inch slices and removed from the bone. In the frying-pan in which the pork has browned the onions and the bacon, cut into dice, are sautéd and sprinkled while cooking with chopped parsley to which pounded cloves of garlic have been added.

After roasting, cut the knuckle of lamb into substantial slices, and having laid a foundation of haricot beans on the bottom of an earthenware casserole, cover it with some slices of lamb, slices of browned pork, some of the browned onions and diced bacon, the strips of lard, and a slice or two of garlic sausage. Lay over this more beans, another layer of meat, and so on, until beans and meat are used up. Then dilute some tomato *purée* with the red wine and stock, season with salt, and pour over the dish to reach to the top of the preparation. Sprinkle the whole with breadcrumbs which will form a lid and to some extent reduce evaporation, and place the casserole in a slow oven where it should cook as slowly as possible for 3 or 4 hours.

Pork, Bacon, Ham, and Sausage

FROMAGE DE PORC

Pigs' heads are extremely cheap and make an excellent brawn. Half a head will provide enough brawn for 8 or 9 people. See that the butcher splits it in 3 pieces, or no saucepan will be large enough to contain it.

½ a pig's head, 2 onions, 3 carrots, 2 small leeks, a few black peppers, a stick of celery, orange and lemon rind, bay leaves, a garlic clove, a pinch of cinnamon. Half a bottle of white wine, a tablespoonful of wine vinegar, 4 hard-boiled eggs, lemon juice.

Wash the pig's head, remove the teeth, singe off any bristles attaching to the skin, and scrape the tongue. Put it in the largest saucepan you have, and add the vegetables, seasoning, wine, vinegar, and water to cover. Simmer the head very gently for at least 3 hours, when all the flesh should leave the bones.

Strain the juice and vegetables through a sieve, remove the fat, and return the liquid to the saucepan. This should be reduced by boiling to ½ the quantity, when it should be capable of setting to a firm jelly.

Meanwhile, remove the meat and fat from the bone, and skin the tongue. Put all meaty pieces on the chopping board, and some pieces of the fat part, and chop or slice into fine slices.

Taste the stock, which should be dark in colour, and add seasoning if necessary. If it is not sharp enough, squeeze in the juice of a lemon and some freshly grated lemon rind. If it is sufficiently flavoured put the sliced meat back into the saucepan, to make sure that there is sufficient liquid to cover the meat, and pour the contents of the saucepan into a large mould, which has been lined with slices of hard-boiled eggs. This not only improves the appearance of the brawn, but the texture.

Put a weighted flat plate on the brawn, and leave it to set in a cold place. Serve it with hunks of rye bread and sliced beetroot, which has been soaked beforehand in burgundy to which a little sugar has been added. The fat which has not been used in making the brawn should be melted down in a slow oven, and will produce a very clear white lard.

HUNGARIAN SWEET CABBAGE WITH PORK

3 small hard white cabbages, 2 lb belly of pork, 6 peppercorns, 3 sprigs of thyme, 1 tablespoonful of plain flour, 1 cup of sour cream, salt, and a little white wine vinegar.

Trim the belly of pork and remove the skin. Put the pork in a stewing vessel with just enough water to cover it, add a little salt, bring it to the boil, lower the heat and cook gently.

Take the cabbages and cut each into 8 pieces; put them in a colander and scald them with some boiling water. When the pork has been cooking for 1 hour, put the scalded cabbage round it and add the peppercorns and the thyme. Simmer until the cabbage is almost cooked.

Then blend the cream with the flour and pour this over the pork and cabbage. Stir well and simmer the mixture for a further 10 minutes. Taste for seasoning and add a little vinegar if necessary. The liquid should have the consistency of a thin creamy sauce. Serve the pork and cabbage accompanied by plainly boiled potatoes and a salad of green peppers.

PETIT SALÉ À LA RATATOUILLE

1 ounce of butter, 2 ounces of plain flour, 4 ounces of pickled pork (breast), 10 potatoes peeled and of medium size, 6 small onions, 1 bay leaf, 2 branches of fresh parsley, 1 branch of thyme (tied for easier removal), 1½ pints of hot water, salt and pepper according to taste.

Melt the butter in a saucepan till light brown, quickly add the pickled pork cut in pieces 2 inches square, brown them, and remove them from the pan. Sprinkle the flour on the melted butter, stirring with a wooden spoon till the flour becomes a light

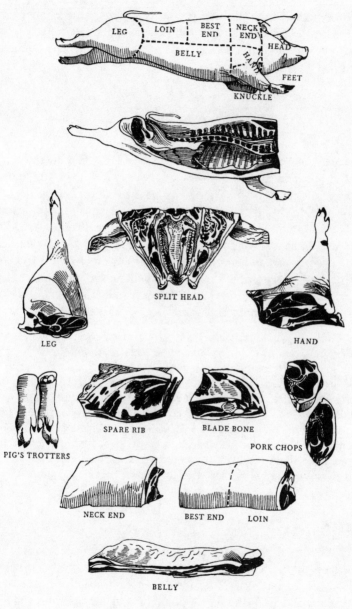

LEG   LOIN   BEST END   NECK END   HEAD

BELLY   HAND   FEET

KNUCKLE

SPLIT HEAD

LEG   HAND

PIG'S TROTTERS   SPARE RIB   BLADE BONE   PORK CHOPS

NECK END   BEST END   LOIN

BELLY

Pork

brown. Add the hot water gradually, stirring all the time; then return the pickled pork to the saucepan, add the potatoes, the onions split in half, the bundle of herbs, salt and pepper. Simmer for 45 minutes.

PORC FRAIS À LA BASQUAISE

1 loin of pork, salt and a little pepper, 3 pints of milk.

Remove the skin from the loin with some fat adhering to it and put it in the bottom of a large heavy pan over a moderate heat to extract the fat. When this has been done, brown the loin of pork in the fat on all its surfaces. Then remove the pork skin. Heat the milk in a separate vessel with salt and pepper added to it and when it is hot pour it over the loin of pork. Adjust the heat under the pan and simmer gently until the meat is tender. Depending on the size of the loin this will take 20 minutes for each pound weight, and 20 minutes over. A piece of loin weighing 4 lb will need 1 hour and 40 minutes' cooking.

Pork cooked in this way can be served with a *purée* of potatoes, and aubergines, *courgettes*, or red pimentoes stewed in butter.

A loin of pork is good simmered in water with herbs and seasoning, and served with a *provençale ratatouille*, a stew in which aubergines, *courgettes*, tomatoes, and artichoke hearts are cut up with onions and a little garlic, and simmered with herbs in olive oil for a long time. This is usually done on top of the stove, and the *ratatouille*, to which some stoned black olives are later added, presents the appearance of a thick sauce in which the vegetables have submerged their identities. It is served alone, or hot with pork, and sometimes with cold roast lamb.

SELIANKA

1½ lb loin of pork, 2 lb *sauerkraut*, 2 onions, 1 tablespoonful of capers, black pepper to taste.

Strip the fat from the lean, cut the meat into cubes of about 1½ inches, and hash the fat. Melt this fat in a pan, removing the frizzled débris, and brown the cubes in it. Put the browned pork in an earthenware casserole.

Slice the onions next and fry them in the pork fat, and while they are frying squeeze the liquid from the *sauerkraut*. This can be done by putting it in a colander and pressing it with a saucer. When the onions are a light brown, put in the *sauerkraut* and cook both together, stirring constantly for a further 15 minutes. Season with ground black pepper and the capers.

Transfer the *sauerkraut* and onion mixture to the casserole containing the pork, mix the contents, put the lid on, and bake the dish in a moderate oven for an hour and a quarter. Serve with potatoes baked in their jackets or plainly boiled and sprinkled with chopped parsley.

BACON AND RED CABBAGE

1 red cabbage of medium size, about 3½ lb boiling bacon, 2 onions, 1 large cooking apple (Bramley), some powdered cinnamon, a pinch of powdered cloves, salt if necessary, black pepper, ½ a bay leaf, some orange peel, a little soft brown sugar, ¼ pint of red wine.

More bacon is specified than is required by 4 people, but it can be served cold later.

Tie the bacon round with some tape so that it keeps a good shape, put it in a pot with plenty of water and bring this to the boil. Adjust the heat and let the bacon simmer for 40 minutes. Take it out and skin it with a knife. Put the skin with some of the fat attached to it in the bottom of another capacious pan over a moderate heat and extract the fat. Then remove the skin. Chop and sauté the onions in the fat, shred the red cabbage, removing the hard core, and put it in the pan. Peel, core, and chop the apple and add it to onion and cabbage. Let these all cook in the fat over a moderate heat, turning them about with a wooden spoon. Then put in the pinch of powdered cloves, some powdered cinnamon, a little mace, the orange peel, and bay leaf. Stir it well and add the red wine. When the mixture is simmering put the piece of bacon on top of the cabbage and other ingredients. Put a lid on the pan and cook for a further hour in the oven. Taste for seasoning and if salt is needed, add some.

HAM OR BACON COOKED WITH CIDER

Choose a piece of ham or bacon of about 3 or 4 lb in weight and soak it for 2 hours. Then put it in a stewpan with cold water to cover it completely. (If the joint is small it is advisable to tie it round with some tape so that its shape is kept while cooking.) Bring to the boil, then lower the flame so that the ham or bacon is simmered rather than boiled. At the end of an hour, remove it, partly cooked, from the water, draw off the skin and put it in a casserole or pan which is just large enough to hold it. Pour over it about ⅔ of a pint of dry still cider (vintage or draught). Put the lid on the casserole, and if it is not a close fitting one seal it down with a flour and water paste or put several layers of grease-proofed paper over the casserole before putting on the lid. Put it in a moderately hot oven for a further hour, when the ham will be cooked. If it is to be served hot, remove it onto a dish, and keep it in a warm place while the sauce is made.

Prepare the sauce by melting in a thick pan 1½ ounces of butter into which is stirred 2 ounces of plain flour. Stirring all the time, let the mixture cook on a gentle heat until it is a light brown colour and smells like hazel nuts. Too high an initial heat precludes – later on – a satisfactory absorption of the liquid, in this case cider, with the flour. When the *roux* has reached a russet hue, take half a pint of the liquid from the casserole, removing the fat, and pour it while still hot onto the *roux*, stirring until the flour and butter paste has absorbed it. Then simmer for seven minutes. This sauce should not be very thick, and if it is, it must be diluted with more of the cider from the casserole. Taste it for seasoning and add a little black pepper. Strain into a sauceboat and serve it separately.

When the ham or bacon is to be served cold it should be left to cool in its own liquor. The liquor is skimmed of fat, and converted into a jelly by dissolving half an ounce of gelatine in a little of the stock, adding it to the rest of the liquid, which is heated, and straining it into a bowl; when it is beginning to set it is painted over the ham. Any jelly that remains is chopped and used with fresh parsley as a garnish for the cold ham, to be served with *sauce ravigote* and a salad of black olives, red pimentoes, and hard-boiled eggs.

SAUCE RAVIGOTE

Hard boil 2 eggs and remove the yolks, which should be pounded in a basin with a little powdered mustard, salt, pepper, and a thread of white wine vinegar. Add olive oil to this mixture little by little, stirring vigorously with a wooden spoon or whisk. When about half a pint has been added and the sauce is not too thick, add to it a finely chopped mixture of parsley, tarragon, chives, and chervil.

Cold ham may also be served with *Courgettes à la niçoise*, little marrows cut into dice, sautéd in olive oil, simmered in a tomato sauce flavoured with garlic, and sprinkled when cold with chopped tarragon.

BOERENKOOL MET ROOKWORST EN AARDAPPELEN
Curly kale with smoked sausage and potatoes

8 leaves of curly kale, 1¼ lb smoked sausage (either one large or several small Frankfurters), 4 lb floury potatoes, salt and pepper to taste, and a piece of bay leaf.

Remove the hard stalks from the curly kale, wash the leaves well, and put them to boil in salted water. At the end of 3 minutes, strain the kale and chop it finely. Clean the saucepan in which it was cooked and put in the bottom of it the peeled potatoes which have been cut into pieces about 1½ inches square. Add a little salt and some black pepper to them, and mix the chopped kale in with the potatoes. Put in the piece of bay leaf and then lay the smoked sausage on top. Just cover the potatoes with water, put the lid on the pan, and bring the contents to the boil. Reduce the heat and cook, stirring occasionally, until the potatoes are well done and the sausage cooked. It may be necessary to add a little water. The final result should be a rather thick stew, a good dish for a cold winter's day.

SAUSAGE WITH LENTILS

1 lb lentils, 1 large onion, 3 tomatoes, 2 red sweet peppers, 1 clove of garlic, 3 or 4 branches of parsley, salt, black pepper, ½ gill of olive oil, and 1 lb small Frankfurter sausages.

Soak the lentils overnight and then put them to boil, with just sufficient water, until they are cooked (1½–2 hours).

Heat the olive oil in a thick pan. Chop the onions, skin and quarter the tomatoes, remove the seeds from the pimentoes and chop them, crush the clove of garlic with a little salt, and put all these ingredients to cook gently in the oil. Add the sausages and then put in the lentils and the parsley finely chopped, with a little salt and some freshly ground black pepper. Cook slowly over a low heat until the lentils are very soft. Serve from the pan in which it was cooked with bread and a crisp green salad.

LIVER SAUSAGE

½ lb liver, ¼ lb dry breadcrumbs, 2 or more rashers of bacon, 1 fresh egg, ½ cupful of stock, a sprig of thyme, a piece of lemon rind, a little sage, ½ a clove of garlic, nutmeg, black pepper, and a little salt.

Put the breadcrumbs to soak in the stock. Remove the veins and sinews from the liver and cut it into small pieces. Take the rind off the bacon and put it together with the pieces of liver twice through the mincer. Take the breadcrumbs out of the stock, strain them over a sieve, and mix them with the minced liver and bacon. Crush the garlic with a little salt and add it with the thyme and sage and the grated lemon rind to the liver mixture. Add a touch of nutmeg, some freshly ground black pepper, and a little salt. The texture will be improved by pounding in a mortar. Finally, break the egg into the mixture and beat it in well.

Grease a straight-sided earthenware jar with lard or bacon fat and turn the liver into it, leaving sufficient room at the top for the mixture to expand. Cover the jar with greased paper and put on the lid, or if there is no lid tie the greased paper down. Put the jar into a pan of gently boiling water so that the water comes ¾ of the way up its sides, cover the pan and let the liver sausage steam gently for 1 hour and a quarter. Alternatively, the sausage may be cooked by standing the jar in a vessel containing hot water in a moderate to cool oven for the same period of time. Serve cold with crisp toast or crusty bread.

Veal

BRACIOLINE DI VITELLO

This is an economical way of cooking veal, which is excellent eaten either hot or cold. The bones, which are removed, will provide good stock for soup.

1 shoulder of veal, ½ gill of olive oil, the juice of 2 lemons, a little salt, a sprig of rosemary, a piece of bay leaf, marjoram, a clove of garlic.

The butcher will probably remove the bones from the shoulder of veal, if asked, but if it reaches the kitchen unboned it is quite easy to do the job. The meat should be kept in one piece and laid flat. A leaf of rosemary is placed on it here and there, the meat being discreetly impregnated with a garlic clove crushed with salt. Then it is rolled up firmly into a good shape and tied with tape. A little rosemary, marjoram, and the bay leaf are crushed and spread on the outside of the meat, which can then be left until it needs to be cooked.

(The bones removed from the shoulder should be chopped into pieces and put in a deep saucepan, covered with water with a piece of lemon rind added to it, a pinch of salt and a few herbs, and the water brought slowly to the boil. Simmer for a long time, 4 hours or more, and when cold the stock will set to a firm clear jelly.)

To braise the rolled veal, heat the olive oil in a very thick pan, put in the veal and seal and brown it. This will take about 20 minutes to half an hour, turning it about. Put the remainder of the garlic-impregnated salt into the pan, together with any of the herbs that may be left over. Add the strained juice of the 2 lemons to the olive oil, adjust the heat so that the liquid is just at simmering point, and put the lid on the pan. The veal will need to simmer for a further 2 hours and this can be done either on top of the stove or in the oven.

Taste the sauce (which will be increased by the juices extracted from the veal) and add a little salt if necessary. The veal may be served hot with its sauce, accompanied by a crisp green salad or a *purée* of spinach. If it is to be served cold, take the meat from the pan, remove the tape, put it in a dish, and strain the liquid over it. This will set to a delicious jelly and the veal will be firm and very easy and economical to carve. Have a chilled bottle of white wine waiting for it.

ESCALOPES DE VEAU PANÉES, SAUCE MADÈRE

1½ lb veal fillet, 2 eggs, a tablespoonful of olive oil, salt and pepper, plain flour, fine breadcrumbs, 2 ounces butter; for the sauce: a small onion, a carrot, 1 ounce of butter, a tablespoonful of tomato *purée*, a concentrated beef cube diluted in ½ pint of water, *bouquet garni*, an ounce of cornflour, a wineglassful of Madeira.

As the fillets of veal take only a few minutes to cook, the sauce must be prepared beforehand.

SAUCE MADÈRE

Melt 1 ounce of butter in a small pan, hash the onion and carrot, put them in the pan, and cook gently. Put in the tomato *purée* and the concentrated beef cube diluted with hot water, a bunch of herbs, and simmer this concoction for half an hour. Mix the cornflour with a little water into a thin cream, and pour it through a strainer onto the sauce, stirring until it thickens. Cook the sauce for 15 minutes, then strain it carefully into another pan. Add the glass of Madeira, and keep the sauce warm while the fillet of veal is prepared.

Cut the fillet into slices a ¼ inch thick, trim the slices into equal shapes about 2 inches wide and 4 inches long, allowing 2 or 3 for each person. Beat the slices. Beat 2 eggs with a teaspoonful of olive oil, a pinch of salt, and pepper. Dust the fillets with flour, paint them with the egg and oil preparation, lay them on a plate of fine breadcrumbs, and turn them, pressing to assure that the crumbs adhere.

Heat a little butter in a heavy pan, and when it is hot put in the fillets, allowing a few moments to elapse while the egg and breadcrumb coating seals, before carefully turning them over. When both sides are sealed, the heat can be reduced a little and the cooking completed.

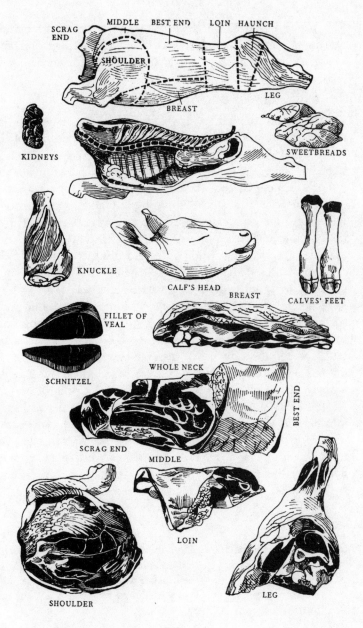

SCRAG END   MIDDLE   BEST END   LOIN   HAUNCH

SHOULDER

LEG

BREAST

KIDNEYS

SWEETBREADS

KNUCKLE

CALF'S HEAD

CALVES' FEET

FILLET OF VEAL

BREAST

SCHNITZEL

WHOLE NECK

BEST END

SCRAG END

MIDDLE

LOIN

SHOULDER

LEG

Veal

Remove the fillets from the pan onto a warmed dish, strain any remaining butter into the Madeira sauce, and serve fillets and sauce separately, with a *purée* of spinach, green peas, or *haricots verts*.

FRICASSÉE DE VEAU AU VIN BLANC

1½ lb of breast of veal from which all the bones have been removed, 1½ oz plain flour, 1½ oz butter, 1 wineglassful of dry white wine, 1 small carrot, 1 small onion, 1 clove, a small leek, a *bouquet garni*, a piece of celery, 1 oz mushrooms or mushroom stalks, salt, pepper, and water, and a tablespoonful of cream.

Prepare some veal stock by putting into a saucepan the bones removed from the breast of veal together with the sliced carrot, the onion stuck with the clove, the leek, the *bouquet garni*, and the celery; cover these with water and bring to the boil. Skim the liquid and put the lid on. Cook the bones for several hours until any meat adhering to them can be easily removed.

1½ hours before the meal, cut the veal into pieces about 1 inch square. Melt the butter in the bottom of a thick pan and sauté the pieces of veal without browning; slice the mushrooms and sauté them in the same pan. When the meat is well sealed on the outside, sprinkle it with flour to absorb the butter. Cook gently without colouring for a few minutes. Then pour on the glass of wine and increase the heat a little. Strain 1 pint of the veal stock into the pan and stir with a wooden spoon until the sauce is well combined. Adjust the heat to simmering point, taste, and add salt and a little black pepper. Cover the pan and simmer for 1½ hours. Just before serving, stir in the cream. Serve the *fricassée* with some boiled *nouilles* which have been tossed in butter.

OSSO BUCO

Osso buco is a speciality of Lombard cooking, a way of preparing a knuckle of veal. The joint can either be cut into slices about 1½ inches thick right through the bone – the butcher will do this – or if a suitable pot is available it can be cut into thick slices as far as the bone and cooked in the following manner:

Prepare a hash of onions, celery, carrots, and leeks, and fry it in butter in an iron pot. Sprinkle with herbs, and lay the sliced knuckle on this vegetable bed, adding salt and pepper. Put on the lid for a few minutes to allow the meat to sweat, but take care that the vegetables don't burn. When they are beginning to brown, pour a glass of white wine over the meat, let some of the liquid evaporate, and then sprinkle the vegetables with a little flour, add a tin of tomato *purée* and some stock, put back the lid, and simmer for 2 hours very gently.

Remove the veal onto a warm dish. Pass the sauce in which it has cooked through a strainer, remove any fat from the surface, squeeze some lemon juice into it, and sprinkle with chopped parsley before pouring it over the meat. Serve the *osso buco* with an accompanying dish of *tagliatelli al burro*, green peas, or plainly boiled rice sautéd for a few minutes in olive oil, and a cheap Tuscan wine, or if you can afford it, a *Valpolicella*.

TÊTE DE VEAU, SAUCE VINAIGRETTE

1 calf's head complete with tongue and brains, 1 large onion, 1 bay leaf, 2 sticks of celery, 2 carrots, the juice of ½ a lemon, several bacon rinds, salt and black pepper, 1 teaspoonful of mixed pickling spices.

For the sauce: 1 small gherkin, 2 tablespoonfuls of finely chopped raw onion, 1 tablespoonful of chopped capers, 3 table-spoonfuls of finely chopped parsley, 1 tablespoonful of olive oil, 2 tablespoonfuls of white wine vinegar, 1 saltspoonful of castor sugar, salt and black pepper.

Get the butcher to chop the head in half and remove the eyes. Soak it in lukewarm water for 2 hours. When it has soaked for an hour, prepare a *court-bouillon* by putting the onion, bay leaf, celery, carrots, bacon rinds, salt, pepper and pickling spices with the lemon juice into a very large pan with plenty of water. Bring this to the boil, and let it simmer with the lid off until the head is ready for cooking.

Remove the brains carefully and put them back to soak. Put the head into the *court-bouillon*, bring it quickly to the boil, and remove scum. Put the lid on the pan, adjust the heat, and simmer the calf's head for 2 hours. At the end of this time test the flesh with a fork and if it comes away easily from the bone remove the head from the stock and keep it warm with a little of the liquid.

Put the brains into a piece of fine cloth or muslin, drop them into the stock, and poach gently for 20 minutes. While the brains are cooking take the meat off the calf's head and cut it into pieces. Skin the tongue and slice it. Put the meat and the tongue with some of the strained liquid into an earthenware casserole and keep hot, until the sauce is ready.

When the brains are cooked remove the fine membrane which covers them. Put them into a bowl with the oil and vinegar and beat them all together with a wooden spoon until the sauce is smooth and of a creamy consistency. Stir in the finely chopped onion, gherkin, capers, and parsley. Add the sugar, a little salt, and some freshly ground black pepper. Re-heat and serve in a sauceboat.

VEAU SAUMONÉ

This recipe comes from the Saintonge area near the mouth of the river Gironde in France. The veal is pickled for a week in a spiced marinade before it is ready to cook.

A thick slice of veal fillet weighing about 2 lb, 2 oz rock salt, 1 oz saltpetre, ½ pint of white wine vinegar, 1 clove and a little nutmeg, 6 shallots, 10 juniper berries, a sprig of thyme, 1 bay leaf, 3 branches of parsley, a few celery leaves, a chopped carrot.

For the garnish: 6 anchovies, 1 tablespoonful of finely chopped shallots, 1 tablespoonful of finely chopped capers, 1 tablespoonful of finely chopped parsley, olive oil, mayonnaise (page 160).

Rub the fillet of veal on all sides with the coarse salt and the saltpetre. Roll it up and tie it into a neat shape. Put the roll of veal into a bowl and marinade it in white wine vinegar with clove and nutmeg, shallots, crushed juniper berries, thyme, bay leaf, parsley, celery leaves, and carrot. Leave the veal in this marinade for 7 days, turning it each day and basting it with the pickle.

When ready to cook, take it out of the pickle, and simmer it in water for one hour. Take it out, remove the tape, put the veal onto a serving dish, and leave it to cool. When it is almost cold, chop the anchovies and mix them with the finely chopped shallots, capers, and parsley, and bind this mixture with a little olive oil. Cover the veal with it, and leave it to cool. Sprinkle over it a few more drops of olive oil and serve with the mayonnaise, or, ungarnished, with *salsa tonnata*. This calls for a dry white Bordeaux wine.

SALSA TONNATA

2 ounces of tinned tunny fish in olive oil, $1\frac{1}{2}$ ounces of capers, 4 anchovy fillets, 2 egg yolks, some chopped parsley, the juice of $\frac{1}{2}$ a lemon, pepper, and olive oil.

Mince the anchovies, the tunny fish, the capers, and the parsley with a *mezzaluna*. Then pound them in a mortar with the egg yolks and a little olive oil, so that the composition is not too dry. Season with pepper and pass the mixture through a sieve into a bowl. Then gradually add olive oil and the lemon juice, until a sauce is obtained of the texture of thin cream.

Poultry . Game . Rabbit : Venison

POULTRY, GAME, RABBIT, AND VENISON

THE atmosphere of economy is temporarily suspended in this section on poultry, game, and venison. Butter, cream – fresh and sour – small measures of brandy and *Marsala*, gills, half pints, and bottles of wine, are specified – not in a spirit of extravagance, but because a farmyard chicken, a young duck, pheasant, or hare are really worthy of them. These dishes represent a concentration of good things, a sheaf of gastronomical experiences put together from the recollections of feasts divided in real life by considerable lapses of time. The occasions are infrequent but splendid. It is because of this that one can afford from time to time to pour a pint of sour cream over a hare or a bottle of good burgundy over a pigeon. But it is only fair to say that particularly in the case of chicken and rabbit, draught or vintage cider can be substituted for wine without a drastic loss of character: for instance, in *lapin sauté au gratin, lapin au riz au safran, poulet sauté à la paysanne,* and *poulet en capilotade.* At the other extreme it should not be forgotten that a platter of oysters is the best prelude to roast goose.

Capon

ROAST AND STUFFED

Prepare a well-fed capon by stuffing it with the following preparation:

4 ounces of fresh breadcrumbs soaked in milk and squeezed dry, 2 ounces of finely chopped *mortadella,* 2 ounces of diced *prosciutto* (Italian smoked ham), 4 shallots finely chopped, 2 anchovies pounded, a tablespoonful of chopped parsley and basil, grated nutmeg, 4 ounces of mushrooms sliced and sautéd for a few minutes in butter, a crushed clove of garlic, 8 black olives stoned and chopped, the capon's liver shredded, 2 red peppers

roasted and chopped, a dessertspoonful of grated sweet almonds, salt and black pepper, 2 eggs, and a little olive oil if the mixture is too dense.

Combine the ingredients in a bowl, bind them with the beaten eggs, and stuff the capon.

Heat some good olive oil or butter in a pan until it is very hot indeed, rub the bird with salt and put it in a baking tin, and pour over it the very hot fat, so that the breast and extremities are seized. Return the fat from the baking dish to the pan again, heat it once more, and turning the capon over, repeat the process so that the back is likewise seized by the hot fat. Then lay some bards of bacon on its breast and a bunch of herbs (parsley, thyme, rosemary), and wrap it up in several layers of greaseproof paper. Lay it on a grid over a baking tin and set it in the lower part of the oven, starting in a moderate heat. When the first sounds of sizzling can be heard, reduce the heat to the equivalent of Regulo 2 on a gas oven, and let the bird cook very slowly for $2\frac{1}{2}$ hours. Use the fat which was originally poured over the capon to roast some potatoes, in the upper part of the oven, if you like. But a capon cooked in this way is better served with *pommes de terre dauphinés*, which are mashed potatoes sieved and combined with a paste of flour and butter, flavoured with nutmeg, moistened with water, and formed into little balls which are fried in hot fat. Have a dry white *Pouilly*, already chilled, to serve with it.

Cockerel and Farmhouse Chicken

The following recipes apply to cockerels and farmhouse chickens. The test of youth is applied at the tip of the breast bone; and confirmed by flexibility in the legs. If less than one year old the tip of the breastbone will still be pliable, the bird being too young for the cartilage to have formed into bone; the legs should be soft and free from scales. If the chicken also has firm plump flesh without too much apparent fat, everything points to a good bird. In youth a chicken has a gelatinous quality which subsequently disappears. The carcase of such a bird will produce a stock which sets into a jelly of its own accord on cooling, but

which has less flavour than a full-grown bird. Young chickens
are spoiled in flavour by over cooking.

The next eight recipes have a certain resemblance in their
method of preparation, the chicken, left whole or jointed, being
browned and then braised with various accompaniments, to
produce a great variety of taste in what the poulterer terms a
'roasting' chicken, as opposed to a 'boiling' fowl.

POULET BÉARNAIS

Cut a young chicken into pieces, remove the skin, and fry the
pieces in pork fat in an aluminium pan. Prepare a foundation of
finely minced onion and grated carrot in an earthenware casserole and transfer the chicken pieces and the pork fat to it.* Add
some squares of lean ham cut from a ¼ inch thick slice, salt,
pepper, a tablespoonful of dry white wine. Put the casserole in
a fairly hot oven, and cook for a quarter of an hour. In the meantime peel three tomatoes, slice them, remove the pips, and crush
two cloves of garlic with the point of a knife. Put these into the
casserole, and proceed with the cooking until the chicken is
tender, about thirty minutes all told.

POULET BOURGUIGNON

Joint a young cockerel and fry the pieces in 2 ounces of butter
with ¼ pound of streaky bacon cut into neat cubes, a dozen
peeled button onions, and a minced clove of garlic in a heavy
pan.* Transfer these ingredients to an earthenware casserole,
add salt, pepper, a *bouquet garni*, and a glass of Burgundy. Cook
for twenty minutes with the lid on in a moderate oven. Then
add a dozen mushrooms which have been sautéd in butter, and
cook for a further ten minutes.

---

* If an enamelled iron *cocotte* is used, there is, of course, no need to do the
preliminary browning in another pan. But when using earthenware on
gas or electric cookers, it is best to preserve them from the fierce heat of
gas jet or hot plate, and the sautéing is, therefore, done in an aluminium
frying-pan.

POLLO COLLA MARSALA

1 chicken, 1 large onion, 2 ounces of butter, powdered basil, salt, 1½ pints of chicken broth (made from the carcase, giblets, onion, clove, carrot, herbs, and stick of celery), a wineglassful of *Marsala*.

Joint a roasting chicken, dividing the legs into two, with two wing pieces and two breast pieces with bone attached. Remove any other meat from the carcase to use later in a *risotto*, and pound the carcase in a mortar so that some chicken stock can be obtained more quickly. Put the pounded bones in a pan, with the giblets, a bunch of herbs, an onion pierced with a clove, a sliced carrot, and a stick of celery, and simmer for 40 minutes.

About ¼ hour before the stock is ready, hash the onion, sauté it in butter in a casserole, and when the onion begins to brown put in the joints of chicken, which have been sprinkled with a little salt, and dusted with powdered basil, and sauté them until they have taken on a good colour.

When the stock is ready, strain it over the chicken joints, put on the lid, and simmer gently till the meat is tender. Put the chicken into a dish, pass the sauce through a sieve, reduce it over a lively heat if it is too thin in consistency, pour in the *Marsala* and stir for a few moments until the sauce comes to the boil, when it should be taken off the heat, a good nut of butter added to it, and poured over the chicken. Serve with boiled rice garnished with sliced aubergines sautéd in olive oil.

POULET À L'ESTRAGON

1 young chicken, ¼ pint of dry white wine, ¼ pint of gravy made from the chicken giblets and neck, 4 branches of tarragon, a little arrowroot with some salt and pepper, 4 ounces of fresh butter.

Put 2 of the branches of tarragon to infuse in some chicken stock, which has been prepared by simmering the chicken giblets in water sufficient to cover them, with a bay leaf, salt, and a bouquet of herbs.

Then melt the butter in a sauté-pan or iron *cocotte* and brown the chicken by turning it about and basting it with the hot butter on all sides. When it is well coloured put the lid on the pan, and cook it either on top of the stove or in a medium oven for about 30 minutes, basting from time to time with its liquor.

When it is cooked, remove it onto a hot dish and keep it in a warm place while the sauce is prepared. Put the pan over a moderate heat and pour in the white wine. Stir well, and scrape the bottom of the pan so that the glazed juices are incorporated in the sauce. Let the wine reduce by half, and then add through a strainer the chicken gravy infused with tarragon. Thicken the sauce with arrowroot mixed to a paste with a little gravy, taste it and add seasoning if necessary, simmer the sauce for a few minutes and pour it over the chicken. Decorate the bird with the remainder of the tarragon leaves which should be blanched in boiling water and coarsely chopped.

POULET À LA SAVOYARDE

This is a chicken braised with *cèpes* or *chanterelles* and its sauce thickened with cream. The use of a small quantity of brandy, far from being an extravagance, does honour to the union of these ingredients. An enamelled iron oval *cocotte* should be used to cook it in.

1 chicken, ½ lb of *cèpes* (*Boletus edulis*) or *chanterelles* (*Cantharellus cibarius*), 4 oz salted butter, ½ gill of brandy, ½ pint of cream, salt and black pepper. (If *cèpes* or *chanterelles* (pages 266–70) are unobtainable, mushrooms can replace them.)

Melt the butter in a heavy pan and sauté the chicken in it. While it is gently colouring, sprinkle a little of the brandy over the chicken, and turn it about so that all sides are browned. Prepare the *cèpes* or *chanterelles*. If *cèpes* are used, the caps must be wiped and sliced, the stems trimmed and chopped up small with a little garlic; the *chanterelles* must have the base of the stalk removed and be rapidly passed through running water to remove any sand attaching to them, being then dried and sliced. When the chicken is golden brown remove it from the pan for a few minutes, and sauté the fungi. After some minutes take them out and swill out the pan with the remaining brandy, scraping the bottom with a wooden spoon to amalgamate the juice, before the cream, which should be warmed beforehand, is added. Put the fungi back in the sauce, place the chicken in the pan, put on the lid, and let it finish cooking gently either on top of the stove or in a modest oven. Baste it now and again. The time taken will depend very much on the size and age of the bird; thirty minutes for a pullet, and 50 to 60 minutes for a maturer bird.

When the chicken is ready (which can be ascertained by piercing the thigh joint with a larding needle; if it exudes a clear colourless juice it is cooked), taste the sauce, season with salt and black pepper if necessary; place the chicken on a dish and serve the sauce separately in a bowl, and accompany with an Alsatian wine.

POULET SAUTÉ BORDELAIS

1 roasting chicken, ½ gill of olive oil, 1 ounce of lard, 8 artichoke bottoms, 20 shallots, 2 cloves of garlic crushed with some salt, 2 tablespoonfuls of finely chopped parsley, ½ gill of stock, 2 ounces of butter, salt, and bay leaf.

Clean the chicken, and make the stock from the neck, pinions, and giblets by stewing them for about 2 hours in a little water, with some salt and a bay leaf.

Cut the chicken into neat joints and melt the oil and lard in a heavy sauté-pan. Sauté the chicken, turning the pieces constantly with a wooden spoon so that all their surfaces are sealed and evenly cooked. Add the prepared shallots to the pan and sauté them. Put on the lid and simmer the chicken and shallots, basting from time to time.

In a separate pan melt the butter and stew the artichoke hearts, which have been blanched for a few minutes in boiling water, gently in it. When the chicken is almost ready, add the crushed garlic to the olive oil and lard.

When the chicken is tender, put the pieces on a hot serving dish, surround them with the shallots and artichokes, and keep the dish warm. Swill out the sauté-pan with the chicken gravy, and pour the resultant sauce round the chicken. Sprinkle the finely chopped parsley over all and serve at once. *Cèpes à la borde-*

laise (page 267) are sometimes served with this dish or it might be followed by a salad of aubergines.

AUBERGINE SALAD

Leave the aubergines whole and bake them in a moderate oven until they are quite soft. Then cut each one in half and scoop out the soft pulp, discarding the skins. Put the pulp into a bowl with some very finely chopped raw shallot, a little salt, and some black pepper, blend in sufficient lemon juice and 2 tablespoonfuls of olive oil. Put the salad in a cold place and stir it well before it is served with crisp bread or toast.

POULET SAUTÉ À LA PAYSANNE

1 chicken, 1 pound of waxy potatoes, salt and black pepper, 4 ounces of butter, ½ a wineglass of white wine, ½ a gill of gravy (made from the giblets of the chicken), 1 bay leaf, 1 teaspoonful of finely chopped parsley.

Cut and joint the chicken into eight pieces and sauté them in 3 ounces of the butter in a sauté-pan or shallow earthenware casserole. Peel the potatoes and cut them into dice of about ¾ inch. Sauté these in the remaining ounce of butter in a separate pan.

When the chicken is sealed on all its surfaces, put the potato dice into the same pan and sprinkle them with very little salt. Put the pan in the middle of a moderate oven with the lid on, and let the chicken finish cooking which will take about 25 to 30 minutes.

As soon as the chicken is cooked put it on a hot dish to keep warm and surround it with the diced potatoes while the sauce is made. Put the sauté-pan – or casserole – on a moderate heat, put in the bay leaf and the white wine, stirring well and scraping the bottom of the pan. When the wine is bubbling, add the chicken gravy and let the sauce simmer for 2 or 3 minutes. Taste it, add whatever seasoning is necessary, and then pour it through a strainer over the chicken. Sprinkle the chopped parsley over the chicken and serve without delay.

This method could also be applied to a very young rabbit or to young pigeon.

POLLO ALLA ROMANA

Italian methods of preparing chickens for the table are often excellent. The birds themselves are usually rather stringy.

Take two small chickens (*poussins*) and cut them through the carcase lengthwise. Sauté them with olive oil, salt, garlic, bay, and thyme in a stewpan with the lid on. Turn them about until they are well browned. Pour off the oil, and replace it by some tomato *purée*, a glass of Madeira, some mushrooms which have been sautéd in butter, the juice of a lemon, and some concentrated stock.

If the chickens are young and tender they will need only a quarter of an hour to simmer in the sauce. Serve them with *tagliatelli al burro* or *lasagne*.

Fowl

The following recipes are not concerned with farmyard pullets, or capons fed for the table, but with the fowl which is more normally within the housewife's budget – usually rather old and tough.

Very old chickens should either be simmered in milk, or painstakingly jointed, sautéd, seasoned, wined, and casseroled to produce the best results.

COLD BOILED CHICKEN

Stuff the bird. An excellent stuffing can be made from breadcrumbs, three rashers of bacon finely chopped, 2 anchovies, a sprig of rosemary, a pounded garlic clove, chopped parsley thyme, and basil, 8 green olives already stoned, the chicken's liver shredded, a pinch of salt, and a pinch of saffron. Thoroughly mix these ingredients, and bind them with a beaten egg. It is a precaution to slip a peeled onion into the stuffed cavity before stitching up the opening, to prevent the stuffing from escaping while it is simmering.

Use the saucepan with a tight-fitting lid, which will just contain the bird. Sever the legs at the joint, as they tend to stiffen and push the lid off. Put in a peeled onion, two carrots sliced lengthways, a stick of celery, a *bouquet garni*, and pour on enough milk to cover the bird. Lay two slices of bacon across the breast and cover the pan. Put a weight on it. Simmer on the lowest possible flame for three hours, and then allow the bird to cool in its own juice. Serve it cold next day.

This way of cooking and cooling produces quite a different result from the dried up ruin of a chicken with which one is too often confronted. The milk stock can be used for a dish of *Maccheroni colla balsamella* (page 99), for *Soupe à la bonne femme* (page 80), or for a Mushroom soup (page 77).

A STUFFING FOR A ROAST FOWL

A lighter stuffing for a roast fowl which is both succulent and aromatic consists of:

2 large cups of dry breadcrumbs, 1 onion, 1 dessertspoonful of finely chopped parsley, 1 teaspoonful of finely chopped thyme, a very little grated lemon rind, salt and pepper, and 3 ounces of butter.

Squeeze the juice from the onion over a lemon squeezer. Put the butter to melt in a pan and meanwhile mix all the other ingredients together. When the butter is frothing put the mixed breadcrumbs, onion juice, and herbs into it. Turn it all about in the butter with a fork and when all the butter has been absorbed by the breadcrumbs the stuffing is ready to be put in the bird.

POULE AU RIZ AU SAFRAN

1 boiling fowl, an onion stuck with 2 cloves, a clove of garlic, two pints of water, a glass of white wine (or wine vinegar), a cube of concentrated chicken broth, salt and pepper.

For the rice: 1 ounce of chicken fat, an onion, ½ pound Italian rice, salt, pepper, saffron, nutmeg.

For the sauce: 1 ounce of butter, ¾ ounce of flour, two egg yolks, and lemon juice.

Simmer the boiling fowl very gently in water to which the onion stuck with cloves, the garlic, the concentrated broth, salt, pepper, and the glass of white wine have been added, with the lid on for 1 to 1½ hours according to the age of the fowl.

When it is nearly cooked, hash an onion and sauté it in the chicken fat in the bottom of a thick pan large enough to take the rice. Before the onion has browned, throw in the rice, turn it about in the fat, and then pour on through a strainer one pint of the stock in which the fowl has been cooking. Add salt, pepper, grated nutmeg, and a pinch of saffron, and cook gently for 25 to 30 minutes, when the rice should have absorbed the stock.

Put the chicken on a dish and keep it in a warm oven while the sauce is prepared with the remaining stock. Melt the butter in a pan, stir in the flour, and keep stirring so that the *roux* does not brown. After a few minutes, strain the stock onto the *roux*, stirring while the sauce boils and thickens. Beat the egg yolks with a little milk, take the pan off the heat, and add a little sauce from the pan to the beaten yolks. Then pour this back into the sauce in the pan, stirring it over a gentle heat while it thickens, but on no account let it boil. Squeeze the juice of a lemon into it at the last moment.

Pour the sauce over the fowl, surround it with the saffron rice, and serve it with green peas, or *courgettes* simmered in butter, or a little dish of *chanterelles* (page 271).

POULET EN CAPILOTADE

Here is a sauce in which the remains of a cold chicken, say about half of it, roasted or boiled, can be served very quickly.

Cut what is left of the chicken into respectable pieces. Hash a large onion and fry it in butter till it is lightly browned. Pour on a glass of white wine and a thread of vinegar. Reduce the liquid. Add two tablespoonfuls of tomato *purée* and a tumbler of broth. Season with salt, a teaspoonful of sugar, and a tied bunch of herbs, and put in the pieces of chicken. Add two teaspoonfuls of capers from which their liquor has been drained, and cook for about ten minutes. Put the contents of the pan into a *gratin* dish, sprinkle with breadcrumbs, and brown under the grill. Dress with *croûtons* fried in butter, and serve with a dish of green peas, or aubergines, when they are in season, sliced and sautéd in olive oil.

Duck

CANETON AU BEURRE D'ÉCREVISSES

This dish originates in the district of La Bresse, one of the richest regions of France, lying to the south of Burgundy, and famous for its grain-fed pullets and superb dishes which often combine unmatched poultry with rich cream, crayfish, and mushrooms. An Aylesbury duckling is the nearest English equivalent to a *caneton de Bresse*. A duckling weighs between 3 and 4 lb; its underbill should be flexible, the webbing on its feet soft, and its breast meaty denoting a well-fed bird.

As the crayfish butter takes longer to prepare than does the duckling the recipe for its preparation comes first.

1 dozen live river crayfish, 4 ounces of butter, and two pints of *court-bouillon* made from: 1¼ pints white wine, 1¾ pints water, a *bouquet garni*, salt, 2 or 3 peppercorns, and a minced shallot simmered together for 30 minutes, cooled, and strained.

Simmer the crayfish in this *court-bouillon*, putting them in when it has reached the boil, and then reducing the heat. They are cooked when they have turned bright red; this takes from 15–20 minutes. Take them out, and remove the tails which are used as a brilliant garnish for the dish. Remove the black eyes, shell the rest of the crayfish, pound the shells in the mortar, and pass them through a sieve. Add the flesh and the 4 ounces of butter, and continue with the pounding until the preparation is smooth. Keep this in a double saucepan over warm water, it must be soft but not melted. Joint the duckling and fry the joints in 3 ounces of butter in a sauté-pan, keeping the pieces turned so that cooking proceeds evenly. This will take about 25–30 minutes. When the meat is tender, serve it on an oval dish, garnished with the crayfish tails, and hand the *beurre d'écrevisses* separately. Such a dish calls for no further accompaniment than hot French bread and a good claret.

CANARD AUX OLIVES

In braising a duck care must be taken to avoid drying the breast. This can be done by barding it and by basting from time to time with the braising liquor.

1 duck, 4 ounces of butter, 2 onions, a stick of celery, 2 carrots, ¼ pint of white wine, ¾ pint of stock, a *bouquet garni*, some bards of fat bacon, salt, pepper, ½ pound of black olives.

Brown the duck in the butter, on all sides, in an enamelled iron *cocotte*, basting with a spoon. Put in the onions, carrot, and celery sliced into four, browning them likewise. These vegetables are to impart their flavour to the duck while it is cooking, and are removed subsequently from the sauce. When bird and vegetables are suitably browned, pour in the wine, reduce it, and add the stock, so that it reaches about half-way up the bird. Put the bards over the breast, put in the *bouquet garni*, cover the *cocotte*, and simmer gently either on the stove or in the oven for about an hour. Baste the bird from time to time.

When it is almost ready, take it out of the *cocotte*, keep it warm, while the sauce is prepared. Strain the liquor in which it has braised into a little pan, removing the vegetables and the *bouquet garni*. Reduce the sauce and add the olives which have been stoned and blanched for a few moments in boiling water. Pour the sauce back into the *cocotte*, replace the bird in it, and let the cooking proceed for 10 or 15 minutes. If you are not satisfied that the sauce is of a sufficient consistency, a little kneaded butter and flour can be stirred in at the last moment while the duck is put on a hot dish to carve, but flour added with butter at the last moment must not be allowed to boil, or the flavour will be spoiled. In any case, this is not usually necessary, the sauce for a braise being half-way between a gravy and a sauce proper.

CANARD AUX NAVETS

Braise the duck in exactly the same way as for *canard aux olives*, but instead of the olives prepare some young turnips, by trimming them neatly, blanching them for 8 minutes in boiling water, and sautéing them in a covered pan with two ounces of butter. In order that they may acquire a golden colour, a little sugar is sprinkled over the turnips, and the sauté-pan is shaken from time to time so that they brown all over. After the reduction of the sauce, the turnips are put round the duck in the *cocotte*, the sauce poured over, and the cooking is proceeded with for 10 to 15 minutes before serving the duck, garnished with the turnips, and the sauce handed separately. Claret is the wine for duck.

Goose

BONED ROAST GOOSE (*served cold*)

1 goose, and for the stuffing: ¼ lb dry breadcrumbs, 2 oz grated suet, grated lemon peel, 1 teaspoonful of finely chopped sage, ½ a clove of garlic crushed with some salt, ground black pepper, 1 yolk of egg, and about ¼ pint of milk.

To bone the goose, if the poulterer will not oblige, lay it down on its breast so that its spine faces upwards, and with a short, firm, sharp knife cut the flesh deeply along the line of the backbone. With the knife lever the flesh away from each side of the backbone until the legs are reached. These are rather difficult, but with a proper knife the flesh can be cut away from the bones and these withdrawn. Proceed in the same way with the wings but remove the pinions completely. When the lower part of the bird is boned, turn it over and continue to remove the flesh from its upper part and breast. Keep the flesh in one piece and in as neat a shape as can be managed. It takes about 20 minutes to bone a goose if one is not accustomed to it.

The stuffing can be made either before the goose is boned or afterwards. Mix the breadcrumbs with the chopped suet, add the grated lemon peel, the sage, the garlic crushed with the salt, and the black pepper. Savour the mixture to see whether the aromatics are well balanced and add more of whatever seems to be needed. Beat the yolk of egg with half the milk and stir it into the dry mixture. Add the rest of the milk, little by little, until the right consistency has been obtained. It should be rather on the firm side, and is improved by being pounded with a pestle in a mortar.

Before putting the stuffing into the goose, its skin must be removed. This is quite easy to do with the fingers, aided, here and there, by a knife. Then lay the goose flesh flat and spread the stuffing over it evenly. Roll it up into a neat shape and wrap the skin all round and over it. Skewer the skin into position, with one or two wooden skewers, and if necessary tie it with string.

The boned goose should be put on a grid over a baking dish, set in a hot oven for the first hour, and basted with its own dripping and turned during that time. The boned goose will take about 2 hours to cook, and the heat should be moderated a little during the latter part of the cooking time. When it is done, it should be put in a cool place to get quite cold, and before serving the skewers and string should be removed. The carving is done by cutting across the goose as in a rolled joint of beef. A salad of chicory dressed with oil and vinegar, a haricot bean salad, and beetroot soaked in Burgundy could be served with it.

The carcase and bones of the goose will provide an excellent stock if broken up and put in a large pot with sufficient cold water to cover them, with salt, 1 small onion, 1 bay leaf, 1 stick of celery, 1 carrot, 1 artichoke, and a small piece of cauliflower. Simmer for at least 4 hours or longer, when the liquid is strained into an earthenware pot and allowed to cool so that any fat may be taken from the surface before it is used as a basis for a soup such as *bortsch*, or stock for *risotto*.

ROAST AND STUFFED GOOSE

1 goose, and for its stuffing: ¾ pound of Italian rice, ½ pound of prunes, 6 finely chopped shallots, 1½ ounces of butter, ½ a powdered bay leaf, grated lemon rind, salt and black pepper, 1 egg, and the goose liver.

The goose should have a plump breast and its feet should be yellow, which denotes youth. If the weather is cold, the goose will be improved in flavour if it is hung for a day or so.

When ready to be cooked, its neck and giblets are put in a pan with a little salted water and cooked gently to provide the basis of the accompanying gravy. The goose liver should be blanched and set aside to form part of the stuffing; the prunes should be stewed until tender, the stones removed, and the fruit coarsely chopped; the rice is cooked in salted water until it is ¾ done, then drained and dried.

To make the stuffing, put the rice in a bowl and mix with it the chopped shallots together with the butter. Chop the goose liver, mix it with the rice, and then put in the chopped prunes. Add salt and pepper, the powdered bay leaf, and bind the whole with a beaten egg, adding some grated lemon rind. The stuffing can be made in advance, the bowl covered with a cloth, and left to combine its flavours overnight in a cool place. Most stuffings are improved in taste if they are allowed some hours in which this combination can take place.

When the goose is to be cooked, put the stuffing into it so that it is well distributed, tie the skin of the neck to the back, and put the parson's nose through a hole in the skin in order to prevent the stuffing from escaping. Cover the breast with strips of fat bacon. Have a good hot oven ready, prick the skin of the goose all over, but don't pierce its flesh, put the bird on a grid over a baking dish, and set it in the oven. Let it cook from 1½ to 1¾ hours depending on its size and keep it well basted with its own fat which will drip down into the baking dish below.

When ready, the goose should be put on a very hot dish, the dripping poured off the baking dish, and the gravy from the giblets added to the residual juices, brought to the boil and simmered for a few minutes. The gravy should then be poured through a strainer into a sauceboat and handed separately.

The bird can be served with apple sauce, or red cabbage cooked in the following manner:

Red Cabbage

1 medium-sized red cabbage, 1 lb cooking apples, 1 lb onions,

2 oz demerara sugar, allspice, two cloves of garlic, a piece of dried orange peel, powdered cinnamon and nutmeg, a pinch of dried herbs, a large glass of red wine, and two tablespoonfuls of wine vinegar.

Shred the cabbage and remove the central core, peel, core, and slice the apples, and slice the onions. Dispose these ingredients in a casserole in layers, starting with a layer of cabbage, then onions, then apples, season with spices and herbs, a little salt, some of the sugar, and repeat the layers duly seasoned until the cabbage, onions, and apples are used up. Then pour on the wine and wine vinegar, add a little water, cover the pan, and simmer very slowly for some hours. This dish has a tartness, which counteracts the richness of the stuffed goose, and a wonderful colour. Horseradish sauce can be used to the same end.

If the rice and prune stuffing is replaced by one composed of breadcrumbs, black stoned olives, three or four anchovies, chopped parsley, diced bacon, hashed onion, and a pounded garlic clove, besides the goose's liver, then a dish of sliced potatoes cooked in the oven (page 115) can accompany the goose.

Another method of roasting goose is propounded on page 56.

Turkey

ROAST TURKEY

Prepare a stuffing of 6 ounces of finely chopped bacon, 6 ounces of loin of pork with its fat, the turkey's liver, 4 ounces of mushrooms sautéd in butter beforehand, a crushed garlic, 8 ounces of boiled chestnuts which have been peeled and sautéd in butter, a small tin of *pâté de foie*, a tablespoonful of chopped parsley to which a leaf of sage is added, ground pepper.

Pound the sautéd chestnuts in a mortar, chop the bacon and pork very finely, shred the liver, and combine all the ingredients together, moistening with a little melted butter if the preparation is too stiff. Stuff the turkey, bard its breast, rub it over with salted butter, and set it in a hot oven, which should be moderated after the first half an hour. Baste the bird from time to time. It will take between 2 and 3 hours to cook depending on its size. About twenty minutes before serving, remove the bacon from the breast. While it is cooking prepare a bread sauce, which is made by sautéing six small chopped shallots in butter until they are quite transparent, adding a suitable quantity of breadcrumbs (at least one pound for four or five people), 1½ pints of milk, some grated nutmeg, a little powdered cinnamon, salt, black pepper, a pinch of sugar, and two ounces of butter, and simmering the concoction in a double saucepan for an hour at least. If the sauce becomes very dense by evaporation and the swelling of the crumbs, add a little more warm milk. Before serving, this quite excellent sauce is improved by stirring in a spoonful of cream. With a rich stuffing, it is preferable to serve some form of potatoes *au gratin* rather than roast, with a green vegetable, and both for the sake of colour and its admirable sweet-sour taste the traditional cranberry sauce (page 236).

If the above stuffing is thought to be too revolutionary, a simple chestnut stuffing can be substituted, which is prepared in the following way:

CHESTNUT STUFFING

2 pounds of chestnuts, 2 ounces of dry breadcrumbs, 4 ounces of butter, ½ pint of good beef, poultry or game stock, ½ a bay leaf, salt and black pepper, and 1 teaspoonful of soft brown sugar.

Slit the skin of each chestnut and either roast them in an oven for 20 to 25 minutes or boil them in water for about 20 minutes. Peel off the outer skin and the bitter, furry inner skin. Put the chestnuts into a thick saucepan with the ½ pint of stock and the ½ bay leaf and simmer gently, stirring now and then, until they are soft. This will take about 30 minutes.

When they are ready, remove the bay leaf and push the chestnuts through a sieve together with any stock left in the pan. Mix in the breadcrumbs and beat in the butter. This is not hard work, provided the chestnuts are hot. Taste the mixture and add sufficient salt, freshly ground black pepper, and the sugar. Stir it all well together and at the last add the well-beaten egg.

This stuffing is admirable with any form of braised or roast poultry.

Pigeon

Pigeon are cheap. Pigeon are tough when no longer young. These two recipes advocate slow cooking to ensure satisfactory results.

PIGEON AUX CHOUX

2 pigeon, 1 medium sized cabbage (red or white), 1 cooking apple, 1 large onion, 2 or 3 rashers of bacon, 2 clove heads, salt and pepper, ¼ pint of red wine or stock (or the equivalent in water to which the juice of half a lemon has been added), a pinch of sugar, 1 bay leaf, a handful of chopped and seeded raisins.

Cut the birds in half down the backbone. Melt the fat from the bacon rashers in the bottom of a thick earthenware pan. Fry the halved birds, basting them on all sides, and then remove them from the pan. Slice the onion, put it into the pan, add the rest of the bacon rashers cut into pieces about 1 inch square, add the crumbled heads of the cloves, the pinch of sugar, and the bay leaf. Slice up the cabbage and remove the hard core. Add the cabbage to the pan with the apple, previously peeled, cored, and chopped. Stir the ingredients, heat the liquor and pour it into the pan. Sprinkle with salt, put the four pieces of pigeon on top of the cabbage, and having put on the lid, cook it either on a modest flame on top of the stove, using an asbestos mat, or in the middle of a slow oven, for at least 1½ hours. If red cabbage is used, the time would be a little longer.

When both cabbage and pigeon are almost ready, put in the raisins, taste for seasoning, and add salt or black pepper if necessary. This method of preparation particularly applies to pigeon past their youth.

PIGEON AU FEU

This is ideally a braise to be carried out in a lidded cauldron suspended from an old-fashioned chimney iron over a wood fire. The cauldron, if not copper, can well be an enamelled-iron preserving pan fitted with a contrived lid.

Remove the fat from a piece of cooked ham, cut it into pieces, and melt it in the suspended cauldron. When it is sizzling, put in the pigeon, which should be ready trussed and stuffed with a lump of butter as large as an egg. Turn it about, brown it, and then remove it for a few minutes onto a waiting platter. Have 2 pounds of fresh carrots cleaned and sliced lengthwise into four, a bunch of herbs which should include parsley, thyme, bay, and rosemary, and two cloves of garlic. Put the garlic into the pot with the carrots and move them about a bit so that they all meet the fat. After a few minutes settle the pigeon on this carrot bed, put in the herbs, and pour a bottle of good red Burgundy onto the bird. If the pigeon's breast rises above the wine, lay a piece of fat bacon on it. Put on the lid, and if it isn't a good fit seal it with a flour and water paste.

Keep the fire going, and adjust the chimney iron if the cooking is proceeding too violently. This pot is a pleasure to watch. The cooking should take about an hour depending on the age of the bird, and it should be served beside the fire on pewter platters with another bottle of Burgundy.

Pheasant

Pheasants require hanging for a period of some days before their flavour, which is of little consequence when fresh, develops its particular excellence. This only takes place when decomposition is in sight, and as the entrails are first affected the bird must be so hung that its innards do not press upon the flesh of the breast lest it become tainted. It follows that the bird must hang, not from the feet or tail, but from the neck, and in a cool and airy situation. One need not wait for the bird to drop onto the paving of the larder floor; the ripe moment is at hand when the leading tail-feather can be easily plucked from the tail. The period of hanging is naturally conditioned by the weather. The age of a pheasant is read at the wing tip; if the biggest feather is pointed the bird is young, if rounded it is already old.

FAISAN À LA CRÈME

1 young pheasant, 4 ounces of butter, 1 onion, ¼ pint of sour cream, a very little salt and pepper.

Heat the butter in a heavy casserole. Sauté the pheasant in it with the onion cut into quarters, turn the pieces about so that they brown without burning and shake the pan from time to time to reduce the temperature while the browning is proceeding. Then lower the heat, put the lid on, and let the pheasant cook for 30 minutes.

At the end of this time, pour the sour cream over the bird, stirring so as to combine it with the butter and juices at the bottom of the casserole. Replace the lid and cook the pheasant for a further 5 minutes in the cream. Taste the cream sauce, add a little salt and pepper, and simmer gently for a minute or so. The pheasant can then be served from the casserole in which it has been cooked, together with a *Médoc* or a *Saint Émilion*.

PHEASANT WITH APPLES

1 young pheasant, 4 ounces of butter, 8 medium sized cooking apples (not too sour), 3 tablespoonfuls of cream, a little salt and pepper, and a pinch of sugar.

Heat 3 ounces of the butter in a sauté-pan, and brown the pheasant on all its surfaces. Meanwhile, peel and core the apples and chop them into small pieces. Melt the remaining 1 ounce of butter in the bottom of an earthenware casserole and sauté the chopped apples in it with a pinch of sugar. When they are a little softened, put the pheasant on top of them with the juices from the sauté-pan and then pour the cream over the bird. Put the lid on the casserole and place it in a moderate oven for about 25 to 30 minutes. Taste the apple sauce and add seasoning. Serve the pheasant from the casserole.

Wild Duck

SALMIS DE CANARD SAUVAGE

Wild duck are usually served roasted; they should not be overdone or they will lose their flavour. It has been said that they should just fly through a very fierce oven and be served immediately, but as we can hardly give a recipe for this, here is one which produces satisfactory results but transfers the call for speed at the last moment onto the shoulders of the cook.

2 wild duck, 2 ounces of butter, 6 shallots finely hashed, salt, black pepper, nutmeg, and allspice, ½ wineglassful of red wine.

Roast the duck in the fiercest possible oven for 8 to 10 minutes. Take them out, let them cool for a minute or so, set them on a board, and with a sharp knife sever the leg joints and remove the legs. Remove the wings likewise. Pound the allspice with a little salt and grated nutmeg, and powder the four legs and four wings with this preparation. Then set the legs on the grill, exposing them first to a strong heat for a few minutes on each side, and then reducing the heat while the grilling is completed. When this is accomplished place them in a fireproof dish to keep warm in the bottom of the oven which will still be fairly hot. Then grill the wings in the same manner, but allowing rather less time, as they are less substantial, and put them into the same dish.

Carve the rest of the two duck into long thin fillets, and lay them in a large shallow fireproof dish which has been buttered and sprinkled with very finely hashed shallots. Sprinkle some powdered spice on the fillets and put the dish in the oven.

Break up the carcases of the birds and pound them in a mortar to release any captive juices. Sprinkle the wine onto the fragments, and strain the resultant juices over the fillets.

Place two legs and two wings at each end of the serving dish, and distribute the rest of the butter over the fillets in the centre. Put the dish under a red-hot grill for a minute or so for the top to glaze but not long enough for the dish to dry. It must be withdrawn the moment the fillets show signs of curling. Serve at once

225

on very hot plates, with an orange salad, from which all pith, skin, and pips have been removed, garnished with black olives.

Rabbit

LAPEREAU AU CIDRE

1 young rabbit, ¼ pint of olive oil, the juice of ½ a lemon, 4 large onions sliced, 2 ounces of lean bacon or ham, ½ pound of peeled and sliced tomatoes, salt and pepper, 1 bay leaf, thyme, ¼ pint of dry cider.

Joint the rabbit into 4 pieces and put them to soak for an hour in lukewarm water to which the lemon juice has been added.

When the rabbit is ready to be cooked, take the pieces out of the water and dry each one well with a cloth. Heat the oil in a sauté-pan and brown the pieces of rabbit. Add the sliced onions and adjust the heat a little. When the onions are soft add the bay leaf, a little thyme, and the bacon or ham which should be cut into small pieces. In 10 minutes or so put in the peeled, sliced tomatoes and stir them in with the rest. Simmer for another 10 minutes, then pour in the dry cider. Let the liquid bubble rather fiercely for a minute or so, reduce the heat and simmer with the lid on until the rabbit is tender. By this time the tomatoes, onions, and bacon will have amalgamated into a dense sauce. Taste the sauce, add a little salt and pepper if need be, and remove the bay leaf.

LAPIN À L'HONGROISE

1 rabbit, ¾ pint of milk, 2 crushed garlic cloves, an ounce of paprika pepper, an ounce of flour, powdered mint, thyme, and marjoram, grated lemon rind, salt and pepper, 1 pound of Danish lard for deep frying, 1 lb of green peppers, 1 dozen black olives (stoned), oil, and lemon juice.

Prepare a salad of sliced green peppers, removing core and seeds, sprinkle with olive oil and lemon juice, and decorate with stoned black olives.

Cut the rabbit into 8 joints and leave them in milk for half an hour.

Mix the flour, paprika, garlic, powdered herbs, and the grated lemon rind in a mortar.

Heat the lard in a small deep pan.

Take the joints of rabbit out of the milk, wipe them, and roll them in the paprika preparation.

When the lard is very hot test it by dropping in a crumb of bread. If it browns and sizzles the frying can begin.

Put in the rabbit joints, three at a time, and fry them for six or seven minutes. The hind legs may require slightly longer. Drain them on blotting paper and place each batch on a dish in a warm oven while the rest of the rabbit is submitted to the same treatment.

Serve the rabbit quickly, with a hot French loaf, the paprika salad, and one of the cheap Hungarian wines which have recently come on the market. The rabbit meat will be as white as chicken, and cooked in this way tastes like it.

LAPIN SAUTÉ AU GRATIN

This dish can only be made with a very young wild rabbit. If possible its blood should be preserved to incorporate with the sauce, which means hanging it by the hind legs soon after it has been shot and attaching a little receptacle, into which the blood can drip, to its nose.

1 young wild rabbit, 1 pound of finely chopped onions, 1 pound of diced potatoes, salt, 2 dessertspoonfuls of dry breadcrumbs, 4 branches of parsley, 1 clove of garlic, 2 ounces of lard, and if the blood has not been kept, ¼ pint of red wine, salt, black pepper, a teaspoonful of wine vinegar, if the blood is used, to mix with it and prevent it from congealing. A teaspoonful of brandy has the same effect.

Divide the rabbit into four by splitting it across the base of the loins, and again down the backbone. Remove the head. Melt the lard in a shallow sauté-pan or iron pan of convenient size. Wipe the pieces of rabbit, and when the lard is hot sauté them till they are golden brown on all sides. Remove the rabbit from the pan for a few minutes while the onions and potatoes are sautéd in the remaining fat, and put in a crushed clove of garlic.

When the onions begin to brown restore the rabbit to the pan, season with salt, lower the heat and add the dry breadcrumbs and chopped parsley, stir the contents of the pan, and sprinkle with ground pepper. Put the blood which has previously been diluted with a little vinegar or *cognac* into the pan; if the blood is lacking, pour in at this point the ¼ pint of red wine. When blood or wine have been incorporated with the ingredients in the pan, taste for seasoning, adjust it if necessary, and put the dish uncovered in a moderate oven for about 20 minutes. A young rabbit prepared in this way tastes very much like a pullet.

If the proper utensil is lacking, this dish can perfectly well be prepared in a heavy aluminium frying-pan, and transferred for the 20 minutes' cooking in the oven to an open earthenware or fireproof china dish.

It requires no accompaniment other than black olives and French bread.

LAPIN AU RIZ AU SAFRAN

1 rabbit, 1 small onion, 1 bay leaf, ½ a lemon, 1 stick of celery, black pepper, salt, water; ½ a bottle of dry white wine; 2 ounces of butter, 2 ounces of plain flour, ¼ pint top of the milk; 1 pound of Italian rice, 1 packet of saffron, a blade of mace, 2 clove heads, a piece of cinnamon, 1 tablespoonful of olive oil.

Joint the rabbit, and soak the pieces in lukewarm water for at least 1 hour. Blanch them by dropping each piece into a pan of boiling water and removing it after a minute or so. Then, put them into a pan with an onion, bay leaf, the juice of half a lemon, a stick of celery, and a little salt, and cover with water. Put the pan on a moderate heat, bring the water to the boil, lower the heat and cook the rabbit gently until the flesh can be removed from the bones, which will take about 1½ hours. When this time has nearly elapsed, bring a pan of salted water to the boil. Put in the rice together with the saffron, mace, clove heads, and cinnamon. While the rice is cooking the sauce for the rabbit can be made.

Melt the butter in a pan and when it is hot stir in the flour and cook both together for a few minutes, stirring all the time, so that the flour does not brown. Then, heat the wine and pour it onto the flour and butter mixture. Stir while the sauce combines, and then add about half a pint of the strained stock in which the rabbit has cooked. Stir again, and while the sauce is simmering gently remove the meat from the bones of the rabbit, put it in an earthenware serving dish, and keep it warm. Taste the sauce for seasoning and add a little black pepper and, if necessary, some salt.

The rice will take about 12 to 18 minutes to cook and as soon as it is ready, drain it over a sieve and return it to the pan in which it was cooked. Sprinkle some warm olive oil into it and mix it in with a fork. Put a cloth over the top and leave the pan in a warm place for the rice to dry.

Pour the cream from the top of the milk into the sauce, re-heat it, and pour it over the rabbit in its earthenware dish. Turn out the rice into another platter, or dispose it round the rabbit.

The rice should be glistening, dry, and golden, with a pleasant aromatic taste. The rabbit should be very white and firm in a rich, creamy sauce. Serve a bottle of white *Chianti* and follow with a *Camembert* cheese.

TERRINE DE LAPEREAU

This *terrine* is prepared with the meat of a young rabbit but the recipe can equally be applied to portions of hare which remain when the saddle has been roasted according to the recipe on page 232. When hare meat is used, it is advisable to increase the proportion of fat bacon, hare being far dryer than rabbit.

> 1 young rabbit, 1 thick slice of fat bacon, 8 rashers of streaky bacon, thyme, 2 bay leaves, a few allspice, salt and pepper, a liqueur glass of brandy (red wine can be substituted *faute de mieux*).

Forcemeat in the proportion of 6 ounces per pound of rabbit meat, made with: dry breadcrumbs, grated lemon peel, thyme, sage, chopped fat pork (or sausage meat), salt, pepper, 1 egg to bind it. (Chopped shallot may be included.)

Joint the rabbit and cut the flesh from the bones in neat strips. Season with salt and pepper, put it in a bowl with the brandy (or red wine), and leave it to marinade for at least an hour.

Prepare the forcemeat in the usual way, but add the brandy or wine in which the rabbit has been soaking.

Grease a large *terrine* with the fat rendered from the bacon rinds and line it with strips of bacon cut from four of the rashers. Spread a layer of the forcemeat on the bottom of the *terrine* and on this put some fine strips cut from the remaining bacon rashers. On top of this lay some rabbit fillets. Cover the rabbit with another layer of forcemeat then some bacon strips, and again rabbit. Proceed in this order until the *terrine* is ¾ full, finishing with forcemeat. Cover the top with the slice of fat bacon sprinkled with a little powdered thyme, the bay leaves, and allspice. Put on the lid, or, if there isn't one, cover with grease-proof paper and tie down. Put the *terrine* in a shallow baking dish containing warm water, and cook in a moderate oven. The time will vary with the size of the *terrine*, but allow from 1 to 1½ hours. The *terrine* will be cooked when the fat which rises to the surface is absolutely clear. If the *terrine* is to be kept for a day or two, some pure lard should be melted and poured over the surface as soon as it is completely cold.

Hare

HARE PÂTÉ

A hare with red fur irresistibly recalls Senator Couteaux and the emotion created by his *Lièvre à la royale*. A Scottish hare of darker hue can be used for the preparation of this *pâté*.

1 small hare, 6 ounces of bacon fat or dripping, 2 cloves of garlic crushed with salt, a blade of mace, two clove heads, 1 stick of celery, 2 bay leaves, salt, black pepper, plain flour, 8 ounces of bacon or ham, 2 liqueur glasses of brandy, 4 ounces of pure lard.

Sharpen a chef's knife and cut the flesh of the hare from the bones. Put the bones in a pan with a little salt, cover with water, and simmer gently for at least four hours. Then strain the stock and leave it to cool.

Put the meat in an earthenware crock, and mix with it the crushed garlic clove, the mace and clove heads powdered, a chopped stick of celery, the bay leaves, and some ground black pepper. Sprinkle over this a liqueur glass of brandy, and leave the hare to absorb these flavours overnight.

Melt 4 ounces of bacon fat or dripping in a heavy pan. Take the hare's meat from the bowl, dry the pieces by dusting with a little flour, and drop them into the hot fat. Stir them about with a wooden spoon, so as not to pierce the flesh, while they brown. Chop the 8 ounces of ham or bacon into pieces about one inch square and put them in the pan. Add the herbs, celery, and any liquor left in the bowl in which the hare stood overnight. Reduce the heat and mix the contents of the pan well together. Heat the hare stock and pour enough of it into the pan to cover the ingredients. Put on the lid and simmer for 2½ to 3 hours when the hare should be as soft as cheese. Strain off the liquor into a bowl and push the meat through a sieve into a mortar. Pound the mixture with a pestle until it is perfectly smooth and even in texture. If the *pâté* is very stiff a little of the liquor may be added to it. Taste it and add seasoning if required.

Grease a number of little earthenware bowls or *terrines* with some of the remaining bacon fat and fill each three-quarters full. Tie a piece of greaseproof paper over the top of each, and put on the lid, if there is one. Place the *terrines* in a shallow dish into which some warm water has been poured, and put it in the middle of a moderate oven for forty minutes, when they can be taken out and the greaseproof paper removed. Dribble a little of the remaining liqueur glass of brandy on top of each *pâté*. Leave them to cool. When cold, melt 4 ounces of lard, pour it gently over the top of each *pâté* to ½ inch deep, to exclude the air. This ensures the safe preservation of the *pâté*, in cold weather, for 7 to 10 days in a cold larder, and longer if kept in the refrigerator.

LEPRE AGRODOLCE

A young hare usually weighs between 5 and 6 pounds, and is improved by hanging for two or three days, according to prevailing weather. It should not be paunched until it is time to cook it.

1 young hare, 1 pint of good beef stock, $\frac{1}{2}$ pint of red wine, 2 tablespoonfuls of stoned Malaga raisins, 2 tablespoonfuls of pine kernels, lemon peel, $\frac{1}{4}$ pint of olive oil, salt, pepper, and 1 dessertspoonful of soft brown sugar, nutmeg, $\frac{1}{2}$ a bay leaf.

Joint the hare into eight pieces. Chop finely the heart and liver. Put all these into a bowl, adding the stoned raisins, the pine kernels (*pinoli*), grated nutmeg, grated lemon peel, pounded bay leaf, the sugar, and finally the red wine and beef stock.

Leave the hare to marinade overnight.

The cooking will take about two hours, so when the time has come, put the oil to heat in a substantial pan, remove the joints of hare from the marinade, wipe each one with a cloth, and brown them in the hot oil. Add some salt and ground black pepper, pour in the marinade with the shreds of heart and liver, raisins, and pine kernels, raise the heat so that the liquor bubbles and reduces a little. Put on the lid, and simmer gently for two hours.

The dish should be served with *tagliatelli* or *lasagne* tossed in olive oil and sprinkled with a little grated nutmeg, and a white *Chianti* from the Antinori vineyards.

Pine kernels can usually be bought at Health Food Stores, they are expensive but a small measure will last a long time.

BARON OF HARE

Soho ironmongers are stocked with chefs' larding needles. The absence of this weapon from the kitchen drawer doesn't exempt a cook from larding; larding carp, larding beef, larding hare can still be done, if less effectively, by cutting shorter strips of pork fat (loin or belly fat) and sliding them into neat incisions made with the sharpened point of a chef's knife. But a larding needle makes a neater job of it, with more even results. Lardoons should be cut about 2 inches long, $\frac{1}{4}$ inch wide, $\frac{1}{8}$ inch thick, and left for an hour or two sprinkled with salt, chopped herbs, and a crushed garlic clove, before use.

Use the hindquarters and the loins of the hare, cutting across the body of the animal close to the shoulder blades. Remove the fine second skin, and lard closely on each side of the backbone inserting the needle about a ¼ inch into the flesh before drawing it through. Trim the lardoons so that all are of equal size.

This is rather an extravagant dish, the larded hare being put in a deep pan with a pint of sour cream and a glass of wine vinegar. Season with salt, and roast in a fairly hot oven, basting the hare from time to time with the cream. After three-quarters of an hour put the hare under the grill to crisp the larding. Put two tablespoonfuls of red currant jelly into the sauce in which it has been baking, stir together, and strain it over the hare before serving it with *nouilles* or a potato *purée*, and perhaps the Yugoslavian wine *Lutomer Riesling*.

LEPRE COLLE POLPETTE

1 hare, 5 bay leaves, lemon peel, 10 garlic cloves, 1 bottle of red wine, ¼ pint of olive oil, bacon rinds or bacon fat; salt and black pepper, 3 ounces plain flour, 10 crushed clove heads.

Cut the meat from the bones and put it into an earthenware crock. The head and bones should be kept for making soup later. Crush the garlic cloves with salt and put this preparation in with the hare, together with the powdered bay leaves, and the grated lemon peel. Pour the olive oil over the meat, and then ¾ of the bottle of wine. Leave the hare to marinade overnight.

The following day render the bacon rinds or melt the bacon fat in a deep casserole, and set it on an asbestos mat over a moderate heat. While the fat is getting hot, drain the pieces of meat from the marinade and roll each in flour which has been seasoned with black pepper and salt. Fry the meat and brown it. If bacon rinds have been used they should now be removed.

Sprinkle powdered clove heads onto the meat, and if there is any seasoned flour left sprinkle it on as well. When the flour has been absorbed, pour over some of the liquor from the marinade, reduce it by raising the heat, and then add the rest of the liquor. Put on the lid, and when the contents are simmering gently put the pot into the middle of a slow oven, and cook the hare for six hours. At the end of four hours, taste the sauce for seasoning and consistency, and add more black pepper, if necessary, and the remainder of the wine ($\frac{1}{4}$ bottle) if the sauce seems too thick.

Serve this wonderful dish with medlar jelly, potatoes in their jackets, and *polpette*.

POLPETTE

3 ounces of fry breadcrumbs, 1 ounce of butter or shredded ox kidney suet, 1 teaspoonful of chopped parsley, 1 teaspoonful of chopped marjoram, 1 teaspoonful of grated lemon rind, 1 teaspoonful chopped wild thyme, 1 egg, 2 tablespoonfuls of milk, salt, a pinch of cayenne pepper, 1 chopped rasher of bacon, with 1 ounce of bacon fat or butter to fry in. Mix the breadcrumbs, suet, and seasonings. Beat up the egg in the milk and bind the mixture. Roll the forcemeat into little balls, the size of a small hen's egg, and fry them in a little butter or bacon fat for about 10 minutes. Keep them rolling in the fat so that they brown evenly. Drop the *polpette* into the casserole of hare just before placing it on the table. All that is now left of the hare are the head and bones which can be made into soup (page 72).

Venison

Venison in any form does not often find its way to ordinary dinner tables in this country, but when it does it is usually a haunch of venison from a fallow deer. Roe deer (*chevreuil*) are more commonly eaten in France, and portions of that animal are normally larded and marinaded a long time before roasting. The flesh of fallow deer has a thick outer coating of hard white fat which is esteemed by venison eaters, and haunch or neck should be hung for a considerable time so that its flavour may develop away from the taste of mutton towards the more interesting taste of game. Venison which has not been sufficiently hung is very tough.

ROAST VENISON

To prevent the meat from drying, the joint is best treated by completely encasing it in a firm dough made from suet, flour, and water, and baked. The dough is covered with greased paper kept in position by string or tape. The parcel of venison is placed on a grid over a baking dish in a fierce oven and baked for a long time. A large haunch, encased in dough, will take between 4 and 5 hours to cook. The hot oven should be reduced in temperature after the first hour. Without this case of dough the cooking time would be less, but the joint would have to be basted frequently to prevent the meat drying.

After this lapse of time, the parcel is undone, the crust removed, the joint dusted with a little plain flour and salt, butter is poured over it on all sides, and it is quickly browned in a hot oven. It should be served on a piping hot dish, and the plates must be equally hot, as venison tends to cool and the fat to congeal very quickly. Mrs Beeton says that 'to be thoroughly enjoyed by epicures, it should be eaten on hot water plates'. These are no longer manufactured, but we found one, a large plate ornamented with a mauve transfer Greek key pattern round the edge and a central *motif* of elegant urns, fitted with a pewter base into which hot water can be poured.

The usual accompaniments of venison are red currant jelly (sometimes melted in a little port), a rich gravy, with *pommes rissolées* and brussels sprouts. A tart gooseberry or quince jelly goes well with this meat, and it can be served with Cumberland sauce or *sauce poivrade*, which is made in the following manner:

Sauce Poivrade

Hash two shallots very fine. Transfer a little of the butter used to baste the joint of venison into a little pan, put in the hashed shallots, a good pinch of ground black pepper, and a tablespoonful of wine vinegar. Reduce by boiling, add the juices from the basting tin, half a glass of red wine, a glass of stock. Reduce again.

VENISON STEW

Cuts of venison unsuitable for roasting can be stewed after a period of hanging. In such a case the piece is divided into suitable joints, rubbed with a mixture of powdered wholespice, ground black peppers, and a little salt, sautéd in mutton fat, and transferred to an earthenware casserole in the oven. When the meat is thoroughly browned, two glasses of red wine or port should be poured over the meat and reduced by rapid boiling. A pint and a half of good stock is heated and added to the casserole, the lid is put on, and the cooking is proceeded with in a moderate oven for a long time, at least 3 hours. The venison is served straight from the hot casserole with red currant jelly or cranberry sauce.

Cranberry Sauce

½ lb cranberries, a slice of lemon peel, the juice of a lemon, a tablespoonful of sugar and a little butter.

Put the cranberries in a pan with only sufficient water to moisten the bottom, put in the lemon peel and the sugar, and simmer very slowly with the lid on for about 40 minutes, by which time the fruit will be pulpy. Beat in the butter, squeeze over the lemon juice, and once it has cooled the sauce is ready.

Cheeses

CHEESES

CHEESE is probably the best of all foods, as wine is the best of all beverages. It is full of nourishment and good to eat on its own. It is made in a tremendous range of types with different flavours and consistencies and in different shapes and sizes. In association with shallots and mushrooms it is an essential ingredient of many cooked dishes which have an improving influence on wine. In its natural state it not only has the effect of clearing the palate but it supports and brings out the flavour of the wine which it accompanies. With bread, butter, and beer, cider, or wine it provides a meal in itself.

Cheese is made from the milk of cows, goats, sheep, mares, and buffaloes. The cheese with the highest food value in terms of proteins, fats, and vitamins is that made from whole milk with cream added, or from cream alone. In France all makers of cheese are obliged by law to indicate the fat percentage per 100 grammes of cheese; thus a *fromage du Monsieur Fromage* bears a 60% in large type on its label, while some of the most celebrated cheeses, *Brie, Camembert, Pont l'évêque, Neufchâtel, Livarot, Port du Salut*, and *Reblochon* come into the category of not less than 40% *de matières grasses* or fat content. A fat percentage of at least 60% entitles a cheese to a 'double cream' qualification, and one of 75% to 'triple cream'. The processes of manufacture, described in interesting detail in *Larousse gastronomique* and other standard works, are widely different, and these account for the varying period of time taken for cheese to mature. A cheese is usually at its best when it is ripe and its flavour fully developed; its taste and smell are indications of its quality, but touch in the case of soft cheeses is a helpful guide.

The best opportunity of enlarging one's experience is when travelling, particularly in France where many remarkable cheeses are local in manufacture, and in Italy where it is possible to appreciate *Parmigiano* as a fine eating cheese before it has matured into the rock-like grating cheese with which we are familiar here, and the sheep cheese *Pecorino* which is remarkably good in Tuscany, as well as the delicate *Ricotta* made from ewes' butter milk, and the buffaloes' milk cheese *Mozzarella*.

There are pleasures to be enjoyed in sampling local cheeses with a carafe of the *vin du pays* in the courtyard of some country inn, pleasures often overlooked by diligent sightseers focused too sharply on visual surprises. The cheeses reserved for export are sometimes specially treated and in many cases it is only possible to form a true opihion of a particular cheese in its own district. Some of the best are unable to stand the hazards of the journey and the selection available in this country is confined to those which can. The Cheese Importers in Jermyn Street only stock twice as many cheeses from nine different countries, including our own, as are produced in Normandy alone. G. Parmigiani Figlio Ltd in Old Compton Street stocks about 28 cheeses, with 13 Italian types. Before the war a London restaurant offered a fairly wide selection as its principal attraction; about 40 cheeses were on sale. But even this comparatively small number of cheeses still provides interesting variety and opportunity, which can be increased by trying to find the right wine to go with a particularly good cheese.

English, Scottish, and Welsh Cheeses

These are mainly eating cheeses of good, sound quality which will provide a simple enjoyable meal if taken with beer or draught cider. But the best English cheese with which to complete a meal is, undoubtedly, a ripe Stilton, and its taste and texture enhance the wine which may be served with it.

Blue Vinny, or Dorset Blue, is only made in Dorsetshire by a few farms and is not usually available in shops, though Harrod's has some from time to time. It is a very hard cheese made from skimmed milk.

Caerphilly was originally only made in Wales, but now it is produced in a number of other districts in Somerset, Devon,

Wiltshire, and Dorset. Made from skimmed milk, it is ready to eat when it is about 10 days old and is a rather refined cheese both in texture and flavour, the latter being mildly sour. It is not of great character but can be used successfully in cooking when a recipe requires a cheese with melting qualities. Primarily an eating cheese, it must be eaten fresh, as it dries up in a day or two.

Cheddar is still made in the Cheddar district of Somerset, but the name covers any cheese which has undergone the 'cheddaring' process, and much of it is now factory made. The best Cheddar is still farmhouse-made from cows' milk during the months May to October, is allowed from three to six months to mature, and is usually ripe at six months. Good Cheddar has a pronounced, benevolent flavour and is of a good round character, and at its best it is a most satisfactory eating cheese. It can be used grated in cooking. *Wessex Cheddar*, a small cylinder in shape, is disappointing in flavour.

Cheshire is made from full-cream cows' milk, and the best still comes from Cheshire. There is a white Cheshire and a red Cheshire, and when the latter loses its colour and develops blue veins it is known as 'blue' Cheshire. Besides being a great rarity, this is also the best, with a sharp tang and a creamy texture. As eating cheese, red and white Cheshire are rather dry when mature with a crumbly grain and an un-sweet flavour. Both can be used in cooking but are better eaten on their own.

Dunlop is a Scottish cheese and is not dissimilar to Cheddar, but it tends to be whiter in colour, has a close consistency, and a mild flavour. A good eating cheese with wholemeal bread or oatcake.

Gloucester is made from skimmed cows' milk. *Double Gloucester* is made from whole cows' milk. Both are hard cheeses similar to Cheddar in their eating qualities.

Lancashire is made in a number of varieties. One of the best known is a fatty cheese with a bite to it which will make an excellent Welsh Rarebit.

Leicester is made from whole cows' milk in the same manner as Cheddar but is flat and round instead of cylindrical in shape. A good eating cheese.

Stilton is made from the richest full-cream cows' milk during the months May to September and is mature after about nine months. It is probably the best of English cheeses and is made mostly in Leicestershire, Rutland, and Huntingdonshire. It has a pronounced flavour when ripe, but some people prefer it in the course of its decay. It is a fine cheese with which to end a meal. It should be wrapped in a napkin and kept not in a cold larder but in a warm, airy room.

Wensleydale is a Yorkshire cheese and there are two kinds. One is 'blue' when ripe and is made from 'double cream' during the months June to September, the other is a white cheese usually made during the winter months and eaten fresh. Both can be excellent eating cheeses with a not very pronounced, slightly sour flavour, a firm texture, rather dry and crumbly when cut.

This does not, of course, exhaust the list of English cheeses. Omissions include the rarer Cotherstone, Double Cottenham which resembles Stilton and Wensleydale, and Sage Derby which is marbled with green veins.

Dutch Cheeses

These are almost entirely cheeses which are eaten by themselves as a part of a meal. In Holland the cheese is often sliced very thinly, laid on top of a piece of white, black, or ginger bread and eaten at breakfast or midday with a cup of coffee. The two kinds mentioned here are the ones most easily bought in this country.

Edam is a round ball cheese, made from cows' milk, with a bright-red skin and a yellow-to-orange interior. It is a simple eating cheese with no marked characteristics save those of honesty and digestibility.

Gouda is not dissimilar to *Edam* either in taste or texture, but is different in shape, being a large or flattened round of cheese. It is a simple eating cheese.

French Cheeses

These are made in such a variety of shapes, sizes, and textures and produced by such different methods that it is difficult to make a selection, but we have listed those which are either obtainable here or those which might interest the traveller in France. French cheeses are, with one or two exceptions, eating cheeses and their usual place in the meal is after the salad and before the fruit or a sweet dessert.

Bleu d'Auvergne is made in the district of Auvergne from a mixture of cows', goats', and ewes' milk. It is usually matured in cellars, and is a blue mould cheese of a similar kind to *Roquefort*. It is rather mild, sometimes a little salty, and dry in texture.

Bondon de Neufchâtel is a fresh, soft, mild cheese made in Normandy; a little sugar is usually added to it when eaten. It is small and cylindrical, measuring about three inches by about two inches in diameter, packed in straw.

Brie is made from whole cows' milk in the Seine-et-Marne area in autumn, spring, and summer. The best *Brie* is made in autumn, and is usually obtainable from November to May. The spring and summer *Brie* is not so good, and rapidly deteriorates in hot weather. It is a flat, round, pancake-shaped cheese, packed on straw. It is ripe when it is soft and just running, has a delicious flavour, and is excellent with white wines.

Camembert is made from cows' milk in Normandy during the summer months when it is at its best. It is also made between November and May, but as the milk is then deficient in cream the results are poor. A real *Camembert* bears the phrase '*Syndicat des Fabricants du Véritable Camembert de Normandie*' on its box; the rest are commercial imitations. It is a first-class cheese when ripe, which moment can be proved by pressing its centre with the fingers when it should be soft to the touch. When immature the cheese is dry, rather porous in its middle, a little salty and uninteresting. When ripe it is soft, slow running, with a bland flavour. When a *Camembert* is over-ripe the cheese becomes not only too soft, but generates gases which have an overpowering smell.

Cantal is made in Auvergne from whole cows' milk. It is a large, hard cheese made in the form of a cylinder, pale cream in colour, with very little smell but a sharp taste in the mouth. It is an admirable, firm eating cheese with something of the character of Cheddar.

Coulommiers is made in Seine-et-Marne of whole cows' milk from October to May. In shape it is a smaller version of *Brie* and in taste it is also lower in stature, but can be eaten with simple pleasure at the end of a meal or with some crusty bread at a wayside picnic.

Coulommiers frais is a soft cream cheese similar in shape, size, and consistency to *Petit Suisse* (q.v.).

Demi-sel is a small, soft cream cheese made from whole cows' milk mainly in Normandy but also in other parts of France. It has a small proportion of salt added to it.

Fromage blanc à la crème is a soft, cream cheese made from soured cows' milk which has been drained and mixed with a little fresh milk. It is served with fresh cream and usually some soft sugar also. It is a dessert, in fact, and not a cheese at all. This can be made in one's own home, and when it has been moulded in a heart-shaped basket it is known as *cœur à la crème*.

Fromage du Monsieur Fromage is a 'double cream' cheese made most of the year in Normandy, and bears a label with '60% *de matières grasses*' on it. It is a very delicate cheese with a dry yet creamy texture.

Le Chabichou is a goats' milk cheese made in Poitou during the period April to December. *Chevret* is made in Berry from goats' milk from April to December. *Fromage de chèvre* is a goats' milk cheese made in Haut-Limousin. *Le Saint-Gervais* is a goats' milk cheese from Languedoc and should be eaten in its own district at the end of a simple meal. *Tomme de chèvre* is a soft paste-like cheese made from goats' milk in Savoy.

These are all small, dried, goats' milk cheeses which are made in the shape of a cylinder, having a rather dirty looking exterior and a rather strong, country flavour in the mouth. It is most pleasant to end a simple bourgeois meal with one of these.

Livarot is made from skimmed cows' milk in Normandy during the summer months. It is cylindrical in shape, rather small and flat, about two inches high and about six inches in diameter, and usually coloured brown or dark, reddish brown and needs to mature. It is not at its best until the period January to March, and after that it begins to deteriorate. It is a soft paste-like cheese and very strong in flavour.

Petit Suisse is a cream cheese made from cows' milk. It is small and cylindrical, usually made in two sizes, and is eaten fresh. It is soft and mild, if a little sour in the mouth. Quite good with fresh strawberries or raspberries and soft sugar.

Pommel is an unsalted 'double cream' cheese which is made all the year round and is always safe to eat.

Pont l'évêque is made in Normandy either from whole or skimmed milk during most months of the year. It is slightly salted and is a square cheese about one inch in depth and about four inches long. It is half soft, medium strong, and varies in quality, depending on whether it is made from whole or skimmed milk. It is a cheese to eat in its own district, where it can be most palatable.

Port du Salut is a whole cows' milk cheese which is made nearly the whole year round in many parts of France, although it originates in Normandy. It is a round, half soft, mild cheese of innocent flavour. It is usually about three inches in depth and about 10 inches in diameter. The best variety is *Notre Dame de Carentan*.

Le Reblochon is made in Savoy from ewes' milk during the period October to June. It is a small, squat, delicious half-dried cheese.

Le Roquefort is made from ewes' milk during the lambing season in the Cevennes mountains and is matured in the limestone caves of the village of Roquefort. At its best it is one of the most enjoyable cheeses for the end of a meal. It is both soft and moist, marbled with blue veins, and has a strong healthy flavour. But in inferior *Roquefort* cheese (and there is much of it in this country) the flavour tends to be hard and raw and so does the texture.

La Tomme is a cows' milk cheese made in Auvergne, and is not at all dissimilar to Cheddar. It is good and satisfactory as a simple meal on its own, and good at the end of a meal.

La Tomme aux raisins (properly *La Tomme au marc de raisin*) is a dry yet soft cheese with an astringent flavour. It is a round flat cheese of about $1\frac{1}{2}$ to 2 inches in depth and about 10 inches in diameter, and its outer surface is thickly coated with dried grape skins. It is a pleasant eating cheese, and keeps well.

La Tomme de Savoie is a medium soft cheese made from cows' milk in Savoy, and is a pleasing cheese.

Le Vacherin is also made in Savoy from cows' milk, and it is a most charming cream cheese which can be eaten with delight.

Italian Cheeses

Italy produces a great number of excellent cheeses but few of them penetrate to the English market, with the exception of *Bel Paese* and *Gorgonzola* as eating cheeses, and very mature *Parmigiano* as a grating cheese for cooking. But some Soho shops stock *Mozzarella*,

Stracchino, Pecorino and some of the north Italian cream cheeses, *Locatelli, Fior di Latte,* and *Pastorella,* as well as other cheeses mentioned here.

Bel Paese is made from whole milk usually between October and June, and is in the form of a flattened cylinder about $2\frac{1}{2}$ to 3 inches in depth, 10 inches in diameter, weighing about 5 pounds. It is rather a soft but elastic cheese of pleasing flavour, which is of an even consistency and gives an impression of sweetness in the mouth. An excellent cheese to eat on a warm day with some good bread and a dry white wine, followed by fresh fruit. It might be described as a sylvan cheese.

Cacciocavallo is a very hard cheese made from cows' milk. The best comes from the district of Sorrento but it is also made in the Abruzzi and Apulia provinces. This cheese varies in weight from about three to ten pounds and keeps well. It has a mild flavour and is a little salty, but excellent if accompanied by an ordinary wine of the country and can be used for grating.

Gorgonzola is made from cows' milk in Lombardy, and has a high fat content. It is cylindrical in shape and each cheese weighs about 14 pounds. There is a white variety, but the one best known out of Italy is a 'blue' cheese. It is strong and can sometimes be rather rank.

Mozzarella is a small round cheese, weighing about one pound, made from buffaloes' milk. Used in cooking it becomes soft and melting. It is one of the constituents of *pizza* or *torta di patate,* as well as forming the main ingredient of *mozzarella in carozza* which can be bought at most *rosticceria* in Italy. It is a little hard, and uninteresting if eaten on its own, due to its very white colour and indefinite character, but when combined with a few anchovies and black olives its quality is enhanced.

Parmigiano (parmesan) is made from cows' milk in the Po Valley into a very hard dry cheese which when mature (*Parmigiano Stravecchio*) and even older (*Parmigiano Stravecchione*) is the best grating cheese for *pasta* and other Italian dishes. It has a black outside crust, and inside is a pale straw colour. It is made in enormous flattened cylinders as well as in smaller sizes.

Parmigiano Reggiano which is even better in taste, with the same texture and shape, is made in a neighbouring district and in cylinders of lesser size. Both these cheeses are matured for at least two years before being sold as grating cheese. But *Parmigiano* and *Parmigiano Reggiano* not more than one year old are splendid eating cheeses. A small *Parmigiano* brought back from Italy will serve first as a remarkable cheese for the table, and when it becomes too hard to cut, will keep for at least a year as a grating cheese. The flavour of this cheese has a definite bite, but is at the same time fragrant and sweet, and it combines extraordinarily well with tomatoes, onions, herbs, and mushrooms, with *pasta*, fish, and meat. It is needed for the Genoese combination of garlic, basil, pine kernels, olive oil, and *Parmigiano* in *pesto* for *minestrone*. It is expensive on account of the time taken for maturing, but, and we must emphasize this, it is economical in use.

Pecorino is made from ewes' milk during the greater part of the year and assumes different forms, a fresh cheese in the form of a small ball, a round flat cheese a little bigger than *Bel Paese*, and larger cylinders, according to its district of origin. G. Parmigiani Figlio Ltd (see List of Suppliers) stock *Pecorino Romano*, *Pecorino Siciliano*, *Pecorino Sardo*. In Tuscany it is one of the best eating cheeses with an excellent flavour. This sometimes reaches Soho during the summer months. In winter *Pecorino Romano* is sold, which has already matured and hardened from an eating cheese to a grating cheese. In this condition it has an affinity in texture with *Parmigiano*, but with a stronger flavour and the kick of a sheep cheese. It is useful as an alternative grating cheese for Italian dishes.

Provolone is a cheese made in the form of a *Mortadella* sausage. It deserves investigation. It might be described as an Italian *Gruyère*, with a rather similar texture but without holes, darker in colour and with its own distinct Italian character. It is cheaper than *Parmigiano* or *Pecorino*, and rather dearer than *Gruyère*. It can be used instead of *Gruyère* for cooking.

Ricotta is a fresh cheese made from ewes' butter-milk, rich and cream-like in consistency. In Italy it is often used in conjunction with sugar, crystallized fruit, and eggs to form the filling for a tart or cake, and it also plays a part in the savoury filling for certain *ravioli* and *pizza* recipes. It is bland in texture and combines and amalgamates most satisfactorily with other ingredients in cooked dishes, for instance with spinach and nutmeg as a stuffing, and with black olives and anchovies and tomatoes in a *pizza*.

Stracchino is a soft, rather glutinous, strong cream cheese which is often used to flavour dishes of *pasta*. When it is subjected to heat it tends to become rather stringy, although its creamy consistency remains. Its flavour is pungent and a little coarse.

Swiss Cheeses

The two cheeses noted below are both fine eating cheeses but they are equally successful in cooked dishes. *Gruyère* is the main constituent of the classic *fondue*, but if cooked it should not be subjected to too great an intensity of heat as it then becomes extremely stringy and unmanageable. Its subjection to heat should be slow, so that the cheese melts rather than cooks.

Emmenthal is made from cows' milk and undergoes the same process as *Gruyère*, but it is a much larger cheese and may weigh anything from 150 to 300 pounds. Because it is a larger cheese it needs more time to make and more time to mature. Nearly all the cheese sold here as *Gruyère* is, in fact, *Emmenthal*. It has a sweet flavour with a distinctive character, is rather hard in consistency, and is very good eaten on its own. It will keep quite well if wrapped in a piece of butter muslin and stored in an airy, but not too cold, room. Its chief visual distinction is its holes and these should not be either too large or too frequent.

Gruyère is made from cows' milk and is a hard cheese with a small proportion of small holes in it. It is made in a circular shape about 6 inches in depth and about 2 feet in diameter. It is one of the finest of all eating cheeses, sweet in flavour and with a wholesome smell. Its only disability is that when cut the outside surface tends to become varnished and very hard. If it has to be kept for a day or two put it in a loosely woven cloth and store in an airy but not too cold place.

Fungi

12

FUNGI

THIS chapter has been written for people who combine an experimental approach to cooking with an interest in natural history. A great many recommendations for cooking commercially grown mushrooms have been given in the text, and it is only to those who have a wider curiosity that these notes are addressed. They are intended to be used in conjunction with handbooks showing coloured plates. A list of such books will be found on page 273.

In this country not many fungi come to market. In France, Switzerland, Austria, Czechoslovakia, Germany, and Italy in late summer and autumn fungi are regularly collected, brought to market, identified and passed by a market official, and exhibited for sale. About a hundred years ago half a dozen species were sold in Covent Garden, but nowadays it is only possible to obtain *Boletus edulis, Cantharellus,* and sometimes *Tricholoma nudum* in one or two shops in Soho and at a greengrocer's in Notting Hill, while *Tricholoma personatum* (Blewits) are found in Midland markets. There are, of course, dried fungi imported from Italy and dried *Boletus edulis,* mostly German, in cellophane packets stocked by many delicatessen shops, which are a useful addition to casseroles, and excellent in soup, but they lose both in texture and in flavour when compared with fresh specimens.

On the whole, ignorance on the one hand and the abundance of fresh vegetables on the other prevents their appreciation in cooking. The widest knowledge and use of fungi is in those countries where winter vegetables are scarce, in Sweden, Russia, Poland, Germany, and Catalonia, or in France and Italy where everything provided by nature is put to some gastronomic use.

Admittedly there is something mysterious about toadstools which Nicander already in 185 B.C. described as 'the evil ferment of the earth'. The fascination of 'deadly poison' with which children are so preoccupied may be partly to blame. Fungi had a strange mutability of colour, the flesh changing colour in many of them when touched or exposed to the air. The speed of their appearance and the rapidity of their decay are rather awe-inspiring. In the pinewoods after a rainy spell in early autumn the bare pine-needle floor can be transformed overnight, littered with a crop of fungi, edible *Boleti* growing side by side with scarlet *Russulae*.

For those interested in the subject but without previous experience the best way of proceeding is to acquire one of the handbooks mentioned on page 273, and set out on a fungus expedition in familiar country, at the time of year – between August and early November – when they appear in quantity. To begin with many specimens may be carefully collected, and taken home to compare with coloured illustrations. In the early stages it is wisest to restrict culinary experiments to those fungi which are easily identified and quite distinct, particularly *Cantharellus cibarius*, *Coprinus comatus*, *Tricholoma nudum* (Wood Blewit), and *Lepiota procera* (the Parasol Mushroom), which are not easily confused with other species.

After a few such expeditions through woodland or in meadowland it will become clear that the same fungus tends to frequent specific situations, and that woodland species are often associated with certain trees. An example of this is *Cantharellus cibarius* (*Chanterelles*) which can often be found on sandy soil at the base of sweet chestnut clumps almost covered by their last season's leaves. But this must not be taken as a rule, because they are also found beneath oak trees on sand, and in association with birches. Mr Ramsbottom has a great deal to say in *Mushrooms and Toadstools* about this vegetable and soil association, and it is by studying such a book that one comes to learn the hunting grounds for the best edible species.

We must emphasize the importance of identifying the species before cooking. It is also essential to confine oneself only to those specimens which are reasonably young, firm, and freshly gathered.

Every book on fungi contains a vivid warning and description of the deadly *Amanita phalloides*, *Amanita verna*, and *Amanita virosa*, and the poisonous *Amanita muscaria* and *Amanita pantherina*. These dangerous fungi make it essential to approach the subject from a very careful and scientific point of view, and no fungus should be admitted to the kitchen without the cook being absolutely certain of its identity. To establish identity it is necessary to check

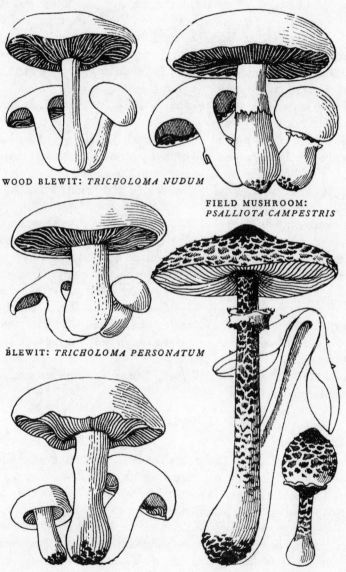

WOOD BLEWIT: *TRICHOLOMA NUDUM*

FIELD MUSHROOM:
PSALLIOTA CAMPESTRIS

BLEWIT: *TRICHOLOMA PERSONATUM*

ST GEORGE'S MUSHROOM:
TRICHOLOMA GEORGII

PARASOL MUSHROOM:
LĒPIOTA PROCERA

every characteristic of a fungus, the shape of its cap, the way the cap joins the stem, the configuration of the gills, the texture of the stem, the presence or absence of a ring, the shape of the base of the stem, and the colour of cap, gills, stem, flesh, and spores, as well as questions of texture and so on. The fungus must also be gathered with care so that the base is intact. In the *Amanita* genus it is possible to leave the volva behind in the earth, and deprive oneself of the obvious means of identification.

From the culinary point of view fungi contain a very high proportion of moisture, and as a rule the method of cooking which most quickly reduces the moisture content is the best, i.e. frying in heated butter or olive oil, soaking in oil and grilling. The fungi which are distinctly fleshy such as *Cantharellus, Morchella, Boletus, Lactarius*, and *Tricholoma* are capable of more prolonged culinary operations, but a large light fungus like *Lepiota procera* (the Parasol Mushroom) should have only sufficient cooking to reduce its water content. If cooking is prolonged, it becomes leathery.

In the following pages we have concentrated on a few genera which repay study, namely, *Agaricus, Amanita, Boletus, Cantharellus, Coprinus, Lepiota, Morchella*, and *Tricholoma*. The genus *Amanita* is included because it contains not only the most poisonous fungi but one of the best species, *Amanita caesarea*, which, though it does not occur in Britain, is often found in the south of France and in Italy.

Agaricus

The characteristics of this genus (whose synonym *Psalliota* has been generally used in this country) are as follows. The cap is separable from the stem. There is a membrane which initially enclosed the gills from the edge of the cap to the stem, and usually leaves its mark in the form of a ring on the stem. The gills are free, thin, and regular. The spores are purple brown, elliptical or ovoid. *Agaricus* is related to *Lepiota*, but distinguished by the colour of the spores.

The genus comprises two groups, characterized by *Agaricus campester* (Common Field Mushroom), and *A. arvensis* (Horse Mushroom), within which there are a large number of species which show slight variations within the type. The division between these two groups is based upon the tendency to a slight reddening of the flesh when bruised in *A. campester*, and a tendency for *A. arvensis* and its associated species to turn yellow, for instance *A. silvicola*, a mushroom of delicate flavour, and the more doubtful *A. xanthodermus*, the Yellow Staining Mushroom which is regarded by many people as being dangerously indigestible. Care must be taken in gathering *A. silvicola* which grows in the same conditions in the woods as the rarer *Amanita verna*. It is distinguished from this poisonous fungus by the *absence of a volva* at the base of the stem, and by the colour of the gills which are pink, not white. *A. arvensis* is the species which is found where there is an abundance of horse manure, and it is this which was originally cultivated.

These fungi are to be sought during August and September in meadows, on golf-links, open pastures, and downland, with the exceptions of *A. silvaticus* and *A. silvicola* which as their names denote are to be found in woodland.

We have already made frequent references to mushrooms, the only fungi free from seasonal limitations owing to their widespread commercial cultivation, and recommendations for their inclusion in many ways, as an ingredient for stuffing poultry, in soups, as a garnish for fish, in sauces for *pasta*, and as an accompaniment for meat. At the beginning of the chapter on AROMATICS the combination of mushrooms, parsley, and shallots called *Duxelles* has been discussed. It provides an ideal bed upon which to lay a fish for baking, or can be used as an omelette filling or stuffing for a small bird.

CHAMPIGNONS FARÇIS   Cultivated or field mushrooms

This is an excellent accompaniment to serve with grilled steak or lamb cutlets. Take about 20 mushrooms of good size, clean them, peel them, and remove the stalks. Put them on a buttered fireproof dish, pour over them a little melted butter and put them in the oven or under a gentle grill while you prepare the stuffing. Hash an onion and sauté it in butter, adding a little chopped ham, the chopped stalks, some parsley or basil. Add a few spoonfuls of meat gravy, season, and let the juice reduce for a few minutes. Lay this dressing on the mushrooms, cover with finely grated bread-crumbs, pour on a little melted butter and brown, the surface of the dish in the oven.

CHAMPIGNONS À LA CRÈME   Small, rounded cultivated
mushrooms

This is the most satisfactory way of preparing the button mush-rooms, *champignons de Paris*, and they should be served on their own after a dish of meat or fish.

Remove the stalks, which can be kept for soup. Sauté the little mushroom heads in olive oil over a gentle flame with a crushed garlic clove and some fresh chopped parsley or basil. Sprinkle with salt. If some of the mushrooms are larger, pour a thread of oil into their caps. Pour over the mushrooms in the proportion of ¼ pint to ¼ pound of mushrooms some single cream, and cook gently for a few minutes, stirring, while the cream thickens. Have some half-inch slices of toasted French bread ready, cut horizontally, ready to receive the mushrooms, and serve very hot, squeezing lemon juice over the cream at the last moment. The proportion of cream to mushrooms is very important. If the cream is used too econom-ically the mushrooms are not properly immersed in the sauce, and the whole point of this simple preparation is lost.

Amanita

The main characteristics of the *Amanita* genus are white spores, white gills, which are more or less free with shorter intermediate gills, a ring on the stem, and a volva or wrapper which completely enclosed the young fungus.

Although a number of *Amanita* species are excellent as food, the genus is held rather in dread on account of the deadly poisonous *A. phalloides*, the Death Cap or Deadly Agaric, as it is commonly called in this country. It is the most dangerous of all fungi. It is essential to become familiar with its characteristics, which are set out in detail in Ramsbottom's *Poisonous Fungi* as there are possibilities of confusing it with *Tricholoma portentosum*, with some of the

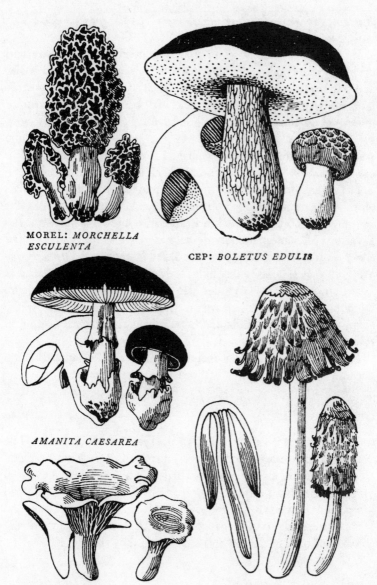

MOREL: *MORCHELLA ESCULENTA*

CEP: *BOLETUS EDULIS*

AMANITA CAESAREA

CHANTERELLE: *CANTHARELLUS CIBARIUS*

SHAGGY INK-CAP: *COPRINUS COMATUS*

Russulae, or with *Agaricus silvaticus*, which all grow in deciduous woods in summer and autumn.

Equally dangerous is *Amanita verna*, which is more rare and occurs in the woods from spring to autumn, particularly on chalk, and *A. virosa* which rather resembles it. There are two further poisonous species, *A. muscaria*, the Fly Agaric, frequently found under beech trees, which is perhaps the best known poisonous species because of its beautiful red cap dotted with thick white warty patches, and *A. pantherina*, the False Blusher, which is rather easily confused with the edible *A. rubescens* (the Blusher).

However, included among this company is the splendid fungus *A. caesarea*, already valued by the Romans. It is not known in this country. Found a great deal in France in the south and east, it has a variety of names, notably *Oronge*, *Oronge vraie*, *Cocon*, *Jaune d'œuf*. In Italy it is commonly found, and is known as *Ovolo*, *Fongo ovo*, and *Bolé*. It is easily distinguished from the poisonous *Amanitae* by its smooth orange rounded cap free from any traces of volva membrane, its substantial volva which remains attached to the stem, and the yellow gills and stem which are normally white in this genus.

We give the following recipes for the sake of interest, and because they can be applied to other substantial fungi.

ORONGES À LA CRÈME   *Amanita caesarea*

This recipe is from the valley of the Garonne in Limousin. The *oronges* are scraped to remove any débris attaching to them, wiped with a cloth and sliced before sautéing them gently in butter for about a quarter of an hour. Fresh cream is whipped up with a little salt, poured over the fungi in the sauté-pan, and when the cream is hot the dish is ready to serve. It can accompany baked fish or be served on its own with buttered toast.

OVOLI IN GRATELLA   *Amanita caesarea*

Amanita caesarea is esteemed in Florence where together with *Boletus edulis* (*Porcini*), it is gathered on the surrounding hillsides and brought in quantity to market in August and September.

The fungi are wiped clean. If they need washing they should be subsequently dried with a cloth. The stalks are removed, the caps are covered with a little olive oil and coarse salt, put into a grilling pan and grilled for a few minutes before being turned over to cook on the other side. They are served as an accompaniment to roast meat.

OVOLI TRIPPATI   *Amanita caesarea*

They are prepared in Tuscany with parmesan cheese, and in this case they are cleaned, sliced, sautéd with butter, salt, and ground pepper, then moved into an earthenware dish, covered with rich gravy, sprinkled with grated parmesan, and browned in a hot oven.

BEIGNETS D'ORONGES   *Amanita caesarea*

The orange caps are cut into slices, put on a plate, and sprinkled with sugar. Two eggs and a spoonful of olive oil are beaten together. The slices are coated in this batter, fried in hot lard, and browned on all sides. When crisp and golden they are removed from the pan, drained on absorbent paper, sprinkled with sugar, and served as a sweet. It is our contention that Orange fritters came into existence through some cook's confusion between 'oronges' and 'oranges'!

Two other species of *Amanita* found here rather resemble *A. caesarea* in their edible substance, *A. spissa*, called *A. épaisse* by the French, which has a good consistency and can be grilled or sautéd, but care must be taken with this species as it has some common characteristics with *A. pantherina*. *A. rubescens*, called the Blusher or Warty Caps, is good, but it too can be confused with *A. pantherina*, although it is recognizable by the pink tinge which colours the flesh when bruised. *A. rubescens* must be subjected to some form of heat before it is innocuous.

Amanitopsis fulva and *Amanitopsis vaginata*, which are allied species commonly found in pastures in this country, are good to eat but have little substance. They are best prepared by sautéing in butter, and served with a little melted butter to which a thread of wine vinegar has been added.

Lepiota

Among the *Lepiota* species *L. procera*, the Parasol Mushroom, is outstanding in size and very easy to identify. It is very large indeed and specimens are often found with a cap as big as a dessert plate. They are fungi of open pastures, downland, golf-links, and sand-dunes, and are not associated with trees at all. In downland situations, they seem to favour the seaward slopes, and can sometimes be seen from a quarter of a mile away.

To prepare them for cooking, the cap should be gently stroked upwards from the margin to the central point to rub off the brown scales, and the actual point of the cap should be sliced off as it is rather leathery. The stalk should be removed, being hollow and fibrous. Divide the cap into segments following the line of the gills without using a knife. Only fresh specimens with perfectly white gills should be used. Stale specimens have already lost a great deal of moisture and are leathery to the touch.

This fungus should be fried quickly in butter. A quarter of a pound of butter should be enough to fry six large specimens. The size is quickly reduced by frying, as the moisture content is higher than in most mushrooms. They can be fried with *Agaricus campester* (Field Mushroom) or with *A. arvensis* (Horse Mushroom), both of which occur in similar situations. The taste of the Parasol is reminiscent of oysters in texture and chicken in flavour. The most agreeable way of serving them is as a dressing for a dish of rice, which provides the best textural contrast. They can also be served with spaghetti, but they should only be incorporated in the sauce after frying for a few moments before the dish is served. They will toughen if allowed to simmer or stew. (The qualities of different fungi soon become apparent in their preparation. The 'substantial' fungi like *Boletus*, *Cantharellus*, *Morchella*, etc., can be subjected to prolonged culinary treatment, while the lightweight large-gilled mushrooms call for rapid evaporation by frying.)

LÉFIOTES GRILLÉS   *Lepiota procera:* Parasol mushrooms

The Parasol Mushroom is esteemed in the remote province of Franche Comté which is rich in many kinds of fungi. Here they are covered with a little oil, their stalks having been removed, laid in a grilling pan, their moisture quickly reduced under a strong heat. They are then served with *gros sel* (page 288) and fresh butter.

Among the *Lepiotae*, *L. rhacodes*, less known than *L. procera*, is also edible. It grows in gardens and clearings in woods, especially pinewoods. Its cap is by no means as large as the giant parasol, reaching about 4 inches across when extended, and its stem is shorter.

Perhaps it is wise to mention the species *L. helveola* which is poisonous, but it is uncommon, and so small that there is no possibility of confusing it with the giant *L. procera* or *L. rhacodes*.

Tricholoma

The genus *Tricholoma* includes a considerable number of firm fleshed fungi, two of which, *T. personatum* (Blewit) and *T. nudum* (Wood Blewit), are well known and marketed in the Midlands.

From the culinary point of view the best are *T. nudum*, *T. personatum* (both of which have been relegated to a separate genus *Rhodopaxillus* on account of their pinkish spore colour and gills which separate easily from the cap, herein differing from the type which has white spores and sinuate gills), *T. Georgii* (St George's Mushrooms), and *T. equestre*. Other species of *Tricholoma* are edible without being particularly worth eating. *T. pardinum* and *T. sulfureum* are poisonous.

T. nudum (*Rhodopaxillus nudus*), the Wood Blewit, is violet in cap, gills, and stem. It is excellent for cooking and has a sweet smell. It grows in humus under oaks or conifers in autumn and sometimes in spring, and is quite common.

It can be prepared and used in the same way as the common mushroom, *Agaricus campester*, and is particularly good sliced, sautéd in butter with chopped chives, thickened with a little flour, cream added, and then piled into *vol-au-vent* cases or served on fried bread.

T. personatum (*Rhodopaxillus saevus*), the Blewit, is a more thick-set mushroom than *T. nudum* with a fawn cap just tinged with violet, a shorter, thicker violet stem, and white flesh. It has a pleasant smell, and though less delicate in flavour than *T. nudum* can be subjected to similar methods of preparation.

It grows in pastures and on lawns, often in large circles, and not in association with trees in autumn and early winter. *T. Georgii* (syn. *T. gambosum* in British text books) is a mushroom prized by the French as one of the most delicate in flavour. It is called *mousseron de la Saint-Georges* and *mousseron vrai*. In French recipe books it is denoted as a rule by the name *mousseron*.

Its cap is variable in colour (white, cream, the colour of chamois leather, or grey), its gills are white when young and later cream. It smells rather of fresh flour. It grows in circles in the field, on the downs where it forms enormous rings, in hedgerows, and on the margins of woods in spring and more rarely in summer. Its frequent variations have led to a division of the species by M. Maublanc into recognized varieties, *albellum* (pure white), *gambosum* (reddish touches to the cap), *graveolens* (bistre-coloured gills), and *palumbinum* (the cap creamy white with lilac shade at the centre).

T. equestre is another good quality *Tricholoma* with an agreeable taste. It is found in pinewoods in autumn. It must not be confused with *T. sulfureum* which resembles it in yellowish colour, but whose gills are far widely spread, and which has a disagreeable smell.

MOUSSERONS À LA CRÈME VALENTINOISE
Tricholoma Georgii: St George's mushrooms

Having gathered a pound of *Tricholoma Georgii* remove any débris that may attach to them. Chop some fat bacon or ham fat into small pieces and sauté them in a pan until they have rendered most of their fat. Remove the fragments, and put the mushroom heads in the pan, with their stalks chopped, and a little collection of chervil, tarragon, parsley, and chives chopped closely. Add the knobs of two cloves crumbled, a grate of nutmeg and of pepper, and sauté the mixture on a low flame. Remove the mushrooms onto a hot dish, thicken the sauce with a little flour and a dessertspoonful of tomato *purée*. Dilute this with a cup of hot milk, and when the mixture has cooked for some minutes add a tablespoonful or two of thick cream. Finish the sauce with a squeeze of lemon juice, pour it over the waiting mushrooms, and serve with fried *croûtons*.

RAGOÛT DE MOUSSERONS   Any species of *Tricholoma*

Blewits, Wood Blewits, and the St George's Mushroom can be prepared in the following way. Slice the mushrooms into substantial pieces, sauté them with a little butter and some lemon juice, covering the pan, for about ten minutes. Meanwhile prepare a sauce by finely chopping a shallot and sautéing it in a little salted butter. Sprinkle the pan with a dessertspoonful of flour, and when the butter has absorbed the flour pour some white wine over it, stirring until a fairly thick sauce is obtained. Pour this over the mushrooms and cook gently for a further ten minutes.

Coprinus

Coprinus embraces many species of which the larger members are edible. They are characterized by black spores and are subject in later stages of growth to autolysis, which is a process of dissolution or deliquescence, and which permits the successful discharge of their spores.

C. comatus, the Shaggy Inkcap, is in fact a common species here, which grows along the borders of lawns, in the neighbourhood of rubbish dumps, and in richly composted ground and gardens in August and early autumn. It is a delicate-tasting fungus which must be picked young. Specimens which have begun to deliquesce should be left behind. It has a sweet smell, white flesh, and white, then pinkish gills which eventually turn black, and is not easily confused with any other species. It has too little solidity for complicated culinary treatment, and is best fried with a little garlic and parsley, basil, chervil or tarragon, in butter, to be served with fish, meat, or omelette.

There is another edible species, *C. atramentarius*, which is much less delicate, and in our opinion not worth eating. It is grey in colour and grows in quantity in gardens and on the sides of roads and paths, and if you wish to experiment with it, only the youngest specimens should be selected.

Boletus

The *Boleti* form a very large group of fleshy fungi which are easily recognizable by the presence of spongy tubes in place of gills. From the culinary point of view they offer the student some of the best prospects with the least amount of anxiety. There is no chance of confusing them with other genera, and they contain only one species which is suspect, namely *B. satanas*, whose greyish white cap with greenish tinge, white flesh, and red netted, yellow swollen stem distinguish it from neighbouring species whose caps are darker and whose flesh is yellow rather than white.

In France the *Boletus* species are popularly known as *Bolets* or *Cèpes* and the species most used are distinguished by some adjective, i.e. *Cèpe jaune* (*B. luteus*), *Cèpe bai* (*B. badius*), *Cèpe roux* (*B. rufus*), *Cèpe comestible* (*B. edulis*), although this last species being the most excellent, both in taste and substance, is often called *Cèpe* which has led to some confusion, and means that many people confine their interest in the *Boleti* to *B. edulis* as being the one and only from the eating point of view.

Our pinewoods, beechwoods, and woodlands generally are well stocked with these fungi in late summer and autumn, up to the first frosts. But it is necessary to keep a watch for them as they seem to provide food for woodland animals, and are rather quick to decay.

There is one characteristic which may put people off, particularly those who have read Victorian books on fungi, in which it was often said that when a fungus turns blue this is an indication of poison. Some of the *Boleti* turn blue when their flesh is exposed to the air. This is particularly the case with *B. luridus*, which has long been believed to be poisonous on this account. The flesh turns from blue to yellow in cooking, and it is in fact perfectly wholesome and good. *B. erythropus* has the same tendency, and so has

B. badius which is a species found on the margin of pinewoods and is of quite good quality.

The most worthwhile species are those with firm flesh, fine tubes, and stems thickening at the base, of which *B. edulis* is typical. In this type the stem is more substantial than the cap, and is the cause of the Burgundian custom of preparing the caps and stems separately. *B. cyanescens*, *B. aureus*, *B. pinicola*, and *B. luridus* come into this category. Then less excellent but quite substantial are *B. rufus*, and its subspecies *B. duriusculus*, which attain a lesser size of cap and longer stem, and *B. badius* which, although attaining a large size, sometimes five or six inches across, has a less resistant texture, and whose tubes in older specimens should be removed before cooking.

B. scaber is good when young; later the cap is rather soft. *B. luteus*, *B. elegans*, *B. granulatus*, and *B. bovinus* are a good way behind both in taste and substance, but are not to be despised. The simplest preparation is the best for these species. They should be fried in oil or butter with a crushed clove or garlic and some freshly chopped herbs, and served on buttered toast or fried bread.

The recipes below can be applied to *B. edulis* and its varieties, and to *B. cyanescens* and *B. badius*.

CÈPES À L'AUVERGNATE   *Boletus*

This is a simple method of treating *Boletus*. Brown the caps in olive oil, and in another little pan sauté the chopped stalks with garlic and parsley. Fill the caps with this mixture, put them in a baking dish, pour over a little olive oil, and bake in a moderate oven for quarter of an hour.

CÈPES À LA BORDELAISE   *Boletus*

This is the most familiar preparation of the *Cèpe*. The fungi are cleaned, and the stalks separated from the caps. The caps are sliced into one centimetre in thickness, sautéd in butter with pepper and salt and a little crushed garlic. The stalks are minced and mixed with chopped parsley, one or two chopped shallots, and sautéd in butter in a separate pan. The sliced caps are laid on a hot platter, the chopped sautéd mixture is sprinkled on top and the dish surrounded by fried *croûtons* with the juice of a lemon added.

CÈPES GRATINÉS   *Boletus*

The same procedure as above, but before serving sprinkle the dish with a little concentrated meat juice, cover with bread-crumbs, pour on melted butter, and brown in the oven.

RAGOÛT DE CÈPES AU VIN ROUGE   *Boletus*

This is a Gascon preparation using one of the local wines, *Côtes du Gers*, *Bigorre*, or one of the *Landes* wines. With us it will doubtless be substituted for a *vin ordinaire* used in the kitchen, or the tail end of a bottle of Burgundy rescued from some more ample occasion. The caps of the *Cèpes* are sliced and browned in olive oil or butter with finely chopped shallots and several cloves of garlic, which can be sliced or pounded before putting in the pan. If there is half a pound of *Cèpes* then half a pint of wine will be needed and the concoction should be allowed to simmer and reduce by at least half. This preparation is used as a garnish for river fish cooked in a *court-bouillon* and served hot, or as an accompaniment to a stuffed fowl.

CÈPES À LA LANDAISE   *Boletus*

This is typical of a district famous for its poultry, where geese are confined and fattened to enlarge their livers, and where a supply of preserved goose, goose dripping, and *Armagnac* is a common-place in every farmhouse larder. Unfortunately most people here only have goose fat for a few weeks after Christmas, when there are no fresh or edible *Boletus*, but it is included for people who can kill their goose in October. The white wine stipulated is one of the best growths in the Landes and will no doubt have to be replaced by whatever white wine is to hand.

1 lb of *Boletus edulis* (*Cèpes*), goose dripping, a liqueur glass or

Armagnac, a glass of *Picpoul* wine, ½ lb lean ham, three shallots, ½ lb tomatoes.

Wipe the *Boletus* with a damp cloth to remove sand or humus. Remove the stalks, scrape them, and chop finely with a handful of parsley and the shallots. Chop the ham very finely and add it to the mixture. Melt the goose fat in a pan, and brown the caps which should remain whole, unless they are very large when they can be sliced into three or four pieces. Peel and slice the tomatoes, remove the pips, and mash them. Put the chopped stalks, parsley, shallots, and ham into the pan with the browned caps. Warm the brandy in a spoon over a flame, set light to it, and pour it onto the caps. When the flames have burnt out, put in the tomato pulp and pour on a glassful of *Picpoul* or whatever white wine is available, and simmer the *Boletus* until the sauce in which it is cooking has considerably reduced. Serve with roast meat.

PÂTÉ DE CÈPES   *Boletus*

Buy some *vol-au-vent* cases from a continental bakery and fill them in the following manner: Put a thin slice of smoked ham on the bottom of the case. Then add a mixture of *Boletus* stalks, bacon, onion, and garlic chopped up very finely and sautéd in a little butter beforehand, on the raw ham, topped with *Boletus* caps which have been oiled and grilled beforehand. Put the filled *vol-au-vent* cases in a baking dish, pour over each a little gravy, sprinkle with parsley, and put them in a hot oven for a few minutes. Serve very hot. Smoked ham sausage from the Ardennes called Lachsschinken is good for this.

CHAMPIGNONS DE PINS GRILLÉS   *Boletus pinicola*

This treatment can be applied to the best *Boletus* species which have both good flavour and texture, although it is specifically used in Provence for preparing the species *B. pinicola* found in pinewoods in autumn.

Remove the stems from the fungi and lay the caps in a grilling pan. Soak them in olive oil and place a little pounded garlic, the chopped stalks, and a sprinkling of salt on the caps. Grill them under a red-hot grill, and serve them on bread fried in butter, or with *croûtons* as a garnish for baked fish.

TO PRESERVE CÈPES

Use only very firm specimens. Clean the fungi, slice the caps and stalks, put them in a saucepan with a few glasses of water, some lemon juice, and salt. Cook for a few minutes with the lid on. Put the fungi into small jars with their juice, seal the top, and sterilize for 1½ hours in boiling water, or according to sterilizing instructions in a pressure cooker.

They can also be preserved in oil. Clean and slice the *Cèpes*, and simmer them for a few minutes in hot oil. Put them into jars, pour over them fresh olive oil, and put one bay leaf in each jar. Then seal the tops, and sterilize for two hours.

Cantharellus

This genus consists of species whose organization is very simple and between whose stem and cap there is no clear line of demarcation. The gills are shallow and blunt at the edge, more like veins than the typical mushroom gill. From the edible point of view the most important is *C. cibarius*, which is widely known and is all the more important to amateurs for being incapable of confusion with any poisonous species.

C. cibarius grows in profusion in open woodland, sometimes in association with birches and chestnuts, and can often be found among the last year's dried leaves at the base of chestnut clumps which are regularly cut for walking sticks or fencing. They appear in July and August and continue through the autumn, and are particularly numerous after rain. While it is usually of an intense yolk of egg colour, the colour is paler in dry weather. They are very easy to dry for winter use. This can be done by threading the fungi on strings and hanging them in a warm place, leaving them on a tray in the airing cupboard, or putting them in the oven when the heat has been turned off after roasting or baking.

They are also good for bottling, and this is the best method of preserving them as drying tends to toughen them. To do this, they should be thoroughly cleaned, trimmed at the base of the stem, and if necessary washed and dried. They are put to simmer with a little butter until they are tender and have produced their own liquor. In the cooking process they reduce considerably in size. Pack them into small heated jam jars together with their liquor and fill up with boiling water if the liquid does not cover all the fungi. Pour over some melted butter, sufficient to make a cover ¾ inch thick, cover with a Porosan cap, and sterilize for 1½ hours in a pressure cooker.

Chanterelles have a flavour peculiar to themselves, rather woody and fragrant.

They are at their best cooked in the same way as *Champignons à la crème* (page 258). If cream is not forthcoming, they can be sautéd in a little butter and simmered for a little while with the lid on, when they will yield a certain amount of their own liquor. This can be used with butter and flour to make a sauce in which to serve the *Chanterelles* as an accompaniment to roast mutton. They are also good to use in a dish of rice, and can be cooked instead of mushrooms to make a soup. Their texture is more solid than mushrooms, and they therefore need to be simmered for a while to become tender. Chopped parsley and butter bring out their flavour.

Morchella

The Morels, of which *Morchella esculenta* (syn. *M. rotunda*) is most commonly found in this country, are quite different in character from the gill-bearing fungi. Their spore-bearing asci are contained in the recesses of the honey-combed surface of the cap itself. They are one of the first edible species to appear in spring, and are to be found in April and May on the borders of woodland, in parks and hedges, and particularly in the neighbourhood of elm and ash generally on chalk or clay. *M. esculenta* is usually ochre in colour while the allied species *M. vulgaris* which has a more pointed cap and is more commonly found in woods is grey-brown, rather variable in tone. Both these Morels are much sought after on the continent. Their hollow caps are specially suited to stuffing, they dry easily, and they have a most delicate flavour.

MORILLES FARÇIES À LA SAVOYARDE

Morchella esculenta: Morels

Remove the stalks, and any débris attaching to the caps. If the caps are not perfectly clean they must be put under a running hot tap for a few seconds and dried. Then stuff them with the following mixture: a few ounces of finely chopped chicken, half the amount of chopped parsley, a little grated nutmeg, the crushed knobs of three cloves, a little salt, a crushed garlic clove, bound with the yolks of one or two eggs. Wrap the stuffed Morels in thin slices of streaky bacon, and sauté them in a little oil or butter, with the lid on the pan, for 10 to 15 minutes, shaking from time to time, so that the bacon is crisp, the Morels tender, and the stuffing has imparted some of its flavour. Serve on toast.

These fungi can be prepared by sautéing the caps in butter, pouring on a little *béchamel* sauce, and thickening this at the last minute with cream. This dish should be served very hot on buttered toast, with a squeeze of lemon juice added at the last moment.

They can also be stuffed with hard-boiled eggs finely chopped, mixed with chopped parsley and crumbs, and put in a small deep sided baking dish, covered with cream, and baked. If this is thought to be too extravagant, a fairly thick *béchamel* sauce could be substituted, the surface sprinkled with fine crumbs and little knobs of butter. Single cream is recommended. A quarter pint to $\frac{1}{4}$ pound of fungi. Morels, chopped and sautéd in butter, are an excellent stuffing for baked or grilled trout.

MORILLES À LA PROVENÇALE

Morchella esculenta: Morels

Heat some butter in a small earthenware dish and fry the caps on top of the stove over an asbestos mat. Season with salt and pepper, sprinkle with a spoonful of flour and a little good *bouillon,* and cook for six minutes. Fry some bread in olive oil in another pan. Mix two egg yolks with the juice of a lemon, take the mushroom pan off the fire, and when it has cooled for a moment add the *liaison* of egg yolks. Heat gently and stir while the sauce thickens, and serve at once on the fried bread.

The fungus groups briefly treated here contain species which are worth looking for, and which can be used with profit in the kitchen. It is hoped that, in spite of portentous nomenclature which cannot be avoided and the rather exacting study which fungi require before they can be safely used for cooking, people will feel slightly less sceptical about the subject after reading this very brief account and set about acquiring some practical knowledge and experience.

List of Recommended Books

Mushrooms and Toadstools, John Ramsbottom (Collins).
Edible Fungi and *Poisonous Fungi*, John Ramsbottom (King Penguin Books).
Edible and Poisonous Fungi (Ministry of Agriculture and Fisheries).
Book of Common Fungi, E. M. Wakefield (Observer Books).
Les Champignons comestibles et vénéneux, A. Maublanc, 2 volumes, 3rd edition, 1946 (Chevalier, Paris).

Vins Ordinaires

13

VINS ORDINAIRES

SOME people have a rather formidable attitude towards wine, giving one to believe that only a few chosen spirits are equipped with the necessary palate, sensitivity, and imagination to appreciate properly its great qualities and to value the extraordinary variations of fragrance, body, colour, and essence that it displays. This attitude comes about because wine is not, now, indigenous to this country; it is partly caused by the rather English preoccupation with exclusiveness and its attendant snobbishness, and partly because the wonderful wines take so long to mature that they are quite outside the range of the ordinary pocket. Because of its peculiar living qualities, subject to countless variations brought about by climate and terrain, and the more or less lengthy period it needs to develop its character, wine demands a devoted lifetime of a connoisseur.

Maurice Healy has summarized the factors that go to the making of a first-class wine as: (1) the soil, (2) the vines, (3) the intelligence and industry of the vine grower, (4) the amount of sun in the year, (5) the amount of rain in the year, (6) the times in the year when the sun shone and the rain fell, (7) the presence or absence of pests and plagues that affect the vine, (8) the skill and intelligence of the man who controls the making of the wine, (9) the care with which the wine is matured in cask before bottling, (10) the judgement and skill with which the bottling is done, (11) the subsequent history of the particular bottle: how often it is moved, whether it is kept in a good or bad cellar, and so on, (12) the care with which it is brought from the cellar to the table, *chambré*, and decanted. All and each of these twelve points are vital to the success of a wine. The pocket vintage chart, published each year by The Wine and Food Society, takes into account all the factors described by Mr Healy and it summarizes by using a system of marks, the drinking value of each kind of wine during the year in which the chart is issued. Here is a copy of one of these charts. It is an invaluable guide.

VINTAGE CHART

YEAR	Port	Claret	Burgundy	Rhône	Rhine & Moselle	Sauternes	White Burgundy	Champagne
1932	1	0	2	3	3	0	2	2
1933	5	5	6	6	6	3	5	5
1934	6	6	6	5	7	5	6	6
1935	7	2	4	3	5	2	5	3
1936	3	3	2	5	1	3	4	2
1937	4	5	5	6	6	7	7	5
1938	5	4	3	5	4	3	4	4
1939	3	2	2	3	3	2	2	2
1940	5	3	2	2	3	3	1	3
1941	4	1	1	3	2	0	1	4
1942	6	3	3	5	5	4	4	5
1943	5	5	5	6	5	6	6	5
1944	4	4	2	3	3	4	2	3
1945	6	6	7	6	6	7	6	6
1946	5	3	4	4	4	3	5	3
1947	7	7	7	7	6	7	7	6
1948	7	6	5	4	5	4	5	4
1949	4	6	7	6	7	5	6	5
1950	6	6	4	6	5	4	6	3
1951	4	3	3	4	2	3	3	2
1952	–	7	7	7	5	6	6	6
1953	–	6	7	6	7	7	7	7

0 = NO GOOD   7 = THE BEST

Reproduced by the courtesy of The Wine and Food Society

On the ordinary level of enjoyment wine is accessible to every-one who has the good fortune to travel in wine-producing districts or the money to spend at home. Although it requires time, money, and attention, those who can afford to start a cellar can supplement their own knowledge by putting their trust in a reliable wine merchant. But it is to those who cannot afford the luxury of an account with a wine merchant, or a long-term system of purchase, or *château* bottled wines, that these rudimentary remarks are ad-dressed; for people like ourselves whose purchases are sporadic and in the cheap wine category, *vins ordinaires* costing between five and nine shillings.

Before embarking on this interesting but limited field we must refer the reader who is seeking a wider understanding of the subject to some of the classic works, particularly to George Saintsbury's *Notes on a Cellar Book*, to Maurice Healy's *Stay me with Flagons*, and to the many books published by André Simon from which much instruction can be gained and into whose pages the subtle pleasures of the palate are distilled. But naturally, the best education is direct experience, and every opportunity to drink first-class wines must be avidly seized whenever it arises, both for their own sake and also in order to experience the delights which wine is capable of giving. The ordinary wine briefly discussed here is on a different level, it does not set fire to the imagination nor does it transform the view. *Vins ordinaires* are a pleasant adjunct to a meal, a modest stimulant, an agreeable taste, which is already a great deal.

Some of the more enlightened wine merchants specialize in a limited range of cheaper wines, for instance, Smith and Hoey Ltd, Dolamore Ltd, Long's Wine House, J. Lyons and Co., Ltd, Layton's, Avery's of Bristol, and Gilbey's, to name only a few, and all supply wine lists on request. A promising field in London is to be found within the limits of Soho where there is a concentration of wine shops with a wide range covering wines, usually blended and imported in the cask for bottling here, from France, Italy, Spain, Algeria, Yugoslavia, Chile, Hungary, Portugal, as well as from South Africa and Australia.

It is important to remember that every bottle bears a duty of about 2s. 2d., a bottling charge of 1s., and on top of this there is the cost of distribution and the profit, so that the actual wine cost of a 5s. bottle is very small indeed. This is why one can expect a noticeable improvement in the quality of cheap wines as the price increases a shilling at a time. In Soho where the labels on the bottles often remain the same the contents change with each new consignment, and if a cheap French or Spanish wine proves to be worth drinking it is advisable to buy a few bottles of it at once, or one may be surprised later on by a change for the worse.

About five shillings is a price that one can expect to pay for ordinary cooking purposes, a white *Coronata* from Parmigiani Figlio, or a stronger Hungarian *Badacsonyi Rizling*, the same price but shipped and bottled by the Hungarian Wine Cellars, Piccadilly; a red Tuscan wine at about 5s. 6d., which is obtainable in many shops in Old Compton Street, is also useful. This is, of course, in the rigid economy category, and starting from 6s. 3d. there is a greater choice of wines which can be used not only for cooking but which are also palatable.

The point must be made here that the better the wine used in the preparation of fish, flesh, or fowl, the better the result will be, and the choice of cooking wine is, again, a matter of what one can afford. In the six to nine shillings a bottle category there are dry white Chilean wines, Yugoslav *Lutomer Riesling*, Spanish white and red *Rioja*, light Portugese *Daõ Clarete*, white Bordeaux, *Rosés* from Anjou and Languedoc, and, better but dearer, *Tavel*, ordinary clarets, *St Julien*, *St Émilion*, and *Médoc*, red *Corbières*, and *Côtes du Rhône* wines, which last usually cost about 8s. Although only a few of the available wines are mentioned here, they are perhaps enough to stimulate investigation. Experiments can also be inexpensively carried out in the numerous little wine bars and lodges in London and elsewhere, where good wine is sold by the glass and one has the opportunity of finding an agreeable wine without first having to purchase the bottle. Country wine merchants might well be pressed to extend the range of their cheaper wines.

It must be common knowledge that white wines of whatever quality should be served chilled. Particularly in summer, they should be placed in a cool cellar for a time or on ice for a short while before serving. But there still seems to be some misapprehensions about red wines and particularly clarets, Burgundies and Rhône wines which must not be warmed by artificial means, but *chambré*.

This means that they should be brought into the room where they are to be served 24 hours before needed, the cork should be drawn an hour before the wine is to be drunk and then replaced lightly in position. Attempts to bring the wine to the correct temperature either by plunging the bottle in warm or, worse still, hot water, or by putting the bottle near the fire all result in ruining the wine. We would not make such a point of this but for an unhappy experience in a very well known and normally respected London restaurant where, not long ago, we had occasion to dine with a Swiss friend. He had recently come from Dijon, and wished to drink a *Château-neuf du Pape*, which he had enjoyed there. The wine was ordered and the bottle appeared and was inspected. The wine waiter vanished and returned with the opened bottle. We cannot forget the look of disappointment and amazement on our friend's face when he tasted it. He was too polite to protest in a foreign country at the condition of the wine, which was positively warm and com-pletely spoiled, and the task fell to us to accuse the wine waiter of putting the bottle in hot water. This he denied, laying the blame on a warm current of air from some imaginary radiator. After a time his misdeed was revealed beyond doubt by the label gently curling off the bottle. He then admitted the crime and for his excuse maintained that, 'English people like their wine warm'.

Red and white wines should be served in glasses which are narrow rather than open at the top; a tulip-shaped glass filled three-quarters full will best contain the wine's bouquet. A salad which has an oil and vinegar dressing impairs the palate and spoils the taste of the wine. An oil and lemon juice dressing has a less un-fortunate effect. Dishes which contain mushrooms and cheese are excellent with wine, while those which contain a hint of garlic need it. It is not necessary to be too nice in the matter of what goes with what when thinking in terms of *vin ordinaire*. The problem of what to serve with the claret or hock only arises when a classic wine is in question, and a great deal has been written about this subject. In the recipes given in this book we have made suggestions here and there when a particular type of wine seems to be called for, or is especially suitable for a certain dish. In the matter of the very best associate for wine – cheese in its natural state – the general principle is to choose a mild cheese to eat with a light wine and a cheese of a stronger flavour to match a heavier wine. André Simon, in his book *The Art of Good Living*, sets down the following wine and cheese associations:

> Claret with *Gruyère*
> Burgundy with *Port-Salut*
> Light tawny Port with Red Cheshire
> Oloroso Sherry with White Cheshire
> Old vintage Port with Blue Leicester
> New vintage Port with *Roquefort*

and there are many valuable discoveries to be made along these or similar lines.

To recapitulate these brief remarks: one should cultivate one's palate. Every opportunity should be taken of drinking wine and, when travelling, of sampling the local wines. One can, for example, get little idea of Italian wines in this country, the ones worth drinking, *Antinori*, *Ruffino*, or *Valpolicella* being relatively dear. Persuade country wine merchants to stock *vins ordinaires*. Never heat wine, heat destroys its qualities. Even an ordinary wine is enhanced by a sound cheese.

Finally, if there is any money to spare from these excursions spend it on a good *apéritif* such as *Dubonnet*, *St Raphael*, *Campari*, on a bottle of good Madeira or on *Amontillado* sherry, rather than on gin, or, and best of all, buy a good *Cognac* or *Armagnac* to set its seal upon a special occasion.

Glossary

14

GLOSSARY

WHEN the scope of this book was first discussed we put forward the revolutionary idea that it should exclude the use of foreign terms denoting culinary practices. It appeared to us that English people were more put off by unfamiliar words than by the practices they ordain, and that a trace of snobbery attaches to their use.

But in the course of time this somewhat puristic idea became blurred and irrelevant. After all, our language already contains many culinary words of undoubtedly French origin, of which the braise, the marinade, the fricassée, and sauté are obvious examples. Why, we wondered, should the casserole be an accepted word, when the *bain-marie* and the *court-bouillon*, for which there is no exact English equivalent, be considered rather affected? And it is hard to decide whether an instruction containing the word *flamber* is more shocking to the English ear than its counterpart 'flare with brandy'.

We have finally reached what we hope is a reasonable compromise in this matter, using foreign words when the English equivalent is too vague or too long-winded, and we were fortified in our decision by no less a man than Louis Eustache Ude. In 1822 in the preface to a new edition of *The French Cook*, M. Ude wrote: 'As several noblemen and ladies of distinction remarked to me that my book contained too many French terms, I have endeavoured in this edition to meet their goodness and liberality towards me by giving translations of such names as were translatable. But I must still observe, as I did in the preceding editions, that Cookery, like fortification, music, dancing, and many other arts, being of foreign origin, its nomenclature is, like theirs, in the language of the people who first cultivated it, and hence the impossibility of transferring to an equivalent many terms in English, so as to convey an intelligible meaning.'

Now, unrepentantly, we have admitted to the text a number of foreign words, usually French, in italics, and hope that anyone who is at a loss for their meaning will refer to the glossary.

Aïoli – a garlic mayonnaise peculiar to Provence.

À la meunière – a method of cooking fish by which it is lightly dusted with seasoned flour and fried in hot butter. Served with finely chopped parsley and a squeeze of lemon juice.

À la poêle – a method of braising using butter instead of *bouillon* or wine; or it may mean a substance cooked in a *poêle* which is usually a round, shallow-sided pan made of iron.

Al burro – refers to a *pasta* dish served with grated cheese and butter.

Al sugo – applies to a dish of *pasta* served with sauce and grated cheese.

Antipasto – Italian *hors d'œuvre*.

Armagnac – a brandy from the district of Armagnac.

Aubergine – the eggplant.

Au gratin – a dish dressed with breadcrumbs and butter or oil, and browned in the oven or under a grill.

Bain-marie – a utensil containing hot water in which bowls or small pans are placed in order to cook or to keep their contents warm: used for sauces, *beurre d'écrevisses*, etc.

Barding – a covering of pork, ham, or bacon fat applied to the breasts of poultry in braising or roasting.

Bards – strips of pork, ham, or bacon fat.

Batterie de cuisine – kitchen implements.

Battuto – a hash of aromatic vegetables and herbs used in the Italian kitchen as a starting point for *risotti*, sauces, and braises.

Beurre maître d'hôtel – butter with finely chopped parsley and a squeeze of lemon juice added to it with pepper and salt, used for fish, omelettes, and steaks.

Beurre noir – butter heated until dark brown and with a little reduced vinegar, salt, and pepper added. A sharp sauce for skate, calves' brains, and sweetbreads.

Beurre noisette – butter heated until light brown smelling of hazel nuts.

Blanching – is a term which includes both boiling and poaching, and is especially applied to the initial cooking of vegetables, sweetbreads, brains, calves' feet, etc., before submitting them to further preparation. In the case of vegetables boiling is maintained; in the case of sweetbreads, etc., after a few minutes the temperature is lowered. Sweetbreads require 20 minutes' blanching before they are ready to prepare *au beurre noir* or in a sauce which uses the blanching liquor as its base. A *liaison* of egg yolks thinned with lemon juice is more suitable than flour for thickening the sauce.

Bouilli – the beef from the *pot-au-feu*.

Bouillon – a clear beef stock resulting from the *pot-au-feu*.

Bouquet garni – usually a sprig of parsley, thyme, and bay leaf, but it can embrace a collection of other herbs.

Braise – a method of cooking substantial pieces of meat, poultry, or fish.

Braisière – a heavy copper or enamelled-iron lidded casserole.

Brodo – soup.

Burro – butter.

Capelletti – small semi-circular envelopes of *pasta* enclosing various stuffings, and used in soup or served with sauce and cheese.

Cassoulet – a preparation of diverse meats, sausages, and preserved goose, duck, or pork combined with haricot beans in an earthenware vessel and peculiar to Languedoc, the Pyrenees, and Alsace.

Caves – cellars or vaults.

Cèpes – one of the best edible fungi, genus *Boletus*.

Chambré – applies to wine which has been brought to room temperature.

Chanterelles – one of the most easily identified edible fungi.

Chinois – a pointed strainer.

Clarified butter – butter whose water content has been eliminated by heating it.

Cocotte – a round or oval lidded casserole in earthenware, copper, ironware, fireproof glass or china, used for stewing, braising, etc.

Cognac – a brandy from the district of Cognac.

Coppa – Italian smoked pork in the form of a large sausage.

Court-bouillon – a liquor consisting of water with wine vinegar or wine, prepared with herbs and aromatic vegetables for poaching fish.

Croûtons – small pieces of bread fried, in the form of squares, hearts, or crescents, as a garnish for soups, *matelotes*, etc.

Daube – a method of slow cooking in a sealed utensil to preserve all the juices of meat or poultry.

Daubière – an old-fashioned copper or enamelled-iron lidded casserole capable of bearing the applications of hot charcoal on its lid.

En daube – see above.

En poêle – see *à la poêle*.

Fettuccine – narrow ribbon *pasta*.

Fines herbes – applies to the fine chopping of fresh herbs.

Fricassée – a stew of poultry, rabbit, or veal enveloped in a fairly thick sauce.

Fruits de mer – small crustaceans and shellfish.
Frutta di mare – small crustaceans and shellfish.

Gnocchi – an Italian form of small dumpling, made with semolina, or potatoes, and flour, usually served with grated cheese and sauce.
Gratin – see *au gratin*.
Gratin dish – a shallow, open fireproof dish.
Gros sel – sea salt.
Gulyas – a Hungarian stew containing paprika.

Hâchoire – a French chopping device.
Haricots verts – French beans.

Kneaded butter – or *beurre manié*. A small quantity of butter into which plain flour is kneaded, which is used to thicken sauces at the last minute.

Larding – the insertion of strips of bacon, pork, or ham fat into substantial pieces of meat, poultry, or fish for roasting or braising.
Larding needle – a special needle for larding meat, etc.
Lardoons – strips of bacon, pork, or ham fat used in larding and usually sprinkled with herbs and seasoned in advance.
Lasagne – a wide ribbon *pasta*.
Liaison – the operation of thickening a liquid sauce with either flour, butter and flour, butter alone, or egg yolks and lemon juice.

Macaroni – embraces all forms of *pasta*.
Maccheroni – substantial forms of *pasta*.
Mandoline – a vegetable slicer.
Marinade – a decoction of wine, herbs, and vegetables, used to tenderize meat or to preserve meat or fish in hot weather.
Marmite – a French stock-pot, tall and cylindrical in form with a fitted lid.
Matelote – a stew of river fish, except the *matelote normande* which contains sole, turbot, brill.
Mezzaluna – an Italian chopping device in the shape of a half-moon.
Millerighi – a form of short *maccheroni* suitable for stuffing and serving with sauce and cheese.
Minestrone – a Genoese vegetable soup.
Mirepoix – a preparation of vegetables, herbs, and bacon or ham, finely chopped and sautéd, sometimes with the addition of wine, and used as the basis of a braise or sauce.

Mortadella – an excellent Bologna sausage which can be used as a stuffing for *ravioli* or poultry.

Mouli (*légumes*) – a device for grating vegetables and making *purées*.

Olla – a large Spanish earthenware pot.

Olla podrida – Spanish version of the *pot-au-feu*.

Paella – a Spanish preparation of rice, originated in Valencia, incorporating a diversity of ingredients usually including both fish and meat.

Paprika – sweet red Hungarian pepper in dried and powdered form, or the vegetable (red or green).

Pasta – embraces all kinds of pastes made from flour, maize flour, or semolina when combined with water into a great variety of shapes and sizes, e.g. *spaghetti, maccheroni,* etc.

Pasta all'uovo – *pasta* made with egg, and when sold commercially its content is 5 eggs to the kilogram.

Past'asciutta – refers to all forms of *pasta* which are served with sauce or cheese as opposed to the *pasta* used for soup.

Pâté de foie – liver *pâté*.

Pâté terrine – a glazed earthenware or china lidded dish in which *pâtés* are prepared.

Pesto – a Genoese preparation of pounded garlic, basil, parmesan cheese, and olive oil, which is added to *minestrone*.

Plat du jour – the special dish of the day.

Prosciutto – Italian smoked ham.

Purée – usually applies to vegetables and fruit which have been reduced to a smooth consistency, which is achieved by passing them through a sieve or *mouli*.

Ragoût – a stew.

Ratatouille – a southern French term for a stew.

Ravigote – a combination of parsley, tarragon, chives, chervil, and sometimes burnet, all finely chopped.

Ravioli – envelopes of *pasta* containing various stuffings and usually served with sauce and cheese.

Rosticceria – an Italian delicatessen shop where one can also eat.

Salami – a type of spiced and smoked sausage.

Salsa – sauce.

Sauté – to stew in butter, oil, or fat. The pan should be kept in movement all the time in order to prevent sticking or burning.

Sauté-pan – a shallow-sided lidded pan which combines frying facilities with those for subsequent stewing.

Scampi – a Mediterranean species of prawn.

Soffritto – under-frying.

Spaghetti – one of the common forms of string *pasta*.

Sugo – sauce.

Tagliatelle – a ribbon type of *pasta*.

Terracotta – baked clay.

Terre cuite – baked clay.

Tortellini – circles of *pasta al uovo* stuffed and served either in soup or with cheese and sauce.

Trattoria – an Italian wine shop-cum-restaurant.

Turbotière – a specially shaped pan for cooking turbot.

Universal Slicer – an adjustable slicer (*mandoline*).

Verde – green.

Vermicelli – a fine string soup *pasta*.

Zabaglione – a sweet concoction of beaten eggs, soft sugar, and *Marsala*, which is served warm.

·>·>·>·> ✳ ·<·<·<·<

ADDRESSES OF SUPPLIERS

Herb Plants and Seeds

Carters Tested Seeds Ltd, Raynes Park, London sw10.
Dobbie & Co. Ltd, The Scottish Seed Establishment, Edinburgh 7.
The Herb Farm Ltd, Seal, Sevenoaks, Kent.
Kathleen Hunter, Wheal Frances, Callestick, Truro, Cornwall.
Sutton & Sons Ltd, Reading, Berkshire.
Thompson & Morgan Ltd, London Road, Ipswich, Suffolk.
Toogood & Sons Ltd, Millbrook, Southampton, Hampshire.

Dried herbs may be got at Culpepper House or in the food sections of large department stores.

Spices

Spices, either in the whole fruit form or in powder, may be bought at large department stores which have food sections and also at such shops as:

The Bombay Emporium, 70 Grafton Way, London w1.
E. Parmigiani, 61 Old Compton Street, London w1. A comprehensive collection of dried herbs is also available here.

General

Army & Navy Stores Ltd, 105 Victoria Street, London sw1, for the food section and kitchen equipment.
Benoit Bulcke, 27 Old Compton Street, London w1, for fresh meat and cooked *pâtés*.
Cadec Ltd, 27 Greek Street, London w1, for all kitchen utensils and implements.
Harrods Ltd, Knightsbridge, London sw1, for their food section, Boucherie française, and kitchen equipment.
Parmigiani Figlio Ltd, 36a Old Compton Street, London w1, for cheeses, delicatessen, and wines.

Paxton & Whitfield Ltd, 93 Jermyn Street, London w1, for cheeses.

Randall & Aubin (London) Ltd, 16 Brewer Street, London w1, for fresh meats, cheese, *pâtés*.

Roche Ltd, 14 Old Compton Street, London w1, for French cheeses, vegetables, and fungi when in season.

Schmidt's (London) Ltd, 41 Charlotte Street, London w1, for German delicatessen.

Selfridges Ltd, Oxford Street, London w1, for the food section and kitchen equipment.

Wm. Whiteley Ltd, Queensway, London w2, for the food section including cheeses.

INDEX

INDEX

INDEX

Books in other Penguin series
are described on the following pages

A BOOK OF MEDITERRANEAN FOOD

Elizabeth David

PH27

This book is based on a collection of recipes made by the author when she lived in France, Italy, the Greek Islands, and Egypt, doing her own cooking and obtaining her information at first hand. In its pages will be found recipes, and practical ones, evoking all the colour and sun of the Mediterranean; dishes with such exciting and unfamiliar names as the *Soupe au Pistou*, the *Pebronata* of Corsica, or the *Skordalia* of the Greeks. Now that food is plentiful again, the author has revised the book to include more recipes from Spain, Provence, Greece, Italy, and the Middle East, making use of ingredients from all over the Mediterranean now available in England. The majority of the dishes however do not require exotic ingredients, being made with everyday vegetables, herbs, fish, and poultry, but treated in unfamiliar ways.

'In *Mediterranean Food* Mrs David proves herself a gastronome of rare integrity. . . . She refuses to make ignoble compromises with expediency. And in this, surely, she is very right. . . . Above all, she has the happy knack of giving just as much detail as the average cook finds desirable; she presumes neither on our knowledge nor our ignorance.' – Elizabeth Nicholas in the *Sunday Times*

ALCHEMY

E. J. Holmyard

A348

From the dawn of history the shining and untarnishable metal gold has exerted its fascination upon man. Very early the idea arose that other metals were either impure or unripe gold, and that therefore by suitable treatment they could be converted into the precious metal itself. Such a belief, the principal tenet of alchemy, led to vast programmes of experiment, from which, after the lapse of centuries, a scientific practical chemistry developed. But the fact that the belief in transmutation was almost universally accepted offered great opportunities to rogues and charlatans. Side by side with honest searchers, therefore, were clever scoundrels who fleeced prince, peer, and peasant by the skill with which they carried out tricks of sleight-of-hand and deluded their victims into thinking that here was an infallible method of acquiring unlimited wealth. Gold was attributed with marvellous therapeutic properties, and many of the alchemists attempted to prepare from it an elixir of life. Others found in alchemical theory a religious or mystical symbolism.